Spiritual Values For Our Time

New and Personal Sources of Meaning and Transformation

NED BELLAMY

www.spiritualvalues.net

Copyright © 2013. Edward J Bellamy
All rights reserved.

ISBN: 1469944871
ISBN-13: 9781469944876

TABLE OF CONTENTS

Introduction: More Life vii

PART ONE: THE QUEST

1) Religion and Family: The Foundation 3
2) A Spiritual Reawakening 13

PART TWO: VALUES (INSTEAD OF BELIEFS)

3) Determining Meaning 21
4) Spiritual Values of One's Own 27
5) Inspirational Ideals: The Meta-Values 35
6) Spiritual Happiness in This World 43
7) Transformation to More Spiritual Values 49
8) Identity As Character 57

PART THREE: FROM HEDONISM TO THE IDEALS OF WISDOM AND PEACE

I   <u>The Ideal of Wisdom</u> 67

9) The Value of Integrity (Instead of Delusion) 75
10) The Value of Discernment (Instead of Ease) 85
11) The Value of Individuation: Accessing Our Whole Psyche 99

II	<u>The Ideal of Inner Peace (and Quietude)</u> 109
	<u>The Value of Equanimity:</u> <u>Accepting the World As It Is</u> 121
12)	Desire for "The Good Life" 125
13)	Less Desire and Aversion: The Value of Satisfaction (with the Present) 133
14)	Our Fear of Suffering 143
15)	Less Hope and Fear: The Value of Trust (in the Future) 155
	<u>The Value of Healing Our Wounds:</u> <u>Accepting Ourselves As We Are</u> 167
16)	The Wound of Shame 171
17)	Healing Our Shame: The Value of Self-Forgiveness... 179
18)	Healing Our Grief: The Value of Gratitude 193

PART FOUR: FROM SELF-INTEREST TO
THE IDEALS OF LOVE & COMPASSION

19)	From Self-Interest to Self-Forgetfulness 209
I	<u>Love in the Family: Marriage &</u> <u>The Gift of Nurturance</u> 219
20)	The Value of Magnanimity 227
21)	The Value of Intimacy 237

II	**Love in the Family: Parenting & The Gift of Generativity** 249
22)	The Value of Liberation: Setting the Children Free ... 257
23)	The Value of Encouragement 269
III	**Compassion for Strangers & The Value of Abundance** 283
24)	Obstacles to Generosity and The Value of Re-Visioning 293
25)	The Value of Interconnection 303
26)	The Value of Equivalence... 311
27)	The Value of (Economic) Justice: Sharing our Treasure 319
28)	The Value of Merciful Service: Sharing Ourselves 331
	Conclusion 341
	End Notes 343
	Acknowledgements 353
	Bibliography 355
	Index of Values 371

INTRODUCTION

More Life

I will encourage you to consider the benefits of a practice of spiritual values as a supplement to your own personal belief system, whether that be religious, humanist, or something in between. I've found that clarifying relevant and useful contemporary values of my own has enlivened my spiritual life and revealed new and rich sources of meaning. This spiritual approach is consistent with other underlying belief systems because it does not take any stand about God or the hereafter, about which I know nothing.

I developed this practice after three decades as a practicing Catholic followed by several years as a Buddhist. In my early forties, prayer and meditation had begun to feel empty, and I'd become ever more dubious about promises of transcendent bliss in heaven or nirvana. After years of religious devotion, I was distracted by more questions than answers; I wasn't growing; and I was still living a ninety-eight percent secular existence.

Spiritually adrift, I awarded myself an indefinite furlough from religious practice. But after only three years, working hard and playing hard didn't seem to be enough. There had to be more to life—and to me—beyond our family and my work, our security and my success. I felt a yearning for a more full and abundant life in *this* world—for me and for others. In short, I'd found religion not *credible* enough, but secularism not *meaningful* enough. Neither could satisfy my persistent longing for more meaning, purpose, and identity.

Meaning. I needed a spiritual life for some of the reasons Garrison Keillor thinks we need poetry in our lives: "The intense vision and high spirits and moral grandeur are simply needed lest we drift through our days consumed by clothing options and hair styling and whether to have the soup or the salad."[1]

Purpose. What was I to *do* with my life? Jesus' and the Buddha's calls for compassionate service certainly sounded good, but I was largely unconcerned with the world beyond. A self-interested life in pursuit of ever more ease and comfort seemed hardly purpose enough. But how could I manage to leave something of value behind when I wasn't even sure what to teach the children about the formation of their characters?

Identity. Who *was* I, anyway? Wanting a more complete life, I knew I would need to grow spiritually, but I wasn't learning, loving more, stretching—*becoming* much of anything. Who did I wish to become?

I cast about in search of an existing spiritual program to find more satisfying answers to these three issues. I was heavily influenced by what I had loved and learned from my religious experiences. The spiritual practice I'll share would have been inconceivable without them. But this time around I needed to start afresh to find a more sustainable path. I found it through turning to spiritual *values* instead of spiritual *beliefs*.

New Sources of Meaning, Purpose, and Identity: Values

Religions, nonreligious spiritualities, and atheism rest primarily upon systems of belief. *A belief is an assent to an explanation.* Examples include explanations about the origin and end of the world or about the purpose of life. Discussions of the beliefs incorporated in the Nicene Creed comprise 242 pages in the Catholic Catechism. I was uninterested in any more beliefs, especially more of my own.

I was drawn instead to a much less frequently used currency of meaning than beliefs. *A value is an assessment of the importance or worth of a thing.* I hadn't found any credible *explanation* about the meaning of life. But I thought I could learn what was most *important* and therefore meaningful to me. I distinguished between two types of values.

- **The Meta-Values: Our Spiritual Ideals.** Personal ideals are our long-term, faraway goals. They inspire our most potent aspirations. Over the centuries, religions have done most of the heavy lifting about humanity's perennial ideals. As both a Buddhist and Christian, I'd always been particularly drawn to four such ideals: wisdom, inner peace, love, and compassion. I define spirituality for myself as the pursuit of greater wisdom, peace, love, and compassion. I will encourage and help you identify the most salient ideals of your own.

- **More Down-to-Earth, Practical Spiritual Values.** But exactly *how* does one actually go about becoming a little wiser, for example? Spiritual values are the virtues and principles that firmly anchor our chosen faraway ideals to our quotidian lives. These values also serve to help define what our ideals really mean to each of us.

New Sources of Spiritual Values

Every religion espouses a constellation of ideals and values, many of which are profound and timeless. But many of the religious values I'd learned had not seemed very relevant or helpful in the conduct of my everyday life. First, many religious values are too ancient, dogmatic, immutable, and exclusive to be adaptable to my circumstances in this culture. For example, most of The Ten Commandments and the Eightfold Path just don't pertain much to the everyday conduct of my life.

Second, it seemed that the Christian emphasis upon salvation for me in the *next* world has minimized the importance of the pursuit of greater spiritual happiness for all in *this* world. Because both Jesus and Paul shared apocalyptic visions of the immanent end of the world, happiness was naturally imagined as an exclusively otherworldly proposition. But I wanted to focus on values to support greater life here. I saw no inconsistency between increased happiness here *and* the promise of happiness hereafter.

Finally, religious values and ideals are focused upon the pursuit of moral righteousness. But most people I know were well trained as children to discern right from wrong. I was more interested in values that might offer better solutions to everyday problems; that is, a more *practical* practice. For example, my practice of the value of *integrity* has reduced my denial and illusion, and the value of *satisfaction* helps to release me from envy and addiction.

More Relevant and Useful Spiritual Values

I became interested in a much broader, more expansive role for spirituality in the conduct of everyday life. I mined two new sources to uncover sixty-four very relevant and useful spiritual values that helped deepen the practice of my own chosen ideals.

1) **Values Chosen by Each One of Us.** I wonder if we have long misinterpreted our religious founders' intentions about dogmatic exclusivity. Are we sure that two thousand years of silent obedience and rote learning have been expected? Is passivity really preferred to co-creating a more vital personal spiritual experience for each of us? I found it enormously useful to create my own collection of spiritual values and I'll urge you to do likewise. Because each individual formulates her or his own, each value will, by definition, be meaningful, reasonable, useful, and relevant—*to each of us.* Our own value system grows organically, based upon the particular needs, roles, and circumstances of our lives.

For example, my spiritual value of *realism* was triggered by a passage from Thoreau and also from my experience as an entrepreneur. My opinions about the value of parental *encouragement* evolved as a widower in my thirties, as a co-parent of seven, and as a grandparent of eleven. The values of *honesty* and *discipline* were influenced by my recovery from addiction.

My spiritual value of *equanimity* is Buddhist, but it was also influenced by s'ome therapeutic work to heal some new grief and old shame. My understanding of the spiritual value of *mercy* was derived from Jesus' Sermon on the Mount, informed through volunteer work locally, in a federal prison, and with the homeless; and overseas, in Tanzania, Honduras, and Guatemala. And so on.

2) **Values Originating in the Contemporary Culture.** To remain important, relevant, and useful, I believe that each new generation should reinvent and reinterpret their own spiritual values. Through reading, conversation, or prompted by personal experience, my choice of values has reflected my culture's postmodern eclecticism. This book features provocative quotations from historians, columnists, politicians, poets, psychologists, and philosophers, as well as from Christian and Buddhist commentators. An example of the contemporaneity of my chosen value system is the last century's discoveries about the psyche. (Aptly, *psyche* is a Greek word to describe "the soul"). Diligent self-inquiry and self-knowledge has been most helpful in my very gradual efforts to increase my own wisdom, peace of mind, and capacity to love.

My Spiritual Values

The following are the values I selected to enhance the practice of my four chosen ideals. Your own list will of course be unique to you, but some of these ideas may prompt more of your own.

I personally define the **Ideal of Wisdom** through the Values of:

Self-understanding	Discernment
Integrity	Novelty
Realism	Humility
Diversity	Holism
Honesty	Synthesis
Uncertainty	Individuation

I best express the **Ideal of (Inner) Peace** by the Values of:

The Past	**The Present**
Healing	Quietude
Regression	Mindfulness
Authenticity	Equanimity
Self-acceptance	Self-discipline
Self-forgiveness	Temperance
Grief	Fortitude
Gratitude	Satisfaction
Shame	Renunciation

The Future
Trust	Prudence
Acquiescence	Letting Go
Suffering	

I understand the **Ideal of (Familial) Love** to consist of the Values of:

Marriage
Self-forgetfulness
Constancy
Nurturance
Feedback
Mediation
Magnanimity
Generosity
Acceptance
Blessing
Forgiveness
Renewal
Transparency
Revelation
Listening
Intimacy

Parenting
Generativity
Teaching
Liberation
Balance
Encouragement
Self-esteem
Competence
Self-confidence

The **Ideal of Compassion** is a compendium of these Values for me:

Abundance
Re-visioning
Interconnection
Equivalence
Imagination
Justice
Redemption
Sacrifice
Mercy
Heartbreak

Personal Transformation

This spirituality of personal values facilitates change and growth. The clarification of our deepest personal values is necessary because our ideals and values simply *don't exist* until they're brought to our awareness. Only after we breathe life into them can the ideals and values we embrace become fertile sources of new meaning; help clarify our life's purpose; and flesh out our intentions about who we wish to become.

A code based upon the ideals and values to which I personally aspire has been far more appealing than dutiful compliance with any institutional code of conduct. And the *process* of the personal design of one's spirituality is itself transformative. Assuming responsibility for selecting my ideals and values was empowering. This process of clarification also unearthed deeper longings and aspirations I thought I'd relinquished long ago. I'd forgotten who I was. Finally, the process of organizing my own values into a manageable, cohesive, coherent, and comprehensive collection was a very effective means to focus my intention and attention. These values have became a spiritual operating manual.

But the ultimate reasons this spiritual practice is effectively transformative is that slowly growing into my chosen ideals gives me a great deal of satisfaction. I love to learn and increase in wisdom; to grow in inner peace has relieved me of life-long anxiety; exchanging love more consistently in my extended families is its own sweet reward; and acting compassionately for strangers simply feels good.

From Me to You

Rather than a quest, the unfolding of my own value system felt more like a labyrinthine walkabout. To help foreshorten and ease your own journey I'll share, through example and story, the lessons I managed to learn—usually the hard way—about personal transformation. We will cover a lot of spiritual ground and delve as deeply as possible into my own process of discovery. Three-quarters of this book is devoted to helping you think about and then develop your own palette of ideals and values.

I'll describe both my problems that gave rise to the need for the spiritual values I've adopted, and the solutions contributed by each new experiment. Some of my circumstances and re-decisions will resonate with you. I'll report more than my fair share of humbling obstacles to growth: my failures, foolishness, delusion, and self-interest, for starters—all reasons that prompted this spiritual quest in the first place. Paradoxically, these dubious qualities are also a testament to the wonders of transformation, which after all, is a large part of the spiritual story.

———

My wish is that you'll find this book to be as I found the spiritual practice described within: personal, relevant, practical, and transformative. I hope it will be a contribution to deepening and sustaining your own spiritual experience..

PART ONE
THE QUEST

CHAPTER ONE

RELIGION AND FAMILY: THE FOUNDATION

In St. Augustine School I seemed to be a little more interested in religious matters than most. I was also more inclined to question religious doctrines more readily embraced by the other kids. I was pleased when chosen in the eighth grade to represent the school in a Diocesan-wide competition. I crammed for three weeks to learn, largely by rote, one hundred pages or so of Catholic catechetical teachings.

Late on the day before the competition, Sister Cecelia handed me two *more* blue mimeographed single-spaced pages and told me to memorize *The Six Supernatural Effects of Sanctifying Grace*.

Following my request for clarification of the unusually obscure theological language, it became evident that the embarrassed Sister didn't understand them very well either. "Young man, just run along now. I know I can count on you to learn them this evening, word for word." Not lost on this fourteen-year-old was the message that obedience trumps understanding. That afternoon, rather than study, I pitched in our final semester's baseball game, which we lost. We also lost the next day's competition in the final round because of my incoherent response to the very question about grace I'd not bothered to memorize. This sort of passive resistance didn't bode well for my religious future.

My religion was a bequest from my mother. She was the youngest of eleven Irish Catholic kids on a hardscrabble Wisconsin dairy farm. I liked being a Christian. Early, my favorite part was my inclusion in God's family as His child, more comforting on most days than membership in my more immediate, earthly family. I loved my prayerful soliloquies addressed to Jesus, more approachable than His Father, and more imaginable than the Holy Spirit. I grew to love the words of Jesus in the Gospels. I re-read them still.

During my first day at St. Michael's College in the University of Toronto, I took two giant steps designed to buttress my faith. I began a long and sweet romance with Mary Driscoll, who inspired me with a religious belief far more resolute than mine. Convinced of God's presence and beneficence since she was five, Mary was a constant source of encouragement in my moments of doubt. Each spring, during final exam months, as a measure of her devotion to God (and mine to her), we began our days gloriously at 5:30 a.m. Mass. The smell of incense and the Gregorian chants in the cloistered Convent of the Most Precious Blood are deeply etched in my bones.

Some Catholics speak of "the spell of the smells and bells," which for me are still calls from home. Some of my Christian friends are among the happiest people I know. I desperately wanted an unconditional and uncomplicated faith like theirs. The pull of those religious voices—the callings I'd heard since childhood—have transcended time. One favorite prayer we taught to our kids often recurs to me, unbidden:

> Lovingly in thy hands, Father Mother God
> I place my life, my will, and all my affairs;
> Guide me, lead me, show me the way,
> *Thy* will be done today.

My second collegiate initiative to reinforce my faith was a bit more problematic. I chose theology and philosophy as major undergraduate courses of study. I loved being a student and the more I learned, the more I sought to understand. I seemed constitutionally incapable of following St. Augustine's simple, but counter-intuitive dictum: "Understanding is the reward of faith. Therefore, seek not to understand that thou mayest believe, but believe that thou mayest understand." [2]

The most highly valued virtue for Christians is faithfulness, but I'd never been convinced of the central proposition of the Abrahamic religions: that faith is inherently of greater value than understanding. I felt frustrated and even resentful being asked to play the game of faith where *all* the cards were turned face down.

My continuing conflict probably stemmed from my mother's unquestioning Catholicism juxtaposed with my father's agnostic doubts about his forebears' Calvinism.

For the next two decades, I devoted thousands of hours trying to pray my way to a stronger faith during Mass, weekend retreats, and parish renewals. I attended church weekly with the family, enrolled the kids in Catholic grammar schools, and even briefly co-taught religious education to public high school kids. But I felt I was holding onto a very high cliff by my fingernails.

Mary

The life that Mary and I led together had been easy and almost predictable. After college we returned to the suburbs of New York City, where we'd been raised. Mary received a Masters degree in Education from Columbia, while I earned law and business degrees at New York University. We married after a courtship of six years. In the manner of many young Catholic couples of our generation, children followed in rapid succession, including three in the first four years. Mary retired from teaching high school English to raise the kids.

Our four children each brought us indescribable joy. Still a morning person, Mary rose before six on weekdays and went downstairs to pray in the predawn quiet. When I awakened the little ones for school, they tumbled down to snuggle like kittens under Mary's ample wool blanket against the morning chill. The conversations about their coming day always ended with this simple prayer: "Dear God, we offer you all our work and all our play today." Many nights, making our final rounds to re-cover the kids and whisper "Sweet dreams" on our way to bed, we reminded each other of our unearned share of the world's great fortune.

On a grey Ohio morning, in the January of her thirty-seventh year, after suffering severe headaches during the previous week, Mary descended into a coma. Before surgeons could gather to intervene that afternoon, an aneurism had caused irreversible damage to her brain.

Six days later, her magical kids (between ages four and twelve) huddled with me in a tearful pile on the living room floor to determine their mother's fate. We talked of brain death and limited options. After each of Mary's shattered children had their say, we agreed to remove the respirator and invite the team from the Cleveland Clinic to fly in and harvest her salvageable organs. But we couldn't decide whether or not to tell Mary's grief-stricken mom and dad (audibly reciting their rosaries upstairs) about Mary's organ donations. D'Arcy, then nine, cast the deciding vote. "I think they'd rather not know now that their daughter will end up all over the Midwest—or God knows where else." We never did tell them; but I hope they would have approved.

Transitions

Mary's death was the pivotal event in her four children's lives *and* in mine, then—and probably still. It was the end of a kind of innocence and joy we'd never know again. Two months before she died, following my first major professional failure, another issue had arisen. The result had been that I finally understood how emotionally wounded I'd been since childhood. Mary and I had been scoping out therapists for me, and I had a lot of work to do.

How could anybody like me—as fundamentally insecure as Mary was confident—ever fill the enormous vacuum in these kids' lives? I had always spent a lot of time with the kids after work and on weekends. I was a good father. But as a parent, I wasn't in the same league with Mary. Without her presence, I couldn't imagine how to help the children continue to develop a self-regard and self-confidence I didn't myself possess. I felt I was in way over my head, but the kids were extraordinarily patient while I stumbled into my new role as mother/father.

We were very slowly healing together, but we were all just winging it. We missed Mary most in church. Then, we all just held onto the most tearful kid tightly and cried as silently as we could. Instead of dealing with my grief, I got very busy. I changed everything that wasn't nailed down. The first change was easy. I interviewed a half-dozen folks for an *au pair*. I asked one candidate, "What brings you to Ohio from Wisconsin?" She smiled and replied matter-of-flatly, "The Lord." I loved her evangelical religious enthusiasm and wanted her around these children. "Joan, you're hired. How soon would you like to begin?"

I also changed my job and three months later, our home. We all moved to Clearwater, on Florida's west coast. All four kids were enrolled in Our Lady of Lourdes grammar school. I stayed as busy as possible. A year after Mary's death, I wrote to our Yankee family and friends about our new lifestyle:

> [There has been] a marked absence of vegetables (they may be cancerous), and casseroles (likewise). On the other hand, paper plates, junk food, fast food, movies, stereophonic rock, and sleepovers

abound. (Who the hell is *that?*). We've fished, for an average cost of $38 per pound; and camped in the deep woods—average mosquito bites per child: 41. We've been sunburned on tennis courts and beaches and even on our house rooftop, where the girls "lay out" in the sun to look especially radiant for that really cute guy in algebra.

Another Change; Another Loss

I also came to grips with another transition I'd managed to avoid as long as I could. For decades, the entire congregation recited the Nicene Creed in unison every Sunday. It's a beautiful prayer summarizing the dogmatic teaching of Catholicism, allegiance to which is the sole prerequisite for membership in the Church. About three A.M. one Sunday, I awoke dreaming of the prayer. I began to recite it slowly. "We believe in one God... He ascended into heaven...we look for the resurrection of the dead..." I was shocked by the truth I'd withheld from myself for so long: I could no longer assent to eleven of the thirteen tenets in this briefest summary of Christian faith. In good faith I could no longer continue to call myself a Christian. I had lost the faith that had nourished me for so long. So, in spite of working at it very hard for a long time, I washed out of my Catholic faith. I was grief-stricken.

I reluctantly joined many others in the generation Carl Jung aptly described: "People no longer feel themselves to have been redeemed by the death of Christ; they cannot believe—they cannot compel themselves to believe, however happy they may deem the man who has a belief."[3] The truth of the existence, nature, and will of God and the issue of life hereafter are surely the most important of all human questions. But for me, after years of inquiry and prayer, all were unanswerable. As an agnostic, I find myself wanting to clearly decide one way or another, to finally gain a sense of closure about these two questions. But I work hard to remain receptive to greater understanding regarding the presence or absence of the Divine.

The reason for my prolonged allegiance to my inherited religion was simply explained: I knew that leaving the Church was going to be more painful than staying. Because I thought then (and now) that all believers are blessed, my primary concern was that I would confuse the kids, whose faith I wanted to nurture. I also anticipated I would feel a sense of failure, disloyalty, and shame for forfeiting the gift of my religious inheritance. And I surely didn't want to acknowledge the feeling of regret for all the "wasted" years of devotion. Another consequence was dealing with the huge disappointment of the Catholics in our extended Irish families, who had been praying for years that I would "just get over my pointless, skeptical streak and climb aboard." All that emotional aftermath unfolded as expected—and then some. There were also several surprises.

First, my grief following the loss of my relationship with the God I had imagined and to whom I prayed for decades was far more painful and extended than I had ever guessed possible. It lasted for four or five years. Paradoxically, I was also surprised by a sense of relief to be finally free of my lifelong, enervating struggle about faith.

I was surprised that I've never experienced a moment of existential despair about my lost hope for a life after death. The kids used to say that "Heaven sounds kinda dull. No TV? Please. I mean, what do you *do* all day? Listen to church music and sermons? Pray a lot? Bowl?" I must have shared their lack of imagination. The loss of the prospect of a comforting afterlife just intensified the importance to me of creating more life in *this* life.

Buddhism

One more change was my decision to explore Buddhism. I was drawn because Christianity and Buddhism are similar in many ways. Both are elegant, formal, and ancient; both stress commitment and discipline; and both emphasize the ideals of love and compassion. I preferred the Buddhists' spare dogmatism and their experiential approach to knowledge. The Buddhist emphasis on inner peace and wisdom contrasted with Christianity's focus on hope and faith. I liked the insightful dharma talks and the glimpses of serenity during sitting and walking meditations. In my late thirties I practiced Vipassana Buddhism in the early mornings at home and during weekend and week-long silent meditation retreats.

But the meditative form felt a little one-dimensional. And it reinforced my introversion—my natural tendency to isolate and disengage from the world. Stephen Batchelor is a British Buddhist scholar who writes, "To put it bluntly, the central question Buddhists have faced from the beginning is this: is awakening close by or far away? Is it readily accessible or available only through supreme effort?"[4] After a few years, I was discouraged by my slow rate of progress, and meditation seemed like too much work for too little benefit. I became dubious about my ability to measure up to the promised rewards of faithful practice. On most days awakening felt *very* far away; and I did not feel then up to "a supreme effort."

CHAPTER TWO

A SPIRITUAL REAWAKENING

A Secular Sabbatical

Two more changes lay in store during this time of transition. First, one step back. After decades of weekly church attendance and Buddhist meditation practice, I awarded myself a religious sabbatical. I embraced a sort of "effortless spirituality." This "no-*practice* spiritual practice" is popular with many friends. They're attentive to their children, faithful to their partners, supportive of their local community, and generous to the United Way. All great stuff. But not exactly a big stretch for them, since they'd been trained and predisposed to be good and decent people all their lives. This *laissez-faire* spirituality required very little time or attention from folks already juggling a full load of career and family responsibilities. After a lifetime of religion for me, this no-practice lifestyle sounded attractive, precisely because it was so easy.

My spiritual sabbatical, then, was a *de facto* secular existence. I worked hard and played hard. I had always embraced most of the secular values celebrated in the larger culture where, "everyone prizes... achievement, affluence, and appearance."[5] Like many contemporaries, I was very enmeshed in these values that provided much of my meaning, purpose, and identity. Much too much, it turns out. I wanted to *Be* Somebody. Becoming anybody would actually do just fine.

I opted very early for the values of success and money. My dad lost his job as a reporter at the *Milwaukee Sentinel* for helping to organize a union. While he searched for work and housing in New York, Mom and her three kids moved in with my uncle's family for several months. Eight of us lived in a three-bedroom shotgun flat in a walk-up tenement in Cleveland. I remember playing in the trash heap out back, and the long waits to use the only bathroom. Later, while Mom and Dad moved our belongings to New York, we three kids spent a fortnight with another relative in Virginia. We stayed on their gentleman's farm outside Charlottesville, complete with staff and swimming pool. Struck by the contrast between these two recent lifestyles, I determined to do what was necessary to secure the more comfortable of the two. I was five years old.

My Primary Secular Values

The Secular Value of Success. Early on in my marriage to Mary, I began working as a commercial banker on Wall Street. Then followed decades of managing regional operations of national home-building companies in Virginia, South Carolina, Pennsylvania, Ohio, and Florida. We hated all that moving about, but I loved the challenge of starting new ventures and managing people. Mostly, I liked the status of running things and feeling important. I hadn't yet understood that the satisfaction of achievement, so wonderful in the moment, would provide no lasting, meaningful legacy. Three years later, who even *remembers* who did what to whom? *I* couldn't even remember.

The Secular Value of Wealth. Six generations of my dad's male ancestors included Protestant clergymen, writers, and journalists. All those professions held great appeal for me at one time or another. However, after college, in one of my life's more dubious decisions, I chose a career as the first businessman on either side of the family. All for the money. I especially wanted to earn enough money to allow Mary and me to see more of the world together. I hadn't yet grasped the wisdom shared by billionaire movie producer David Geffen: "Anyone who thinks money will make them happy doesn't have money."

Renewed Spiritual Yearnings

Our secular drives are instinctive shouts, but our spiritual longings are whispers, and consequently often unheeded by people like me. In an episode of the sitcom *Seinfeld*, Kramer asks, "George, don't you ever yearn for anything?" George replies, "No. But I crave constantly." Although I stayed very busy during my spiritual time-out, my life was only half-full: the secular half. Was this all there was? Feeling some depression and meaninglessness, I wondered if I was sleepwalking and missing something: more joy, more fulfillment. A conversion event, it wasn't. Rather a gradual, nagging yearning for more. . *life.*

I thought I'd put these inconvenient spiritual longings on hold a few years earlier. But I gathered now that these yearnings were too deep to be extinguished by distracting myself within the whirlwind of the secular culture. In my early forties, after Mary's passing, I was surprised by the continuing influence of my old religious experience, which reawakened existential questions about meaning, purpose, and identity, to which secularity couldn't provide sufficient answers.

Three Spiritual Specifications

Two years into my secular sabbatical, I was amazed to arrive at the following conclusion: To be fulfilled and happy I would need to practice some kind of spirituality that would be relevant, useful, transformative, and therefore sustainable by me for the long term. I gathered the energy and desire to launch one final spiritual quest in search of a new way to satisfy these three simple criteria.

Relevance. To sustain my interest, I needed sources of spiritual teaching that were responsive to my circumstances in my contemporary culture. I was inspired by the life and writings of Lincoln and Gandhi as much as by the compelling stories of St. Francis.

Utility. It was too much to expect that any institutional church could be responsive to my idiosyncratic "real world" problems. But I needed a more detailed instruction manual than the catechism to help me make better spiritual use of my life.

Transformation. If I wanted a more complete life, I was going to have to begin to grow and change.

I didn't wish to return to my old practice of either Christianity or Buddhism, but I couldn't imagine that religion would never be some part of my life. I still attend church services or a Buddhist sangha regularly. My religious life deeply (and often unconsciously) informed this new spiritual practice. I've gained a new appreciation for the spiritual awakening they both quickened in me; for religions' insistence upon disciplined practice; for their emphasis on solitude and silence; for all my spiritual ideals and about a third of my spiritual values; for religions' insistent call to transformation; and for their emphasis upon character formation. Without my previous immersion in those two rich and elegant traditions, the spiritual practice I will share shortly would have been much more problematic.

PART TWO
A SPIRITUALITY OF VALUES—NOT BELIEFS

CHAPTER THREE

DETERMINING MEANING

> I say that religion is not about believing things. It's ethical alchemy. It's about behaving in a way that changes you, that gives you intimations of holiness and sacredness.
>
> —Karen Armstrong, *A History Of God*[6]

Meaning Based Upon Spiritual Beliefs

One source of meaning is based upon our beliefs: our cognitive assent to explanations. Religions and atheism both rest upon a system of beliefs. A Korean Zen Buddhist master first raised the issue of the reliability of existential belief systems for me. At the end of a week-long meditation workshop at the Omega Institute, one of three hundred participants asked him to explain, "the meaning of life and our role in it." Crashing his walking staff atop an amplified podium, he shouted to one and all:

> 'Why, why, why?' Have you all learned nothing? You Americans make awakening *so* difficult. I have a question for *you*. Why do you waste your lives with these incessant, foolish questions? The answer to all of these questions has always been, and must forever be, the same: 'Don't know! Will never know!'

Meaning Based upon Spiritual Values

Another source of meaning is based upon our values. Instead of a cognitive assent to an *explanation,* a value is an emotional assessment of *importance.* What is important to me is meaningful. The existentialists urged us to create our own meaning in the world. Jean-Paul Sartre said, "It's up to you to give [life] a meaning, and value is nothing else but the meaning that you choose."[7] We have as many sources of meaning as we have values, a word I will use throughout as synonymous with "ideals, virtues, and principles."

I wanted to find different ways to deal with ideas like spirituality, happiness, inspiration, meaning, purpose, and identity, that would be less reliant upon unverifiable beliefs. I'd always found what others valued (believed *in*) to be more revealing, interesting, and consequential than their beliefs *about* something. Belief seemed twice removed from reality; but one's principles seemed more thoughtful and less speculative to me.

When talking about spiritual subjects with our adolescent kids, we noticed that values were likely to lead to discussions, while beliefs led to debates. I agree with the Unitarian Universalists, who embrace members with divergent beliefs. "If you and I ask each other what we believe, all too often we will end up arguing. However, when we ask one another what we truly value... we don't argue. We listen. We connect."[8]

Our endless conflicts about belief systems are exemplified by the political and legal arguments surrounding U.S. immigration policy. Because he was very knowledgeable and an advocate, a friend was asked to contribute to such a debate. Dave declined, but offered a story instead.

> As a freshman at Louisiana State, I was flat broke and happy to find work at a minimum-wage job in a nearby sawmill. I bunked there with twenty-seven other hands, all undocumented Mexicans. We taught each other Spanish and English and became good friends.
>
> During my undergraduate years and a few years thereafter (since I was stationed in a nearby Air Force base), I helped each of them navigate the tedious paper chase required for U.S. citizenship. By 2004, twenty-four of them, and thereafter, everyone else in their immediate families, had become U.S. citizens.

You could've heard a pin drop. Instead of arguing in favor of his *beliefs* about U.S. immigration policies, Dave spoke of the *value* of U.S. citizenship—to him and to his naturalized friends. This value was not particularly well argued. It was much more than that. It was a profound statement about him and an inspiration to the rest of us, regardless of our beliefs.

Values: Secular or Spiritual?

Since I'll be referring to "spiritual" or "secular" values, it's time to define our terms. The objective of both our secular and spiritual motivational systems is the pursuit of more life, by increasing the happiness—or by decreasing the suffering—of all. Secular and spiritual happiness are two complementary objectives. Since both are indispensable for our and others' life enrichment, I find it useful to consider the secular and spiritual as equally important. But they are also alternative ways of responding to life's challenges, each competing for our time, energy, attention, and allegiance.

We're both apelike and angelic. The *secular* goal for most of us in the West is *the* good life. The *spiritual* goal is *a* good life. The *secular* is defined by *Webster's* as both "living in the world" and "the absence of religion." The secular is material, practical, worldly, ordinary, quotidian, and routine. Because it is the normal mode of our lives for most of us, comprising perhaps 98 percent of our attention, it is also culturally reinforced. On the other hand, the *spiritual* is much less frequently experienced and often cast as otherworldly and counter-cultural.

The *secular* is anchored in matter in the largely visible world. The *spiritual* is more concerned with the unseen—with timeless and universal ideas (like character, transformation, redemption, virtue, or meaning). Robert C. Fuller writes: "We encounter spiritual issues every time we wonder where the universe comes from, why we are here, or what happens when we die."[9]

The secular motivation arises mostly from our instinctive drive for self-preservation, achieved through our self-aggrandizement and self-interested hedonism. Hedonism is the pursuit of ease and comfort and the avoidance of pain—physical or psychological. The *spiritual* is a wish to fulfill a fainter, and largely unconscious, yearning for some kind of faraway perfection. This longing may manifest in a vision, including, for example, the Beatific Vision or Nirvana.

A more concrete way to distinguish between these two motivational systems is to contrast their representative ideals. Both our secular and spiritual ideals are important—but also very different from one another. Examples of *secular* ideals would be, "fame, reputation, family honor, social standing, eminence in a profession or sport."[10] Spiritual ideals are different. For example, I've defined *"spirituality"* for myself as the pursuit of the four ideals of wisdom, inner peace, familial love, and compassion. I therefore consider all aspects of my life pertaining to these four ideals to be spiritual subjects.

Another concrete way to describe the difference between the secular and spiritual is by contrasting examples of values. Some values are clearly *secular*, like subsistence, romance, thrift, entertainment, consumption, health, education, longevity, industry, and of course, my personal favorites of success and wealth. Just as clearly, *spiritual* values like integrity, magnanimity, mercy, humility, or acceptance are of a very different order.

Summary

We distinguished beliefs from values as different sources of meaning and purpose. Beliefs and values will both always be indispensable guides. They are distinguishable, but intertwined. For example, one of my beliefs is that values are undervalued by most of us today.

Besides our emphasis on values rather than beliefs in the pages that follow, we'll stress four other aspects of the spiritual life that are less emphasized by much nonreligious spirituality and most religions. These include a focus upon: happiness in this world rather than the next; transformation instead of transcendence; personal instead of institutional responsibility; and contemporaneity to complement more ancient sources of wisdom. I view each of these as perfectly consistent with more traditional views. Just like the richness of balancing secular and spiritual motivations, these different interests and positions can enrich, enhance, and help define one another.

CHAPTER FOUR

SPIRITUAL VALUES OF ONE'S OWN

> Three things are necessary for the salvation of man: to know what he ought to believe; to know what he ought to desire; and to know what he ought to do.
> —St. Thomas Aquinas[11]

The Ease and Comfort of Orthodoxy

In the closing ceremony of a weeklong retreat with a couple hundred seekers, a panel of seven elderly, contemplative monks from different religious traditions answered one final question from the assembly: would they share with us their understanding of

God's will for them. Because, all told, the panel of holy men had been meditating for about three hundred years, I was shocked by the responses of all seven. One after another, each acknowledged that he had *no idea* of God's will for him. About then, I decided that in order to determine my own life's purpose, I'd probably better plan to be on my own.

Christians and Buddhists are aptly described as followers, disciples, petitioners, or obedient servants. As such, I was certainly influenced by opinions like those of St. Thomas above, stating what we all *ought* to believe, desire, and do to achieve salvation. I'd inherited many of my core beliefs. Baptized a Christian as an infant, I became confirmed as a "Soldier of Christ" when I was still playing Cowboys and Indians in the seventh grade.

A year later, I attended a college debate about Senator Joseph McCarthy with my parents. Because of the pride I felt for mom and dad's display of courage when shouted down by the conservative anti-Communist crowd, I embraced their political progressivism, about which I knew next to nothing. So, by age fourteen, I'd inherited my parents' religious *and* political belief systems exactly as bequeathed, with nary the first question.

As an adult, I adopted other institutional answers and agendas as well. Compliance was expected and also much easier than creating my own beliefs. For example, I'd acquiesced to the unspoken, but rigid, protocol governing those of us who majored in philosophy and theology in Catholic universities of my day. Acceptable academic performance required substantial agreement with opinions expressed in the *Summa Theologica* of St. Thomas Aquinas. Period. I'd sold my soul for lousy B-pluses.

My first job after business school was with Chase Manhattan Bank, then a primary lender to South Africa during the most heinous years of apartheid. Focused upon learning corporate finance and cash-flow spreadsheets, I managed to minimize this corporate malfeasance. At lunchtime, my faint pangs of conscience couldn't compete with my hunger pangs. I crossed protest marchers' noontime picket lines to forage at the hotdog stand across the street.

Mark Twain noted the main difficulty with adapting to others' beliefs:

> In religion and politics, people's beliefs and convictions are in almost every case gotten at secondhand, and without examination, from authorities who have not themselves examined the questions at issue, but have taken them at second hand from other non-examiners, whose opinions about them were not worth a brass farthing.[12]

My lifetime of accommodation to institutional orthodoxy showed more than a lack of courage; it showed a lack of imagination. Taking an independent path and actually thinking *for myself* had rarely occurred to me either during my initial (or subsequent) twenty years of life. I likened my institutional compliance to F. Scott Fitzgerald's self-described life. He reported that he had always let others do his thinking for him. "... So there was not an "I" any more. It was strange to have no self."[13]

Whose Responsibility? An Awakening
Pluralism is the great "ism" of our time.[14]

For a long time, I'd studiously avoided any thought that I might need to fashion my own spiritual practice. To this Catholic lad, such a notion sounded chillingly heretical, stirring images of hellfire and Inquisitional torture. "You're kidding, right? Design a spiritual practice better suited to what is most important to *you*? Just who the hell do you think you are?" This question was followed after a while with a whispered rejoinder that began, "But why not?"

Why not a spirituality designed by—and for—each one of us? Why not a practice responding to our particular life, with its unique patchwork of issues, problems, enthusiasms, doubts, capacities, passions, needs, challenges, and beliefs? I'd learned a rather unflattering lesson from my failure to regularly maintain the practice of my two religions. Whether due to a lack of enthusiasm or to my passive resistance, I didn't have sufficient interest to persevere for the long run. I learned that I could only sustain a spiritual practice if I wholeheartedly embraced it.

Why not begin with a blank tablet and selectively incorporate as much of the ancient religious and the contemporary nonreligious values most important to me? Beyond obedience, to what end are we to use our creativity, imagination, insight, and aspirations? What if the Hopi exhortation is correct, and "We are the ones we have been waiting for?" I'd relied on others' maps on my past two spiritual journeys and now I wanted to survey the territory from scratch; to explore uncharted ways to a more fulfilling life of my own. There were two consequences of my decision to forge my own way.

SPIRITUAL VALUES OF ONE'S OWN

A Rebirth. I started listening to my own spiritual voice, one I hadn't heard since I was a child. Finding my voice felt like recovering a part of myself; like being born again. I realized that my heart's deepest desire was to grow and become more of *myself*. Lee Robinson's opening stanza in *The Rules of Evidence* resonated:

> What you want to say most
> Is inadmissible.
> Say it anyway.
> Say it again.[15]

A Personal Investment. I became much more invested in the longevity and success of a spiritual practice I had authored. I owned it then. Therefore I was especially motivated to practice it and make it work.

I ended up by defining spirituality for myself as the practice of my most important spiritual values and ideals. I would examine an eclectic cross section of values. These would include many I inherited from religion, sometimes adapted to be more relevant and useful in my life.

Whose Spiritual Values?

My initial step on this quest was to conduct a rigorous search for a pre-established collection of values I could adopt as my own. Over the centuries, there have been many systems of "virtue ethics," the first of which was taught by Aristotle. All have been based upon his assumption that practicing certain values will result in leading a good life. Through the centuries, subsequent ethical systems featured values selected by the founding teacher as the most critical (to him).

To my surprise and disappointment, I was never able to find any lists of *other* people's virtues, values, or ideals that were very resonant or meaningful *to me*. Ancient systems of religious values seemed to focus on morality—right conduct—that were either too broad, like "Thou shalt not kill"; or too narrow, like dietary laws about fish and pork. I personally believe that we've absorbed most of those moral lessons well enough. I was more interested in a set of values to promote—not more moral precepts—but more life and happiness for all.

Aristotle's values of magnificence, pride, and good temper; or Abraham Maslow's self-actualizing "Being Values" of beauty, uniqueness, order, perfection, effortlessness, and playfulness all sounded great, but weren't particularly important to me. On the other hand, many of the virtues and ideals most important to me weren't found on other's lists. By their very nature, other peoples' lists, including my own in this book, are most effective when used as thought-starters, as fingers pointing to the moon. But other folk's choices, (including one website with three hundred and forty-seven values from which to choose), themselves are not the moon.

Forging a personal spiritual practice of my own chosen values turned out to be the single best decision of my life. I recommend that you consider clarifying and adopting spiritual values of your own, for several reasons.

Personal Meaning. If created and customized by each of us, the practice of our own values will, by definition, be credible, relevant, and useful—to us.

Creativity. Personalizing and organizing these ideals and values was a creative and imaginative act. Most of my spiritual values literally didn't exist until I paid attention to my need for them. Turns out, my deepest values, principles, and ideals were covered by years of indifference or distraction. They were not lying about, to be easily dusted off and displayed. To plumb the depths of my value system, I needed to turn inward and burrow down. Soul searching was an inward quest, requiring challenging introspection that often led to psychological insight.

Contemporary Inspiration. The Bible had been the primary source of inspiration for my great-grandfather, the utopian author Edward Bellamy. He and his children had memorized (and could recite verbatim) hundreds of New and Old Testament passages. But most of our post-college-educated kids don't read the Bible. What will serve as spiritual inspiration for *their* children's children? Richard Foster writes in *The Modern Spiritual Formation Movement:*

> We reject the heresy of the contemporary. The people of God throughout history instruct us in the way of the eternal... We learn from Moses. We learn from Luther. We learn from Joseph of Aramathea. We learn from Catherine of Genoa.[16]

I respectfully, but wholeheartedly, disagree. I've embraced many of the ancient values, including, for example, the

Christian cardinal virtues. But because I need to avail myself of as much knowledge as possible, I have chosen not to ignore the fruits of a few thousand years of more recent sources of wisdom.

CHAPTER FIVE

IDEALS: OUR INSPIRATIONAL META-VALUES

> Man would not be man unless he idealized, unless he constructed ideals of a deliberate and imperative character that guide his life and give it a feeling of urgency as well as direction... Ideals can enrich meaning by bestowing great importance upon virtually anything we do or feel. We [are] guided by ideals that have elicited our love.
> —Irving Singer, Professor of Philosophy, MIT[17]

Our ideals lie along a wide continuum, from the more self-aggrandizing (like becoming a big league third baseman or accomplished guitarist); to more spiritual, noble, or humanitarian goals. As a teenager, reading my utopian ancestor's *Looking Backward,* I was struck by the motivational power of Edward Bellamy's ideals of equality, socialism, and democracy. But rather than the creation of ideal communities, I became more intrigued by the power of ideals, both secular and spiritual, to inspire individuals to transform their personal lives.

I once felt hopelessly inadequate in the face of Jesus' call to "be therefore perfect, even as your Father, which is in heaven, is perfect." (Matthew 5:48) I now understand his invitation as a reference to our deep need to aspire, to idealize, and to exceed our human constraints. The call to perfection comes not from a challenge or command from beyond us, but from an internal yearning to exceed our grasp. Ideals are *our* faraway voices calling from our future. I wanted to create at least a part of my future that would not be constrained by who I've been in my past. And I wanted to find a spiritual vision compelling enough to inspire me to lead a consistently more spiritual life.

Four Ideals

All values are meaningful, but our ideals are the most meaningful values of all. The first step in uncovering my own spiritual value system was to determine the values writ most large—the few overarching ideals which stood out as the most motivating and resonant to me. The examples of two religious friends made this search for my own sources of inspiration a lot easier.

One man is a Quaker who devotes a couple of days a week to preparing and serving food to the homeless and another five days a month sharing a Quaker-based program of nonviolence in the nation's largest federal prison. His preeminent ideals are peace and justice and his most important value is service. Another friend was a Catholic and daily communicant, who died suddenly in his early fifties. John was an extraordinary father, whose five children each spoke about their dad at his funeral. The kids told stories of John's parenting: his constancy, gentleness, magnanimity, and encouragement that embodied his ideal of familial love.

Both these men were inspired by specific ideals derived from their religious beliefs. Their example reminded me that our religious founders have already done most of the heavy lifting in this matter of spiritual ideals. One morning in church, I was struck by the similarities between Paul's Epistle to the Corinthians and the Buddha's teachings on compassion. On the title page of my King James Bible, I scribbled the following pair of columns of the Buddhist and Christian ideals that had always meant the most to me. I later distilled them to my chosen four meta-values, the ideals of wisdom, peace, love, and compassion. These four became the cornerstones and definition of my own spiritual practice and formed the outline of this book.

MY OWN SPIRITUAL IDEALS

<u>Personal Awakening</u>   <u>Interpersonal Ethics</u>

Peace   Wisdom   Love   Compassion

ARE BASED UPON RELIGIOUS SPIRITUALITY'S IDEALS OF:

Christian Attributes	Peace	Omniscience	All-Lovingness	Mercy Of God:
Buddhists' Far Goals:	Non-Attachment	Enlightenment	Loving-Kindness	Compassion

Because Buddhists worship no God, their ideals personify the ideal *man*—the Buddha. Christianity's teachings are considered revealed truths about God, but these truths also reflect the most profound and deepest of our ideals. Heather McHugh writes in *A Physics:*

> ...We put [God] well
> above ourselves, because we meant,
> in time, to measure up.[18]

Simply striving to measure up to my chosen ideals has become my ongoing spiritual practice.

Unfinished Business

Why these four ideals? As they must be, my choices are deeply personal, born of my own history and nature. I chose these four ideals as my principal sources of inspiration because they each have a distinguished genealogy in the world's great religions, although my interpretation and adaptation of them is different in several respects. Mine are earthbound ideals, focused upon my aspirations for *this* world. Also, they tend to be broader and more inclusive than the religious ideals that inspired them.

But in addition, I chose them because I'd struggled with each of them all my life and had work to do in these four areas. My selection of *wisdom* was influenced by my long debate between understanding and faith, my study of philosophy, and by my practice of Buddhism. I also felt a need to re-examine the many ways I surrendered my integrity in favor of more comforting beliefs, fearful of confronting more of the truth about myself and about life.

I chose inner *peace* because my anxiety (largely work related) had shredded my peace of mind for years. I was always moved by the serenity prayer my mother taught me from her time in Alcoholics Anonymous, though it felt for years like an elusive possibility. To make room for greater peace of mind, I hoped to heal some old wounds caused by shame and newer wounds caused by later losses. It was clear that my ability to manifest more peace in the world was dependent upon a gradual evolution toward greater inner peace.

Familial *love* was naturally pivotal to me as a single parent and member of several large families. I'd been both my most loving *and* my most irritable in the safe bosom of my families. And far too often I was settling for mediocrity and half-heartedness in my relationships with siblings, in-laws, and extended family members. How was I to better love?

Choosing *compassion* as a spiritual ideal was the easiest decision of all. I'd spent a lifetime being too busy to serve strangers. Who are these others, and what are they to me? How was I to be of use to the poor?

Ideals Are Inspirational

Our chosen ideals are a source of spiritual energy capable of inspiring our greatest devotion. They inform, empower, and transform us. The commitment I feel to my chosen ideals seems similar to the Buddhist call to "pay homage to the Buddha, to the Dharma, to the Sangha." The practice of my ideals gives me pleasure. This is not complicated: We avoid doing chores, but happily do that which we love. As a kid, I loved to play baseball and I hated ballroom dancing lessons. I still play ball every chance I get and rarely dance. I simply wish to become a little more wise, peaceful, loving, and compassionate more than I happen to want anything else.

Over To You

Questions. Clarissa Pinkola Estes has said, "Asking the proper question is the central act of transformation."[19] I've shared my ideals in order to prompt your thoughts about what is most important to you. I personally ended up with four spiritual ideals. You might be happier with three or six. Spend a period of quiet time to begin to formulate your ideals. You're looking for your strongest needs and heart's desires. It's the heart we're after. You may wish to start by asking yourself questions like these:

- Who do I wish to become?

- What do I really care about?

- How can I expand my spiritual experience?

- How can I open my mind and my heart?

- What interests engage me the most?

- What do I need to redeem, heal, amend?

IDEALS: OUR INSPIRATIONAL META-VALUES

- For what do I need to forgive myself?

- What do I love?

Some other questions or exercises:

Notice the sources of your ideas for possible ideals: family or religious instructions, a book, a sermon, a life-changing or life-threatening experience. Identify the key influences on your inner life.

A contemporary school of "intuitive ethics" (at Moralfoundations.org) recognizes a cluster of five foundational values they found are common to all cultures: caring, fairness, loyalty, respect, and sanctity. Abraham Maslow named the dozen ideas he thought were the most important to self-actualizing people. These were "The Being Values" of truth, beauty, goodness, freedom, life, uniqueness, justice, order, perfection, effortlessness, playfulness, and self-sufficiency. Do any fit for you or trigger other ideas?

Your ideals may be found among the burning issues of the day, like these: world peace, freedom, ecology, the right to life or to choice, humane incarceration, animal rights, homelessness, feminism, global warming, the alleviation of hunger, education, maternal and child health, equality, child welfare. Are any of these, or others, crucial to you?

Sometimes your interest in an ideal may be relatively recent. For example, the following ideas mostly became gut issues for me only as I grew older: animal rights, infants, families, foreign aid, poverty, world hunger, Africa, Latin America, migrant farm workers, permaculture, community gardens. Take time to make your own list, and add to it as realizations come to you. They may coalesce into an ideal or two.

Other starting points to think about your most important ideals might be ideas like these: charity, community, connections, faithfulness, freedom, harmony, honor, justice, nonviolence, service, truth, and unity. Which of these, or others, does your heart long to encourage or promote?

CHAPTER SIX

SPIRITUAL HAPPINESS IN THIS WORLD

> 'Does God really exist? How does He exist? What is He?' are so many irrelevant questions. Not God, but life, more life, larger, richer, more satisfying life is, in the last analysis, the end of religion.
> —Quoted by William James[20]

A World Apart: From Transcendence to Transformation

The ancient religions are pathways to eventual blessed transcendence: the promise of everlasting life for Christians; and for

Buddhists, the opposite promise—the cessation of eternal, reincarnated life. After my doubts about eternal life, I became very interested in learning the contemplative method of Centering Prayer from the abbot of a Trappist monastery in Spencer, Mass. Three years later, a few miles away in Barre, I learned the insight meditations of Buddhism.

I'd been seduced and enthralled by reports from novice meditators similar to the following one written some years later. "For the next five months, I lived in a state of uninterrupted deep peace and bliss… I spent almost two years sitting on park benches in a state of the utmost joy."[21] These kinds of reported experience sounded to me like a lot of spiritual bang for the buck. Learning to practice mystical contemplation sure looked like the least effortful, and occasionally glorious, option of choice. But after a while, I began to understand that although Christian contemplative prayer and Buddhist meditation could be lovely, I didn't seem to have the meditative skills or patience to make either of these my primary practice. As a work addict and single parent with four kids, I may not have been the most likely candidate for contemplative success.

An even bigger obstacle than my immersion in the secular world, however, was my expectations that meditation *should* yield blissful results and offer an escape from more mundane challenges to spiritual growth. What I'd *wanted* was a spiritual practice that was transcendent, comforting, easy, solitary, elegant, orderly, and occasionally blissful. What I *got* was most certainly not that. I came to understand that my life's purpose, my spiritual path, was not transcendence to a more sublime, peaceful place. Rather, my lot was to work towards transformation and growth in *this* world.

My relinquishment of the dream of a more transcendent spiritual life began the new challenge of finding more meaning and value in this world by paying closer attention to my mundane, everyday circumstances. The idea that the secular world might favorably inform and influence our spiritual lives is a departure from most religious teachings, which segregate the sacred from the profane. Further, religions position themselves as not only distinct from, but also *above*, the ordinary world. But I think that spirituality is most needed *beyond* the walls of the cathedral, in the cauldron of the world where we spend the vast majority of our time. A spirituality of this world is, by its material circumstance, experiential and interactive. It is the source of two particular blessings.

1. *This World as a Source of New Spiritual Values*

One spiritual advantage to be mined from attending more closely to the circumstances enveloping and engaging us in this world is ironically found in the very personal problems presented in our quotidian life. These personal challenges, in turn, trigger our awareness of the need to search for spiritual values that offer new and better solutions to our old, recurring problems. These dilemmas then become opportunities for solutions and growth. In my case, if these issues pertain to any of my four ideals of wisdom, peace, love, and compassion, I would consider these new values spiritual. For example, practicing the spiritual value of magnanimity has helped to reduce my resentment with my partner; and more faithful attention to the value of satisfaction has moderated both my experience of desire and envy.

2. *This World as a Source of New Spiritual Rituals*

> The more engaged we are in the material world, the more spiritual we will be. The more spiritually awake we are, the more generously we will engage material existence."
>
> —Thomas Moore[22]

Alan Jones, a British Episcopal priest, courageously talks about the challenge of living a spiritual life in the midst of a secular world. He reports that he is "a believer" for about thirty seconds each day, when he is *very* still in prayer. The rest of the day he is an atheist. Before he dies, his aspiration is to double his faithful devotion—to one minute each day.[23] If we can learn to more seamlessly integrate the spiritual into the tempo of our everyday lives, we can celebrate our spiritual role more frequently. I don't know what the right balance between the spiritual and secular hemispheres will eventually be for me, but I know that two or three percent of my waking life was far too little to accomplish any meaningful spiritual growth.

To restore more balance between my secular and spiritual lifestyles, I tried (and failed) in my thirties to increase my time spent apart from the world, in cloistered prayer and meditation. For me, a much better strategy has been to look for spiritual experience beyond the cloister, a practice imbedded in the everyday and everyplace. Gandhi's idea resonates: "My life is my prayer."

―――

Religious rituals have long been understood as choreographed, liturgical, ceremonial, formal, and solemn rites. In my case, the repetition of the elegant religious rituals had lost some of their emotional impact. I wanted to celebrate new daily rituals in, and not removed from, the world. Being more grounded in the everyday has increased my attentiveness to my sensate environment that can provide immanent occasions for new kinds of rituals: the spontaneous celebration of life most immediately at hand.

These rituals are not scheduled events, but spontaneous experiences that generate, as traditional rituals do, possibilities for deeper insight and feeling. Such peak experiences are not limited to the sight of tall ships under full sail or the predawn sound of roars of howler monkeys. Just pregnant, magic moments in a child's question; or in our kitchens or soup kitchens; in a therapist's office; or in the wilderness—all as sacred as those in a priest's confessional.

These experiences *change us* because they open our minds and hearts. In these moments, when I most fully appreciate the worth of this world (or a small part of it), I feel humility, awe, gratitude, wonder, delight, poignancy, or even laughter. At an American-Albanian wedding reception, we joined four hundred and fifty other celebrants in endless rounds of spiraling dancers, moving to entrancing village music, in eye contact with one, after another. The ritual of the folk dance surely felt as loving, inclusive, joyful, intimate—*sacred*—as the archbishop's Solemn High Mass two hours earlier in the magnificent gilded basilica.

These experiences *are changed by us* into something holy. Teilhard de Chardin taught that the individual soul is impelled to "undertake to divinize, transform, and complete the world to… 'subject a little more matter to spirit.'" [24] When we stop to notice beauty, love, loss, history, kindness, or suffering, we extend the reach of the sacred to spiritualize our tiny part of our gravitational world. Thomas Moore writes, "Our natural tendency is to seek spirituality in the thin air of abstraction rather than in the concrete life all around us..."[25]

CHAPTER SEVEN

TRANSFORMATION TO MORE SPIRITUAL VALUES

The most radical division... of humanity is that which splits it into two classes of creatures: those who make good demands upon themselves, piling up difficulties and duties; and those who demand nothing special of themselves, but for whom to live is to be every moment what they already are, without imposing on themselves any effort towards perfection; mere buoys that float on waves.[26]
—Jose Ortega y Gasset, Spanish philosopher

Challenge

After a round of golf or a photography shoot, when others are recalling the great shots that bring them back to their most satisfying moments, I'm making a list of things I need to do to repair my iron play or nighttime exposures. The challenge to "make good demands upon" myself was first delivered in the fifth grade by Sister Mariam Joseph, who was, hands down, the most demanding and most memorable of my teachers. A conversation in Abraham Verghese's novel *Cutting For Stone* reminded me of Sister's challenges to constantly improve us. The young protagonist in the novel has asked a nun who mentored him about choosing his life's work. She replies:

> What is the hardest thing you can possibly do? Why settle for *Three Blind Mice* when you can play the *Gloria*? ... Not Bach's Gloria. Yours. Your *Gloria* lives within you. The greatest sin is not finding it, ignoring what God made possible in you.[27]

By my forties, I'd already had more than my share of comfort and ease in my spiritual life. Søren Kierkegaard was surely writing about me: "They have changed Christianity into too much of a *consolation,* and forgotten that it is a *demand* upon men."[28] I felt stagnant, a little bored, and ready for more challenge. I chose to practice a spirituality that would be challenging enough to change—and not merely comfort—me. This commitment to personal change sounded straightforward enough. But all change is hard, and spiritual transformation has been no exception.

The Comfort Zone: The Enemy of Change

In the field of adult development, the primary challenge is to close the gap between what we all *want* to change and what we *actually do* change. Even when the stakes are higher than discarded New Years' resolutions, most of us fail to make real and lasting change. Following a stroke or heart attack, in the face of certain prospects of an earlier death, six of seven patients are unable to execute doctor-recommended lifestyle changes like non-smoking, exercise, and weight control.

As hedonic creatures, we prefer to devote most of our time and attention—secular and spiritual, psychological and physical—snuggled safely inside our comfort zones. My previous three years of practicing the culture's "effortless spirituality" had been an example of an appealing comfort zone. The comfort zone is our state of regression: our place of rest; the status quo, home, inertia. In our wealthy culture, much of our hedonic pain is more psychological than physical. And today, our pleasure most frequently consists of our personal comfort and ease. Bill Bryson notes in *At Home* that the idea of comfort was not even introduced until 1770. Since then, the broad availability of comfort has hijacked our lives. Bryson writes, "If you had to summarize it in a sentence... the history of private life is a history of getting comfortable..."

In addition to our strong instinctive preference for the ease, familiarity, and ingrained habits of our comfort in the status quo, each of the changes we make to a new, spiritual value must overcome three other obstacles. The first is *myopia*, the tendency of most of us to place a higher value on the short term and to therefore procrastinate about more valuable longer-term options.

The second difficulty is our natural *risk avoidance*. Trying a new, untested spiritual value is a risky proposition because it may well have worked for one writer, or friend, or saint, but not work well for us.

The third obstacle to personal change is our *aversion to loss*. Transformation is hard because we never want to let go of anything—yet are challenged to abandon everything. The adoption of a new spiritual value always involves relinquishing some cherished aspects of our old behaviors. We may need to leave behind a relationship, a habit, our skepticism, or our independence.

The Process of Spiritual Transformation

"Attention is the cardinal psychological virtue. On it depends the other cardinal virtues, for there can hardly be faith nor hope nor love for anything unless it first receives attention."[29] This means paying closer attention to our feelings, beliefs, pleasures, hurts, and attitudes often just under the everyday level of awareness—in our personal unconscious. The sequence of transformation seems to follow an introspective path something like this:

- We are mindful of our commitment to pursue our chosen ideals.

- We notice a current attitude or behavior or emotion that is inconsistent with the pursuit of the ideals we've adopted. It could be delusion, reaction to loss, addictions, stress, resentment, lack of generosity… My usual problems often festered until I was finally ready to acknowledge the need for a new direction. For example, for years I minimized the costs to my family (and to me) of my compulsive overworking. And I disturbed my own peace of mind by avoiding, rather than dealing with, the early deaths of two women I had loved most in the world.

- We become more clear about the advantages and costs of staying in the old patterns as well as those involved in changing our response and adopting a more spiritual value.

- We come to realize that the self-inflicted problems and self-constructed obstacles we've created by this old, tired response may be optional and unnecessary.

- We explore alternative ideas for responses more likely to further our chosen ideals. Some of my spiritual values were learned through personal experience. Most often, the sources of my spiritual solutions were authors, monks, therapists, parents, colleagues, or friends.

- We sort out an alternative value that would both ease our problems *and* further one of my spiritual ideals.

- We experiment living with them, one at a time.

Over to You: Clarifying Values of Your Own

First and foremost, this is a book of values. Spiritual values are both a set of principles *and* practical solutions to problems. Shortly, I'll begin to describe my process of discovery of each of my sixty-odd spiritual values. Because the spiritual values most useful to us are so idiosyncratic, my own process of selecting values was largely a solitary and interior one. The discussion of my values is offered as a stimulus to jumpstart your own collection.

As you read about each of them, you may want to make margin notes about any of the spiritual values I chose that might be useful to help you deal with issues in your life. You'll certainly want to add values of your own that better correspond to your chosen ideals and life circumstances. This process of selecting and then winnowing down your values shouldn't be rushed. Perhaps the best way to describe the clarification and arrangement of our personal values is "chaordic," which is described as "the process of order emerging from chaos." As you read on, just let it evolve.

The first source of chaos is our memories. Awareness of our core values are subject to the laws of entropy—they become disordered and then forgotten over time. I was amazed at the number of values (like humility and equality, for example) I had learned as a child, but had not thought about for decades. In this process, specificity is challenging, but critical. "We are searching for the power inherent in simply naming things, for that which we cannot name is lost to us, and that which we can name is coaxed to life."[30]

To be most useful, a personal list of spiritual values needs to be comprehensive—but also concise enough to be manageable. You may select subsidiary values that help define and nest inside a more general one. You can anticipate an ongoing tension between a complete list versus one selective enough to effectively focus your attention. After adding values to my own list, I had to combine some and cull others, like distilling a broth or chiseling a stone sculpture.

Some ways I organized my own values may be helpful to you:

- Spiritual values are subsets of the particular spiritual ideal they promote.

- I've adopted every spiritual value by growing into it a little at a time.

- The spiritual values I've chosen are the ones I've most *needed* to work on (and have therefore been the ones yielding the greatest rewards).

- I had embraced some values for many years; more often, I identified others I intended to adopt from that point forward.

- I tapped three different sources of values. The first are so universal as to be thought of as innate components of our human nature or of the natural law. The source for another group of values was one or another of the ancient religions. A third source has been the last century or so of our larger culture.

CHAPTER EIGHT

IDENTITY AS CHARACTER

> Morality is character. Character is that which is engraved.
>
> —Søren Kierkegaard[31]

Identity

Espousing the spiritual ideals and values most important to me created new *meaning*. For my life's *purpose,* I simply chose to live a more spiritual life by working to realize more of those ideals and values. My third existential decision was about my *identity*: to learn more about "Who I am."

We each lead lives so varied and disparate that any comprehensive look at our many facets is too broad and fragmented to be meaningful. Our second eldest child, Siri, recently wished me a happy birthday with a note that began: "There are so many Neds: athlete Ned, photo Ned, silly dressing Ned, diet Ned, travel Ned, movie Ned, humor Ned, animal lover Ned, donuts are food Ned, baby lover Ned...." There followed a list of 45 more, and she said she, "was just getting started... Happy birthday to all these Neds and more!" We're all multifaceted. To cope with this diversity, we compensate by constricting our self-definitions in our resumes, in which we concentrate on only a few select aspects of our universe: professional titles, achievements, schooling, family—all bereft of any nuanced view of what makes us who we are.

Character

I wonder if a better source of our identities might be our character. Character is the sum of our secular and spiritual values and ideals. The formation of our character is the end and objective of transformation. Character is that which a person has held most dear, stands for, believes most worthwhile. Character is a pattern of behaviors and attitudes that describe a unique person with unique contributions. A distinguishing trait shared by people of character is a resolute alignment with their principles. The alternative is to "leave impressions not so lasting as the imprint of an oar upon the water."[32]

The notion of character emanated from the feudal age of French heroic tales of chivalry. The ideal knight possessed the virtues of integrity, chastity, fairness, and generosity. He personified honor, valor, bravery, and gallantry. This martial pedigree accounts for the curious fact that since the end of the Victorian period, active military officers are the few people who still seem to use the language of character. They articulate fierce, holy words, like *honor, duty, courage, sacrifice, valor, loyalty, devotion, ideals...*

Today, in the general culture, the notion of character has been replaced by the idea of personality, first celebrated ironically as the key to a successful sales career by Willie Loman in *Death of A Salesman*. Describing some students he interviewed at Princeton, journalist David Brooks writes in *The Atlantic:*

> ...It's hard to imagine what it would be like to be a Saint, but it's easy to see what it is to be a success... When it comes to character and virtue... suddenly the laissez-faire ethic rules: you're on your own, Jack and Jill. Go figure out what is true and just for yourselves....[33]

Character Formation through Disciplined Habits

How do we form the spiritual habits that create character? I'd noticed during my secular sabbatical that in this period there was no spiritual program or process in my life–no *practice*. I watched my own intention and the kids' spiritual attention become more occasional, and then simply vanish, swept away in the undertow of the secular culture. I began to understand the biggest cultural challenges to practicing a more spiritual life were not atheism, fundamentalism, or even lost faith. The problems were more insidious—and included apathy, distraction, and sloth.

"Aristotle believed that we should practice living by the virtues, making them such a consistent part of our behavior that... we become the virtues... If we act justly again and again, eventually we will become just."[34] The virtue of discipline is required to persevere in the habitual practice of spiritual values and engrave them in our everyday routines. For years, I'd taken for granted the benefits of responding to the demands of Jesus and the rigorous lessons of the Buddha. Another beneficial legacy of my once religious life had become apparent.

In Zanzibar, I was inspired by contemporary religion's most effective spiritual habituation. Muslims begin each day with the muezzins' five a.m. call to prayer from public address systems atop the forty-eight mosques in Stone Town. I was very moved watching the disciplined devotion of tens of thousands of men, women, and adolescents. They streamed like flash floods through narrow bazaars and medina alleyways, in both directions, ten times a day, every day—for their lifetimes.

Habits Require Attentiveness

Inspired as I was by the display of Muslim devotion, I well knew I was not prepared to replicate it. I had tried a practice of intensive and disciplined prayer and meditation and failed to persist in the practice. Yet I realized that my spiritual growth was going to require *some* kind of regular prompts to counter the incessant distractions of my secular life. Spiritual life in a secular world seems like a garden planted in the wilderness. A spiritual garden, like all gardens, represents that which Michael Pollan describes below from *Second Nature*.

> [A garden is] a kind of ecological vacuum, which nature will not abide for long. Most garden plants are, let's face it, nature's weaklings... The forest is so vigorous... that a single season of neglect would blast my garden back to meadow... It requires continual human intervention or else it will collapse.[35]

Short Term Attention. Bill Plotkin, in *Soulcraft,* says that we each harbor an image inside us that makes sense of all the other images in our life. For me, one candidate for an idiosyncratic image was that of a serpent who reappeared for a while in many dreams. Another image was a chrysalis, the symbol of metamorphosis I once chose as the name for a business. But soon after my collection of values was clarified, I chose the mandala as my most salient image. Driven by the dictates of readability on a standard page, I distilled about a third of my chosen values and incorporated them on a drawing. I update them to include the values I'm finding the most challenging at that time.

A Sanskrit word meaning "sacred circle," mandalas engage our imagination to help synthesize and focus our fragmented attention. The holographic diagram of my personal values and ideals serves as a tool of self-discipline, a reminder, a checklist, a summary, a visual aid, a target.

The mandala can be imagined as a static snapshot or as a dynamic illustration of growth over time. I also imagine it as the psyche (the soul); a character wheel; a compass to orient me; an operating system; and even a garden to plant, nurture, and harvest.

I imagine my secular values lie inside the circle of my spiritual values, because they are instinctively more insistent and usually pre-conscious. God or Spirit could be included on a mandala drawing in two different places. If a transcendent reality, a deity could be represented beyond the outside edge of the mandala, representing infinity. If imagined as immanent, Spirit could occupy the center of the drawing. And, of course, Spirit can be drawn in both places.

A Soul's Compass
CHARACTER WHEEL

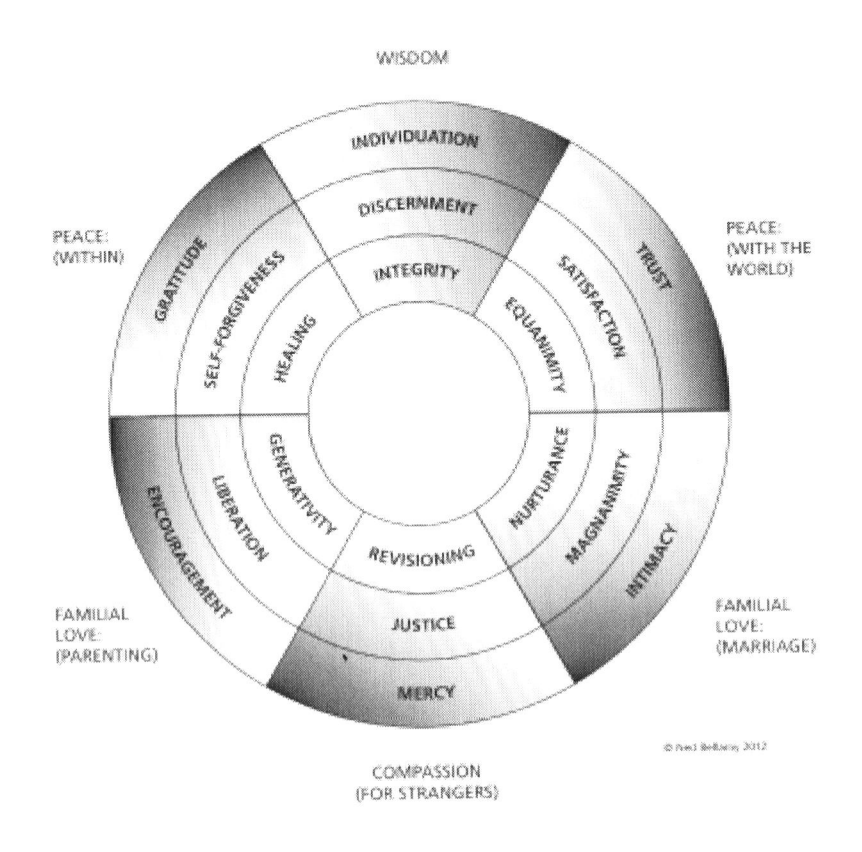

Long-Term Intention. Unlike the conversion experience of being "born again," this sort of transformation to the regular practice of our spiritual values is not a sudden baptismal infusion of Spirit. For me, it's more like hundreds of small insights, decisions, and behaviors, one spiritual value at a time, until they become habituated.

With powerful binoculars and six people pointing to him from our canoe offshore, it took fifteen minutes for me to locate a large sloth in a tall Amazonian tree—in plain sight. Like other predators, I was predisposed to detect movement, and there was almost no movement to detect. I still wonder at the imperceptibility of his locomotion. Sometimes living a more spiritual life feels that gradual—and as well camouflaged.

Three Characters

Though the word "character" is no longer part of our daily lexicon, we still know character when we see it. At a recent family wedding, I was reminded how much I admire the values and ideals of my brother-in-law. As head of a neonatal unit in a New York teaching hospital, John used his unusual combination of diagnostic and leadership skills to help save the lives of hundreds of premature infants. But people respond to John mostly because of the strength of his character. Upon his retirement, scores of the resident pediatricians he had trained came together to recount stories of the values he stood for and had imparted to them all: his devotion as a parent, a steadfast religious faith, a clear medical ethic, a genuine interest in the lives of his staff, and the quality of his mentoring, all imbued with loyalty, kindness, compassion, and humility.

Another friend was a committed Baptist, but no one, including his family, had ever imagined the full extent of his evangelical commitment. During her eulogy for him, his wife shared a discovery made two nights earlier about her partner of fifty years. When she was selecting her husband's clothes for his burial, she came across a folded note in the toe of a rarely worn dress shoe; she said the shoe was so formal it was only suitable to be buried in. The yellowed note consisted of a handwritten list of names of ninety-four men with whom he had shared his faith. She realized the small checkmarks next to some names indicated those who had become active Christians, as a result of his intercession. As she scrolled down his secret list, she realized he'd scheduled breakfast and luncheon dates for the day he died with two of the twenty-nine people whose names remained unchecked. I was reminded in that packed church of the words of psychologist James Hillman: "People who have left remain as a force of character."

On my father's ninety-second birthday, his five children and a few other family members gathered to deliver our eulogies to him in person. While he could still hear it, we wanted to share what he had meant to us—what we'd learned from him, thought he stood for, made him unique, made him "a character." Two grandchildren serenaded him with old Presbyterian spirituals and original rap music. I spoke to him of his abiding good nature and sense of humor; his wisdom and erudition; his egalitarianism and liberalism; his redemption after fifty years of alcoholism; his long service to hundreds of folks in AA. Some of what we said surprised him; many of our stories amused him. But mostly, his rheumy eyes sparkled with tears of gratitude. He realized that we really had known and seen him and valued his legacy.

Over to You

Numerous books about mandalas are available, including *Creating Mandalas* by Susanne Fincher. *Google Images* has a website that illustrates shapes available to combine with a circle. They have sides or points varying from three through eight (triangles, squares, pentagons, hexagons, heptagons, and octagons) to accommodate the number of ideals you may choose.

PART THREE: FROM HEDONISM TO THE IDEALS OF WISDOM & PEACE

The two largest obstacles to spiritual growth are my hedonism and my self-interest. Here in Part Three, we'll deal with the first of these challenges. My hedonism most often takes the form of my desire for short-term comfort and ease, or my fear of emotional discomfort. This combination of desire and fear inhibits my pursuit of wisdom and peace. I'll share the spiritual values that interdict my hedonic drives and free me to more frequently practice both these ideals.

I THE IDEAL OF WISDOM

For Christians, wisdom is described quite narrowly, as a gift from the Holy Spirit to help us discern the revelations and will of God. I much prefer a Buddhist definition, which casts a wider net: "Wisdom is the ability to understand 'deeply the truth of how things are.'"[36]

A Deeper Wisdom: The Value of Self-Understanding

The Psychological Life. After a century of useful discoveries, the psyche's central role in our lives is still often unacknowledged by many, including some humanists and religious people. The psychological notion of the unconscious is seen by humanists as a threat to the power of reason, which they regard as the keystone of human progress. For Christian churches, the unconscious is a threat to the power of our will, undermining the notion of our ultimate responsibility for sin.

Often, Eastern religious monks have also been dismissive of the need for modern Western psychological insight. Following five years of intensive meditation practice in India, a prominent American spiritual teacher described a humbling experience a couple of years after his return to the States. He acknowledged that enlightenment had *not* prepared him to cope with a series of chaotic, failed love relationship that ended with a nervous breakdown in his California hot tub. He subsequently addressed these issues through psychotherapy.

The last century's psychological discoveries have dramatically increased our understanding of human nature. Since my spiritual practice is focused on humankind in this world, I decided to learn as much as I could about the psyche. Thomas Moore, a therapist and former monk, writes, "In the modern world we separate religion and psychology, spiritual practice and therapy…[But] psychology and spirituality need to be seen as one."[37]

My recovery, therapy, meditation, and writing have all helped further my self-understanding. Experience has convinced me that the relative health and strength of our psyche is the single largest determinant of both our secular and spiritual well being and happiness. For example, my delusions had been obstacles to further wisdom. Reducing my anxiety increased my peace of mind. Psychological wisdom helps us to understand others, and therefore affects our practice of the ideals of love in our families and compassion beyond them.

I THE IDEAL OF WISDOM

A Broader Wisdom: A Larger Canvas

The Exterior Life. The Merriam-Webster dictionary defines wisdom as "the ability to judge soundly and deal sagaciously with facts, especially as they relate to life and conduct." The vast majority of the wisdom we assemble over a lifetime concerns exclusively secular matters, which are not of concern here. But secular and spiritual subjects seem to overlap more frequently in the contemporary world. Are the following examples, instances of secular or spiritual wisdom—or both?

The new narrative of creation and the end time, once the exclusive province of religion, are now stories told by scientists. All these great myths require faith of one kind or another. The new story is founded upon the discoveries of the last half-century in cosmology, astronomy, chemistry, geology, physics, biology, and archeology. I'm personally inclined to believe the story of the Big Bang. But the explanation certainly *sounds* less comprehensible and more speculative than Genesis or the Revelation story of Saint John the Divine. The entire universe was created, not by God in *seven days,* but by protons and neutrons in *three minutes*? Yikes.

Solomon's great wisdom was most famously applied in a very mundane adjudication of a civil dispute between a pair of mothers both claiming an infant as her own. This religious lesson began as a very practical and secular legal matter. As culture becomes more complex, the interface between politics and ethics requiring *both* secular and spiritual wisdom seems more intertwined. Aren't subjects like euthanasia, the death penalty, animal rights, family planning, gay marriage, ecology, immigration, and stem cell research all practical political and legal problems *as well as* ethical issues requiring spiritual discernment?

More Sources of Wisdom: The Value of Diversity

In an effort to provide more informed and reliable grounds for my own beliefs, I try to access diverse sources of my personal experience as well as others' experience.

Varied Personal Experience. According to Webster's, "Understanding is the power to render experience intelligible." Diverse experiences for me have typically included travel, work, play, and volunteering, as different from one another as possible. I've always learned more from construction crew members, orphans, villagers, and inmates than from other corporate types like myself. Direct experiences like these are most trustworthy of all. Ultimately, my own decision about religious belief was based upon a single undeniable facet of my personal experience. After thousands of hours in prayer and meditation and years of study, I'd never *experienced* the slightest intuition, sense, or awareness of God's existence or presence. Not the first inkling. Bonhoeffer was right. "An abstract belief in God is not a genuine experience of God."[38]

Long before détente, I arranged a romantic wedding anniversary celebration aboard my imagined version of the Orient Express, a ride on an overnight luxury train between Prague and Budapest. Turned out, this luxury train hadn't been painted in a half-century nor cleaned in years. The dining car had been bolted shut for a long time due to food rationing. The "Express" was boarded five times that night by Communist border guards. Demanding identification, they handcuffed and hauled away dozens of people in their pajamas. Romantic, indeed. Only after that sleepless *experience* did I understand how bankrupt Communism had been in Eastern Europe for decades.

I THE IDEAL OF WISDOM

Eclectic Evidence from Others. I became unwilling to rely on any single religious or nonreligious source claiming the exclusive truth about anything, whether about one subject or many. Rather than limit my spiritual sources to those that were ancient, immutable, exclusive, and final (i.e. closed), I explored more eclectic sources of wisdom. I believe that my most valid beliefs are likely to be those based upon the widest and deepest understandings of our objective and subjective worlds. The spirituality presented in this book refers to sources that are religious and secular, ancient and contemporary.

Opening ourselves to more varied reading patterns is an easy way to learn from others' experience. I have highlighted some books in the bibliography I found of particular interest. For example, *Scripts People Live* was the first book that revealed the impact of psychological matters in my families. At the moment, the night stand includes books as varied as *Steve Jobs*, *Gaia's Garden*, *The Wisdom Jesus*, and *The African Experience*.

In Africa for a couple of months, I attended twenty lectures on bio-intensive gardening, pastoralists, Big History, game reserve management, slavery, Islam, animal tracking and behavior, rural poverty relief, geology, archeological sites, Swahili, East African bird life, water management, HIV prevention... I loved the diverse points of view and learning of the direct experience of so many others about Africa.

Summary

The Value of Self-understanding. My spiritual ideal of wisdom encompasses both my interior and exterior worlds. For most of us, increasing our self-understanding is the harder task, which we'll return to frequently in the balance of the book.

<u>The Value of Diversity.</u> The two primary sources of wisdom for me are experiential and eclectic: both my experience and the experience of others gleaned through conversation and reading.

CHAPTER NINE

THE VALUE OF INTEGRITY (INSTEAD OF COMFORT)

> ...[W]e must be totally dedicated to truth. We must always hold truth, as best we can determine it, to be more important, more vital to our self-interest, than our comfort.
> —Scott Peck, *The Road Less Traveled* [39]

Enchantment: Hedonism and Our Comforting Delusions

Our beliefs are extremely powerful, because as Anton Chekhov has written, "Man is what he believes."[40] The extent of our wisdom is based upon the quality of our beliefs about ourselves, others, and our world. There are innumerable reasons for distorted beliefs, but I want to discuss the single most pervasive one: our instinctive hedonism. We desire to tell ourselves good (i.e., comforting) news and fear to let ourselves know of the bad. These desires and fears keep us in a fog of delusion.

Delusion is a combination of illusion and denial, which have a causal relationship. The more I deny one aspect of discomforting reality, the more I'll need to replace it with a soothing illusion of my own making. We delude ourselves about objective and exterior reality, as well as about ourselves. I'll share in the chapters that follow many of the ways I've personally done so.

But perhaps the most familiar illustration of how extensive are the routine lies we tell ourselves (and therefore, each other) may be the following perennial public policy debate. Both political parties promote their most favored and unaffordable programs: for progressives, the eradication of poverty; and for conservatives, an impenetrable national defense. Both have always been based upon the *illusion* of inexhaustible, Rumplestiltskin-like wealth and the *denial* of the need for sacrifice through other budget cuts or tax increases to pay for either (less than both) initiative(s).

Another, less public, example. Many friends insist that people with more positive and optimistic attitudes will generally enjoy longer, cancer-free lives. This belief is *illusory* because its proponents *deny* the published research, to wit: "There is no evidence that... positive characteristics like optimism or spirituality... can prevent any illness or help someone recover from one more readily."[41]

THE VALUE OF INTEGRITY (INSTEAD OF COMFORT)

Commitment To Truth: Why Bother?

I have a dear friend who would argue: "Why *not* live with beliefs about the future that make us feel good, precisely *because* they make us feel good? Life is hard enough. What's the harm in opting for beliefs that give us the highest order of comfort?" (To which I might reply by asking if we should also believe in Mother Goose?)

During recessions, retailers frequently threaten to withdraw their advertising expenditures unless their local newspapers refrain from publishing negative economic news that discourages consumers. *The New York Times* publicly responded to its own advertisers, thusly: "[Our newspaper's] master is reality… it is its duty to look bad news in the face."[42] But why *should* we choose "to look bad news in the face?" Why adopt beliefs based upon our informed impressions of the objectively real? Why try to understand more of the truth, even when the belief is not comforting and the learning is not easy?

The Foundation of Wisdom: The Value of Integrity

The components of integrity include good faith, truthfulness, and realism. Integrity is the good-faith attempt to determine as much of the truth as we can, as best we can. I find the most compelling description of integrity are these words of John Huss, a Czech reformer, burned at the stake in 1415.

> Seek the truth,
> Listen to the truth
> Teach the truth,
> Abide by the truth and
> Defend the truth unto death.[43]

The alternative to integrity—bad faith and lying to oneself—is, by definition, inconsistent with the spiritual ideal of wisdom. For example, I showed *bad* faith by convincing myself for too long that I believed in God, and did so for the wrong reasons: because I was supposed to; because belief felt good; because I hated to quit anything; and because I wanted to hedge my bet on the possibility of a hereafter.

It took decades to understand how seriously I'd compromised my integrity during this extended period of conflicted faith. My denial compromised my conscience. In the end, I was lying to others and myself. And for what? Finally, I had to choose between losing my religious faith or my good faith. I had to change my focus from the comforting eternal *benefit* of remaining a Christian to the immediate *cost* of staying: my integrity.

The Value of Realism. What do we mean by "the truth?" Thousands of books have dealt with that question more competently than I. But for me, the short form definition is summarized in this comment from Scott Peck: "Truth is reality... Mental health is an ongoing process of dedication to reality at all costs."

The polarity of the real and ideal can be synthesized. The most useful idea is one that both inspires us to reach for an ideal *and* works in the world. My most satisfying job was with a Rockefeller-family-owned, Latin American development company. It was founded upon an inspiring *ideal:* to invest capital in emerging countries only in financially sustainable—*practical*—projects designed to relieve economic bottlenecks. For example, the company founded the first concrete ready-mix company in Chile and the first modern supermarket in Venezuela.

Martin Luther King was an idealist, but I've been most impressed by the gritty, realistic blend of economic and social activist work he planned and executed. With little money, credibility, or support from whites, he engineered a yearlong public-bus boycott, a sit-in protest against segregated store restrooms, and a sympathy strike for garbage workers. These were banal and hardly inspirational, but *very effective*. King, Mandela, and Lincoln were realists. Gandhi insisted that he was first, a politician.

It is especially necessary that a spirituality of ideals be grounded in the real. Anchoring ourselves firmly to our direct experience of "life as it is" avoids the fanciful illusions and naïve optimism of many New Age beliefs, about which one commentator asked: "Please. *Give me some facts!* Is there any material plane verification for the phantasmagorical assertions that we make?"[44] Thoreau encouraged us to build castles in the air, but only *after* we build foundations under them. Realism is important to me because this spiritual practice is designed to help me more wisely deal with *practical* problems.

Some Practical Advantages of A Commitment to Truth At Any Cost

About fourteen years ago, the AIDS epidemic in Tanzania was a terrifying dragon, slowly awakening, but still largely hidden in the culture's deepest shadows. Because this new disease was usually fatal, even the medical profession in the country's second largest city preferred to avoid dealing with it for its first few years. Moma Elizabeth, pregnant with her third child, had a discomforting premonition about an unhealed lesion on her thigh. She was a well respected traditional healer, but for the next six months none of her medical friends (in and out of the public health system) was willing to administer the HIV blood screen to her. One finally admitted, in response to her persistence, "Elizabeth, forgive me, dear friend. But if the results of the test were unfavorable, I couldn't bear to deliver the awful news to you."

Years later, in a workshop in Arusha, she confided: "I sensed these dear friends were killing me. In desperation, I went to a member of another tribe, no friend of mine. Her clinic confirmed that my fear was founded. I was devastated and prepared the children for my death." Moma was unable to save the first two of her kids who, it turned out, had been infected since birth. They died a few months after their father, who had infected other women in town as well. Nevertheless, Elizabeth told us that she is forever grateful to the one person who overcame the cultural conspiracy of silence and denial, "to share a gift in such short supply in those darkest days—the truth."

Elizabeth shared three reasons for her gratitude. First, after learning of her diagnosis, by delivering her baby by Caesarian section, she was able to save her from infection. Next, she developed a regimen of holistic fruits, vegetables, and herbs that saved her own life, and subsequently hundreds of other women under her care. And finally, "since I couldn't save two of my own," she became determined to undertake the task of saving as many of the kids in her hometown she could.

THE VALUE OF INTEGRITY (INSTEAD OF COMFORT)

It took almost a year to convince the first high school student to be examined. "He was dying alone at home in great pain and shame for many months, not of AIDS, but of third stage syphilis. Then ten girls in his class finally relented to be tested, eight of who tested for STDs. "Thereafter, most of the kids came in to our clinic to learn the truth about themselves. HIV was everywhere, of course. But we've been able to save very, very, many of the children we diagnosed early enough."

Knowing the truth is often necessary for our peace of mind. In spite of the fear of possibly learning disturbing news, sometimes we're hungry for the whole truth. We want to know whether our parenting is too strict or too lenient; whether we've saved enough for retirement; or if we've offended a friend in some way. In Rwanda, for fifteen years, the last surviving member of a Tutsi family searched to find just one Hutu in his village willing to tell him the truth about the circumstances of his father's violent end and the whereabouts of his remains. Asked why he persevered for so long, he answered, "I must know the truth, however painful, before I can consider forgiveness or reconciliation. And I must bury my father so he may finally rest."[45]

Telling ourselves the truth is great practice for honest relationships. If I'll lie to myself because the truth is too discomforting, why would I feel obligated to speak the truth to others, often with more unpleasant consequences? Lying makes intimate relationships impossible, including the one with ourselves. Because lying also dishonors the listener, it violates our love. My preference for telling myself more of the truth originated in the addiction recovery programs' ethos of "rigorous honesty" in our dealings with others. This critical discipline had been especially important for addicts like me, who had long ago become accustomed to lying to ourselves.

The absence of rigorous honesty is hardly conducive to greater wisdom and a more spiritual life. Ninety-one percent of us lie regularly to others, and twenty percent lie every day. Lying to others, like lying to ourselves, is insidious. In business, we slant résumés, press releases, advertising, and even financial statements. We cheat on exams and reporting to the IRS. Many euphemisms reflect the absence of rigorous honesty in our communication with each other. To avoid unpleasant truths, we prefer language like "right-sizing" for layoffs of thousands of people; or "collateral damage" instead of speaking of numberless maimed women and children.

Seeing more of the truth saves us from ourselves. Sooner or later, delusion will cost us. The theologian and scientist Teilhard de Chardin emphasized the consequences of not seeing clearly:

> *Seeing.* We might say that the whole of life lies in that verb… [T]o try to see more and better is not a matter of whim or curiosity or self-indulgence. To see or to perish is the very condition laid upon everything that makes up the universe…[46]

When I started a new business of my own in my forties, a less comforting, but more truthful, appraisal would have revealed that the new company had insufficient cash, and I had insufficient talent, to weather the first economic stiff breeze. Upon our subsequent failure, my delusional thinking about our chances of

THE VALUE OF INTEGRITY (INSTEAD OF COMFORT)

success had cost investors, suppliers, subcontractors, customers, and me a lot of money. Charlie Munger is Warren Buffet's only business partner. He advised his fellow wealthy investors in an Annual Meeting:

> This love of truth…this ethos of not fooling yourself, is one of the best you can possibly have… The reason it works so well outside science is that it's so *rare* outside science. You have a real advantage if you get good at it.

In January of 1977, while our new house was under construction in Warren, Ohio, Mary took Galen, then almost three, to scope out the elementary school. Christina was teaching a class as a volunteer and saw Mary in the hallway with her snow-suited little one in tow. Christina assured Mary that she knew a lot of " the family stuff "in the area and jotted down her phone number on a shard of paper. Mary saved that scrap of connection and six months later called Christina as the moving van pulled out. Our families became good friends. Eight months later, Christina assisted on the altar at Mary's funeral service.

Three years afterwards, Christina and I married. We blended her three delightful kids with my four, and settled in Clearwater. The kids fit together by their ages like a dovetailed joint: Galen, Eric, D'Arcy, Hilary, Ted, Siri, and Marc were then respectively seven, eleven, twelve, thirteen, fourteen, sixteen, and nineteen years old. I had told myself that this whole Brady Bunch thing was going to be a piece of cake. No sweat. I didn't want to know about the inevitable difficulties stemming from seven largely adolescent kids and the merger of two mature families with different and entrenched routines, senses of humor, boundaries, histories, and personalities.

Had all nine of us taken the time to anticipate and talk about some of the predictable, inevitable friction points, we could've hashed much of it out, saved a lot of heartache, and avoided lots of unnecessary tears. (And arguments about closet space, boyfriends, laundry, borrowed sweaters...) My delusion far exceeded the bounds of excusable romantic naiveté. It was irresponsible.

CHAPTER TEN

THE VALUE OF DISCERNMENT (INSTEAD OF EASE)

> No man ever became wise by chance.
> —Seneca[47]

Hedonism: Easy Does It

In the last chapter we noted our strong hedonic preference for beliefs that promise more *comforting results*. Here, I'll address another hedonic preference that also undermines wisdom: the tendency to embrace the *easiest process* by which to formulate our beliefs. Predictably, the combination of the easiest *means* to embrace the most comforting *results* creates a set of beliefs based upon distorted perceptions of reality.

Learning more of the truth can often be difficult, frustrating, and time-consuming. Earlier, we spoke of the easiest ways to adopt entire belief systems: as children, through inheritance from our parents; or as adults, by riding the coattails of a pre-existing group's ideologies. Here, we'll look at three ingrained habits of laziness that distort our beliefs, both secular and spiritual. I need to periodically check to see if I'm in the midst of repeating my old, easy habits that shortchange my increased understanding. Thinking about our thinking, a process called meta-cognition helps us compensate for the tendency to drift toward ease. Following are several values I've found most helpful to minimize some old habits of mind inimical to greater wisdom. Together, they help define what the value of discernment means to me, as well as help me to practice it more skillfully.

1) *Openness to Novelty: New Truths (Rather than Intransigence)*

> As soon as you begin to believe in something, then you can no longer see anything else... The truth you believe in and cling to makes you unavailable to hear anything new.
> —Pema Chödrön[48]

The *easiest* strategy of managing our existing collection of beliefs is to avoid learning anything new. Clinging to the status quo requires only that we not change our minds about any existing belief or opinion. In a Tampa workshop, author Terry Hershey told a story illustrating our bias against admitting new information into our familiar frame of reference. "A hunter was trying out his new retriever for the first time. To fetch the birds, the rookie birddog ran *on top* of the water's surface. Amazed, his owner motioned the neighboring farmer over for a more objective, second opinion about his newly prized dog. After several demonstrations, the neighbor had seen enough. 'I don't believe new dog of yours can swim a lick.'"

If new learning is hard, unlearning is much harder. Not *one* legislator changed his mind during the well-argued and exhaustive Clinton impeachment hearings. Consistency, loyalty, and predictability are comforting ordering devices that often persuade us to leave our existing beliefs well enough alone.

The Willingness to Change Our Minds

If we allow ourselves to see the world in a fresh way, new attitudes, responses, and outcomes may result. Anne Wilson Shaef wrote, "differences challenge assumptions." The smallest change in perspective can yield much greater clarity. The trigger could be a snippet of an article, a conversation, or a friend's problem. A change of *place* might do the trick. Photographers learn that the most visually interesting vantage point could be just two yards to the right. Hoisting a five-year-old Honduran upon my shoulders to watch the annual La Ceiba parade altered his sightline by a mere four feet. But his delight indicated that seeing his first parade was a lot more informative than listening to the previous four.

A change of *time* can also bring a fresh view. As a liberal, I'm embarrassed to report that it took half a century for me to even be willing to really listen to the point of view of conservative writers. And only now can I recognize the spiritual benefits made possible by growing older. For starters, these benefits include the easier embrace of my impermanence, imperfection, and insignificance.

Jungian analyst Robert Johnson describes a technique used to teach debating students the validity of more than one side of every question. Five minutes before an hour-long debate is scheduled to begin, the debate teams are instructed to argue the side of the argument opposite to the one they've spent *three weeks* preparing. As an occasional debater, I can assure you that such a role reversal would have made me completely nuts in law school competitions. No wonder we find it so hard to reverse our positions on issues we've justified for *three decades*.

Fallibilism is defined as an openness to additional arguments or experience that might serve to revise our current point of view. It implies the free admission that our beliefs may be mistaken. Asked whether he'd be prepared to die for his beliefs, the philosopher Bertrand Russell replied, "Of course not. After all, I may be wrong."[49] I hold that most of our beliefs should be considered provisional—probabilities and possibilities—rather than certainties.

But changing our mind requires an acknowledgement that we were once wrong, which I for one am usually very reluctant to do. Lincoln is a refreshing exception to our usual reticence to change. He admitted to changing his position frequently and argued that adaptability was not a fault, but a virtue. "... I don't think much of a man who is not wiser today than he was yesterday."[50]

2) Humility: Less Truth (and Less Certainty)

> Only reason can convince us of these three fundamental truths, without a recognition of which there can be no effective liberty: that what we believe is not necessarily true; that what we like is not necessarily good; and that all questions are open.
> —Clyde Bell

The *easiest* (quickest and simplest) attitude to adopt about any belief is certainty. The closure of certainty just feels more satisfying than ambiguity. But as post-modern people, we share more modest assessments about our abilities to know The Truth, much less The Whole Truth. In addition to the fact that we each make lots of mistakes, other factors modulate our claims of certainty:

- **Our understanding changes.** Scientific facts we once thought were reliable have been upended in the last half-century. The more we learn, the more we learn the extent of our ignorance.

- **Reality changes.** We've learned that over the long term, absolutely everything, including solid matter, changes. And change in the short term is epidemic. Of the 193 nations in the world today, 103 didn't exist in 1960.

- **Our perspectives differ.** Perspectivism is the observation that each person's perception of "the truth" is partially dependent on our unique personal histories and viewpoints.

- **Unintended consequences afflict all future projections.** We are simply unable to forecast the outcome of complex social plans or policies. For example, following the discovery of the New World, the citizens of the Old developed a fondness for some of its bounty, which required large plantations and intense manual cultivation. Who could have guessed the unintended consequences of Europeans' craving for four apparently trivial and innocuous luxuries—sugar, coffee, tobacco, and rum?

- First, there was the enslavement of eleven million Africans and the suffering of millions more of their bereft family members over four hundred years. Second, there were the deaths of millions caused by the addictive overuse of sugar, tobacco, and rum. Tobacco alone killed one hundred million souls in the developed world in only the 20th century.

Uncertainty

I think wisdom is increased through questioning and agnosticism, which is the acknowledgement that sometimes the right answer is "I dunno."

Questioning. Scott Peck said, "The path to holiness lies through questioning *everything*."[51] In my thirties I was invited to join a men's Bible study group with eight evangelical Christians. After listening for six weeks, I questioned (very artfully, I thought) the leader's authoritative (and, incidentally, preposterous) literal interpretation of one or another Old Testament text. My friend and sponsor was discreetly informed that my very occasional questions were likely a sign of the devil's work. For them, the idea of asking questions as a devil's advocate, to encourage debate, was interpreted, like all other matters, quite literally. I was more amused than insulted when advised that my continued presence would be a matter of grave concern. Upon taking my leave, I may have mentioned that I certainly hoped a bona fide agent of the devil would be a more formidable Biblical scholar than I.

Agnosticism. Sometimes the only available truth is to admit not knowing. The absolute certainty expressed by some about the nature and will of God has sounded to me like the opposite of faith. It implies a claim to know the unknowable and explain the unexplainable, and thereby trivializes life's most profound mystery. On the other hand, epistemic humility, the admission that "I don't know" is often misinterpreted as a sign of incompetence, accounting for its rarity in corporate boardrooms and politicians' press conferences. Once again, Lincoln is my spiritual teacher. Though his understanding of the national crisis of slavery and the war clearly surpassed that of every other contemporary commentator of record, the person responsible for solving the crisis was nevertheless able to acknowledge:

> I do not know but that God has created some one man great enough to comprehend the whole of this stupendous crisis from beginning to end, and endowed him with sufficient wisdom to manage and direct it. I confess that I do not fully understand and foresee it all.[52]

3) *Synthesis: More Truth (Instead of Dualism)*

Dualism: half-truths. Most of us perceive in terms of opposites. The Book of Genesis, for example, is structured entirely around sixteen dualities, including the sun and moon, Cain and Abel, rest and work, eastward and westward, the garden and the desert.

Our binary facility, originating in our brain's left hemisphere, is an important survival tool. Dualism simplifies and organizes information that helps us to respond more quickly.

But this polarizing bias inhibits our wisdom. First, we split life into polar fragments and miss reality's continuous gradations. For example, the polarity of "good and evil" distorts and clouds our understanding. Objective reality is *neither* good nor evil and all humans are *both* good and evil. Second, we devalue one or another polarity. "Separate but equal" is an unnatural idea to us. The polar structure that provides our fundamental *frame of reference* seamlessly evolves into a *frame of preference*. We normally prefer light to darkness, heaven to earth, beauty to plainness, more rather than less, ours to theirs, the sacred over the profane.

The Value of Holism: More Whole Truths

Although most of us think dualistically, we also have a drive for interrelatedness and inclusiveness. The good news is that the right hemisphere of our brain has the capacity to respond to this yearning for coherence. It connects fragmented parts of our experience and searches for similarities, connections, and wholes. The bad news is that the brains of most contemporary adults are left dominant and so are more inclined to favor dualistic half-truths. Nevertheless, we should work to rebalance our mental propensity to polarize because:

- *Some polarities can't even be understood except in relation to each other.* These are ideas like liberalism and conservatism, theism and atheism, success and failure, waxing and waning, systole and diastole, creation and destruction. We've noted earlier

THE VALUE OF DISCERNMENT (INSTEAD OF EASE)

that secular and spiritual motivations are best defined (and only understood) through a contrast of their differences.

- *Holistic thinking allows a more balanced perspective.* I'll continue to emphasize the currently less popular aspects of spiritual practice in order to compensate for the natural tendency to deflate one pole or inflate another. For example, stressing the earthly rather than the mystical and the soul rather than Spirit mitigates a culturally imbalanced view *and* deepens my own understanding of spirituality.

- *Holism adds richness and nuance to our understanding.* The awareness of two polarities together is often more interesting and thought-provoking than segregating these pairs of ideas.

The Value of Synthesis

How can we promote more holistic thinking? If we're to become more whole people, seek more of the whole truth, and work toward more whole relationships, our task is to synthesize the parts of wholes, using methods like these:

Plurisignation. We *can* think more frequently in terms of "both/and" instead of "either/or." All of us are both masculine and feminine, generous and selfish, in need of both comfort and challenge. In a prison workshop, one participant who understood plurisignation better than the rest of us, introduced himself as "Double Down Dave, because there are two people inside me—one good; and one bad." His evangelical mom, who took the boys to church three times a week, raised him in poverty. When he came of age, his father drafted him to learn the family business. The Honduran drug business. He still feels pulled asunder by his loyalty to both parents and what they each represent to him.

Peripheral Vision. My best understanding of Alaska was obtained through the panoramas seen from single-engine aircrafts. From that height could I appreciate the rugged wilderness of the last American frontier; the edges of glacier, ocean, land, and sky; the majesty of Denali; and the numberless hues of brown (including bears scouring through fall grasses for groundhog canapés). Perhaps the only value shared by the proponents and opponents of legalized abortion is their passionate interest in reducing unwanted pregnancies. If both sides can widen their vision, this common ground may some day provide a basis for some cooperative policies or programs.

Balance. Aristotle taught us to discern and practice the behavior that is intermediate between the extremes of too much and too little in matters of art (symmetry), ethics (prudence), appetite (moderation), and nature (equilibrium). As a novice permaculturist, I'm amazed by the number of variables that must be balanced (and re-balanced again and again) for gardens to prosper. And does not every parent constantly seek the golden mean *between* being too permissive and too strict?

Periodicity. We can synthesize by *alternating* our expressions of a polar pair—one before or after the other. A friend acknowledges that sometimes he is extraordinarily generous *and* other times is compulsively penurious. We might feel bitter grief now; and sweet gratitude later for what we once had. We may set strict parenting rules about the TV on weekdays and lenient rules for weekends. Many of us pursue success and work in the earlier stages of our lives and practice more community service later.

Paradox. We *can* think paradoxically. Work can be play; we can think with our hearts; and less can be more. We can aspire to love our enemies. Transformation itself is paradoxical; we accept our imperfections as earthen beings while we pursue impossible spiritual ideals calling us to greater perfection. At the funeral of a young mother, dozens of stories celebrating this child/woman's death and life produced laughter and tears, in equal measure. Our hearts were shattered *and* full. Philosopher Charles Handy, in *The Age of Paradox*, forecasts that even in commerce, paradox has become a necessary strategy:

> More than ever, organizations need to be global and local at the same time, to be small in some ways but big in others, to be centralized some of the time and decentralized most of it. They expect their workers to be both more autonomous and more of a team, their managers to be more delegating and more controlling... In short, they have to reconcile what used to be opposites, instead of choosing between them.[53]

Kramer

The doorway framed the full moon
that summoned you out last night
to hunt behind the house
in the killing fields,
bathed in light.

Your half-eaten morning offerings
of rabbit, squirrel, and rat were met
for years by disapproving sighs,
though you and I well knew
what we're both bred to do.

You straddled two worlds as easily
as you soared between the highest
canopies of the live oaks.
One twin, the eight-pound,
tortoise shell beauty,
obsequious for our touch;
the other, the panther
only bivouacking with us
dreaming fitfully at our feet.

I found your clasped collar
far beyond the fence today.
The silver bell round your neck
was meant to even the odds
for your innocent prey.
But proclaiming your presence

THE VALUE OF DISCERNMENT (INSTEAD OF EASE)

> in the moonlight also evened
> the odds for the hungry
> coyotes last night.
>
> My dear Kramer.
> Your ferocity and your tenderness
> prompted me to honor my own.
> Little one, I miss you both tonight.

Discernment vs. Ease: A Summary

In my life, the value of discernment is described and expressed in these three ways, themselves values. The subsidiary ideas are the steps I've used to help realize each value.

<u>The Value of Openness to Novelty</u>. New information and experience entails fallibilism, the admission that our belief may be wrong.

<u>The Value of Humility</u> about our imperfect perception of truth, implies that sometimes we question our understanding and acknowledge not knowing

<u>The Value of Holism:</u> looking for the less favored side of the moon to see more of the truth.

<u>The Value of Synthesis</u> counters our predisposition to think dualistically, through:

> Plurisignation: the perspective of "both/and" instead of "either/or";

Peripheral Vision: the long view that incorporates more of both polarities;
Balance: Aristotle's golden mean;
Periodicity: One thing; then another;
Paradox: All at once: inside out and upside down.

CHAPTER ELEVEN

THE VALUE OF INDIVIDUATION: ACCESSING OUR WHOLE PSYCHE

Blinders

Improving our ability, through discernment, to think more clearly and rigorously is one way to improve our understanding, and consequently the quality of our beliefs. But thinking is only one of four psychological faculties that help us learn. These faculties of thinking, feeling, sensation, and intuition are illustrated below. The problem is that we generally tend to utilize only two of these and repress the other two, for our lifetimes. In very approximate terms, this means that most of us, most of the time, understand about half of what we might—about others, the world, and ourselves. Ours becomes a skewed perspective, about as effective as swimming with only one arm (in very small circles, I imagine). In my case, I used only my head.

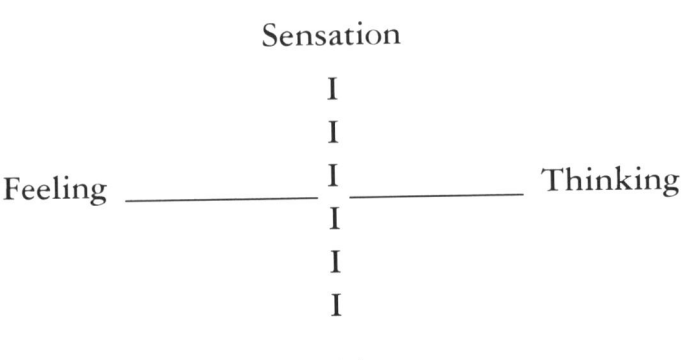

```
                    Sensation
                       I
                       I
         Feeling _____I_____ Thinking
                       I
                       I
                       I
                    Intuition
```

Intuition or Sensation

Ludwig Wittgenstein, a philosopher, of all people, advised that whenever possible, "Don't think, look."[54] Sensation anchors us to a firsthand and fresh experience of life. Thus, sensation is the most trustworthy foundation and standard of any belief. Yet I rarely bothered to use my senses. I was actually fatigued by too much sensory overload. A walk through a busy shopping mall or three floors of a museum would eventually induce a numbed, trancelike state.

At dawn, in a two-hundred-year-old cemetery in North Carolina, Christina knelt in the dew to make rubbings of gravestones of four soldiers who died in a skirmish during the Cherokee "Indian Removal." While standing there, I found myself mentally revising a poem I'd left hopelessly wound around a verbal axle two days earlier.

THE VALUE OF INDIVIDUATION: ACCESSING OUR WHOLE PSYCHE

Thinking or Feeling

According to the Myers-Briggs personality indicator,[55] a psychological test based upon Carl Jung's work, my predominant "guide to judgment and evaluation" has been *thought* (as opposed to *feeling*). This means I "use detached analysis and logic to arrive at decisions." My training in philosophy involved deductive and abstract reasoning processes. Business and the law are populated with men like me. I believed feelings were an irrelevant detour in problem analysis, decisiveness, and judgment. Further, I was convinced that when making necessary "tough-minded" personnel decisions, feelings were actually a liability.

Wholly reliant upon my intellect, I'd severely suppressed my innate capacity to feel. My feelings were limited in their breadth and depth. I had a host of pleasant feelings, but my negative default emotions lay in a narrow band of anxiety, frustration, resentment, and shame. I also didn't let myself feel very deeply. When others were in crisis or consumed by sadness, I'd often disassociate and observe from a safe emotional distance. After all, I told myself, *someone* had to make the arrangements or feed the children. For years I wrote dispassionately while my emotional facility lay dormant.

Several people in my life, including Mary and some of our kids, modeled a much more balanced integration of thinking and feeling. Hilary, for example, earned a magna cum laude at Wellesley, a Rotary scholarship, and a graduate degree in public health from UNC. But Hilary's friends remind us that, in spite of her intellect, she always has *felt* deeply and *lived* with her heart. She cried easily and her laughter has filled our house.

A more public exemplar of the integration of thought and feeling was Abraham Lincoln. While president, his capacity to feel deeply and even weep in public didn't diminish his remarkable intellectual capacity.

> He had a deeper and surer feeling about his own reason and vision in the face of chaos… If not arrogance, a cold self-assurance… a refusal to say Yes… until he had tested those proposals in the fire and the ice of his own mind and heart in long deliberations.
> —Carl Sandburg[56]

Since I couldn't *think* my way to actualize my buried emotional or sensate potential, I assumed I'd never to be able to access those two sides of these oppositional polarities. I'd accepted my lopsided personality as good enough and genetically inevitable.

The Conscious and Unconscious

Until midlife, I'd also largely ignored one more polarity about which both Freud and Jung had developed useful theories: the unconscious realm lying beneath our level of awareness. I had been aware of their psychological discoveries, but as a practical matter, I felt I was largely in control of most of my mental, emotional, and motivational life. It never occurred to me to consider that the personal or collective unconscious could become a source of wisdom or inspiration worthy of attention.

THE VALUE OF INDIVIDUATION: ACCESSING OUR WHOLE PSYCHE

Jung noticed that that during the second half of their lives many of his patients revived some of their two atrophied capacities and restored greater balance between all four faculties. He called this process of allowing our repressed faculties into awareness "individuation." Individuation invites us to use all the psychic tools at our disposal. Comprehending in more manifold ways doubles our ability to absorb and process information.

Thankfully, my unconscious was a lot less resigned to settle for half a life than I had been. Apparently, my conscious intuiting and thinking modes were not vital enough to satisfy some part of my soul. At some unknown level, I yearned to experience more of life, but I couldn't consciously imagine what that might look like.

Dream Work: Exploration of a Brave New World

During a two-year stretch in my early fifties, I had a dozen astounding night dreams, as vivid now as they were then. This dream world was much more powerful—joyful, playful, beautiful, terrifying—than my intuitive and intellectual waking life. These dreams were so emotionally and visually compelling that even I, a master of denial, couldn't ignore their messages. The dreams were urging me to reclaim my dormant, unconscious capacity to feel and to sense more of my interior and exterior life. These dreams felt like an invitation to resuscitate a part of my soul. They were life-giving.

A recurring image in each dream was water, which I learned was a symbol of transformation. The most dominant image was serpentine: very large *Technicolor* serpents in every dream. These were all lethal creatures that produced the strongest possible feelings. Each dream began with terror in the immediate presence of these primordial creatures; progressed through wonder and awe at their beauty and power; evolved to delight; and ended in joy and gratitude. I rarely felt these emotions in my waking state.

In these dreams, my two long suits—my intellect and intuition—were out of their element. Both were useless, irrelevant, consistently unreliable, and *wrong*. My intellect and intuition had repeatedly misjudged the risk and reward of interacting with these prehistoric creatures. I'd begun each dream trying to kill each of them with a sword and then struggling to hold the snakes at bay—even though none had menaced me in any way. Finally, exhausted from grappling with them at arms' length, I very reluctantly had to release them.

Then, in slow motion, the animals began to interact pacifically with me; to coexist in my psyche and in my life. The yellow and gold anaconda, two feet in diameter, coiled around my feet. He had formed a defensive—not offensive—perimeter around me. Others, released from my death grip, wanted only to play. In the deep jungle, a deadly six-foot caramel-and-cream mamba danced around me like lighted electrons. Like all emotions, these dream creatures were spontaneous, unpredictable, unbidden, energizing, uncontrollable, and vital. I've never felt so alive. I felt grateful for my primitive, magical friends. Without a mentor since my late twenties, I began to imagine these serpents as teachers. And muses: my poetic imagination and feelings seemed to be more accessible for my prose writing.

THE VALUE OF INDIVIDUATION: ACCESSING OUR WHOLE PSYCHE

The serpents were also messengers and guides. The night before I departed for a two-month visit to Central America, Christina awakened with a start, having dreamt I was drowning. Weeks later, snorkeling in fifteen feet of water off the Honduran islands of Cayos Cuchinos in the Caribbean, I became mesmerized by another serpent, this time a tawny, five-foot eel with leopard-like rose medallions. Reminded of my previous dreams, I felt strangely moved and even entranced. She undulated slowly along the bottom of the coral, leading me to follow her a substantial way back toward the shore.

Crestfallen when she finally disappeared into a hole in the coral floor, I surfaced to notice a swift island current that had ushered my half-dozen younger colleagues a couple of hundred yards further away, in deeper water. Three strokes after I began the long swim to join them, my right hamstring began to cramp. With startling clarity, I recalled Christina's dream. I turned around for shore, favoring one leg, and swam against the outbound current, wind, and tide, and landed fifteen minutes later on the beach, exhausted, and very relieved.

Postscript

More Feeling. My hedonic aversion to painful feelings certainly hasn't disappeared, but the dream work signaled that it was nigh time to deal with a host of other emotions, like melancholy, nostalgia, generosity, empathy, tenderness, gratitude, sadness, regret, grief, shame, sweetness, and all the rest. I was "practicing" feeling. The dreams helped, and so did grief, meditation, and therapy. Many of the feelings were painful, but they served to open my heart and increased my capacity to love. My increased interest in feeling also opened a new way of understanding the world. I'm also appreciating the wisdom inherent in stories, especially Christina's. A workshop leader for years, Christina is a great storyteller.

More Sensation. I still avoid shopping malls like the bubonic plague, but I'm generally thrilled by my newfound exploration of the exterior world. Possessed of no discernable talent, I've nevertheless experimented with stone carving, line drawing, and painting with acrylics and watercolor. Macro-photography is an exact discipline, insisting upon close attention to the details of my sensate environment. Inshore fishing from a kayak in Florida's Gulf of Mexico, (allegedly) brimming with gigantic trout and redfish, is a visual and tactile treat.

The eight Guatemalan family members and four dozen farm animals with whom I lived for a few weeks felt more vital, noisy, stimulating, and fun than our mile-long street in suburban Clearwater. My visit with them offered a time and space for a heightened awareness of sensations as simple as rain, sun, shade, food, the eyes of children, landscapes, butterflies, monkeys, moths, birds, and fish. I thrived on this more immediate, chaotic, muddy, compelling life. In the old days, I wouldn't have had sense enough to take the time and effort to welcome this much enriching chaos into my closed-off world.

Over To You

To increase your self-understanding, as well as an awareness that not everyone processes information the same way, you might consider taking the Myers-Briggs survey, published by CPP Inc. It's useful to grasp how you and others unlike you perceive the world and make decisions. Two million people use this psychometric questionnaire every year. You can learn more about it from the website *MBTIComplete.com.*

II THE IDEAL OF INNER PEACE (AND QUIETUDE)

We have two needs for peace and quiet. The first is for solitude, very tricky when carrying electronic devices connecting us to the whole world. The second challenge is even more daunting: to quiet the interior distractions originating in our own psyche.

Daydreaming: Stereophonic Mind Games

During a weekend Buddhist meditation retreat, I jotted down the following notes after the first break. Note that all the following mental static occurred while I was earnestly trying to avoid letting my mind wander. When I noticed I'd begun to think, feel, or imagine something other than the inward and outward movement of my breath, I returned my attention back to my breathing. I invite you share this profound meditative experience.

Pillow under my right knee—ah, better. Sweater off, or sweater on? Make up your mind, already. Christina *really* wants another puppy; might be fun. The newest engine noise sounds ominous: how much this time? You *can't* possibly be hungry. That Buddhist nun is stunning; how old is she? Forty-five, fifty-five? Hard to tell with her crew cut. Find a cheaper pool cleaner at *Home Depot*.

Wish I could pronounce these Pali chants—I sound like an idiot. While I'm squirming around like a hamster back here, the big guy in front of me hasn't moved a muscle. A cardinal? migrating already? I need to photograph that teal bamboo branch. Remember the kayak fishing presentation at two this afternoon. God, I loved those horses in *Cavalo* and the music at *GarageMahal* last weekend. Pick up a box of *Keebler's* crackers for Carol. Rewrite the first section of the most recent chapter; it still sucks.

This same gal is coming in late, *again*; why all these noisy, grand entrances? Wonder how Margaret's neurological check-up went. Whatever you do tomorrow in front of all those people on the first tee, do *not* slice the ball into the pond—again. Ah, the bell. Sweet. I really need to pee.

Just brilliant. I also jotted down the full orchestra of feelings accompanying those thoughts: annoyance, wonder, attraction, resentment, blame, curiosity, shame, impatience, concern, appreciation, inadequacy, anxiety, frustration. In addition, my imagination had produced kaleidoscopes of images for the subjects out of eyesight, including the faces of the people I thought about, the food I described, the golf course, even a cute chocolate Labrador puppy...

It Gets Worse

Steady flows of *unconscious* thoughts, feelings, and images occur during a great deal of our waking life. Like trout running below the surface of a stream, only occasionally they splash into view. Because this noisy sideshow is such a constant feature of our mental lives, I wasn't even aware of this pandemonium until I began to meditate.

I know: hearts beat, fingers grasp, and brains think. And our personal unconscious can be very useful as a sorting and organizing tool. I'm reminded to call one of the kids, or pay an overdue invoice, reach out to a client, or check on the pool pump. But it's one thing to remind ourselves to pick up a quart of milk. It's another to prepare the entire shopping list, revise tomorrow's "to do" list for the third time, and... The mind is far too omnipresent for our own good.

During the meditation I catalogued above, I was working hard to avoid all that daydreaming. Normally, my mind games are even speedier and louder. And they become even more hyperbolic and distracting if I'm stressed by job hunting, caring for sick kids, stewing about an argument, running late, meeting a deadline, screwing up at work, worrying about money...

> On average, throughout all the quarter-million responses from more than 2,200 people, minds

were wandering 47 % of the time. The heart goes where the head takes it, and neither cares very much about the whereabouts of the feet. I find it kind of weird now to look down a crowded street and realize that half the people aren't really there.[57]

Most important, the research study referred to above also found that, "over the several months of the study, the more frequent mind wanderers remained less happy than the rest." Eckhart Tolle believes that 80 or 90 percent of our mindless streams of thought are a waste of time.[58] Most of our mental chatter is like watching TV for an extended period: pretty much crap. Who really wants to spend their time, their life, in such a way?

The extent, constancy, volume, and turbulence of this unconscious stream is a great obstacle to peace of mind. We've seen that this mental chatter is time-consuming and distracting. But because it's involuntary and constant, it's also compulsive. It's obsessive too, since we're often recycling the same old beliefs, beefs, stories, feelings, and thoughts—over and over again.

Avoidance

I wanted to try to understand the reasons *why* I might carry on these endless, largely stupid inner monologues. I hoped these motivations might hold the key to reducing them. Here's what I noticed:

Mind games help me try to manage an unmanageable world. Measured by the amount of time we spend in front of our big screen TVs and small-screen devices, we clearly *prefer* to operate

II THE IDEAL OF INNER PEACE (AND QUIETUDE)

in our mental, mediated world rather than deal with the real one. By programming and setting our desired levels of mental streaming, we have some degree of *control* over our mediated reality in two ways.

Programming Content. Our experience of the exterior world and of our psyche in the present moment is spontaneous and beyond our control. On the other hand, our internal monologues are predictable, familiar, and comforting, not unlike a sit-com.

Stimulation Control. Reality is often either too tedious or too stressful for our personal taste. I'm sure that my mind is so active in meditation because I fear that attending only to the present moment will bore me to death. I think Susan Ertz must have had me in mind when she wrote that "'millions long for immortality who do not know what to do with themselves on a rainy Sunday afternoon.'"[59]

Mind games help distract me from my existential limitations.

My Ordinariness. As a descendant of seventy-nine billion ancestors, awash in a sea of seven billion souls, I desperately want to be someone memorable or at least—noticeable. To be somebody. Because we think of ourselves and our surroundings most all the time, these mind games reinforce the delusion that we're the center of our world.

My Impermanence. Our streams of consciousness are a source of constancy, allowing me to imagine that my mind (and therefore my life) is a continuous, substantial, and permanent phenomenon. Recalling the past or thinking of the future helps me to more easily imagine my longevity as extending long before and after this meager moment. A month before her death from brain cancer, our dear friend reported her mind's frantic efforts to extend an illusion of constancy. Mary Ann noticed that in the daytime, "I try to hold my fragments of thought together to share them with my next visitor. But they escape like mists and find their way into open drawers and disappear forever." But in the nighttime, other thoughts repeated themselves obsessively and went round and round for hours. "No matter how hard I try, I can't stop them."

To reduce all this unconscious chatter, I'm challenged to accept two realities. First, that regardless of my efforts to manage my mediated version of it, the exterior world beyond me is ultimately unmanageable. Second, that I'm just very temporary and very ordinary, after all.

Accepting The Present Moment

But if I were to allow myself to stop my comfort zone's stream of unconsciousness, what in the world is left? Only my unveiled impression of the present moment. Since the present moment is all there is, our ability to be aware of it determines how much of life we'll experience. We pursue ideals in the present. *Wisdom* is derived through insight from experience, which happens only now; *inner peace* is serenity in this moment; and *love* and *compassion* are enacted in the moments they occur.

Thinking, feeling, and imagining are critical to us, but if we use them to replace our direct *experience* of reality, they become

II THE IDEAL OF INNER PEACE (AND QUIETUDE)

obstacles to any prospects for inner peace. All these obsessive and myopic thoughts drain our energy and attention from a larger life, beyond these mind games. Poet Wesley McNair photographs one such present moment:

> ...In the deep moment of his looking
> and her looking back, there is no future,
> only right now, all, anyway, each one of us
> has ever had, and all the two of them,
> sitting together,...right now will ever need.[60]

The Value of Mindfulness: Becoming More Quiet

We've spent decades habitually distracting ourselves from ourselves and from the present. How can we ever hope to lower the noise level that separates us from furthering our ideal of peace? How can we still our psyche's constant, disruptive, interior rock concert? We can't stop the mind. But, paradoxically, by increasing our awareness of it, we *can* lessen the amount and intensity of the unconscious chatter. If we're willing to pay attention to the static, we can diminish it. To increase our consciousness about our unconscious streams of thought, feelings, and images, I've experimented with these three routes, well-traveled by others.

First, we can learn to distinguish between our experience and our thoughts about our experience. Just noticing that a thought is not the same thing as experience is an act of awareness.

> The aim is to bring a fresh awareness to everything
> we do... Alone or in company, resting or working,
> I try to maintain that same careful attention. So

when I go to get milk, I will notice the scratching sound of the leaves on the sidewalk as well as my anger and hurt at what S said.[61]

In these brief spaces *between* our mind's interpretations of reality, through thoughts, feelings or images, we can momentarily experience the reality itself. This exercise develops our concentration and ability to hold our attention in the present—and away from our mind—for longer moments. Eckhart Tolle assures us that awareness of the spaces *between* our flow of thoughts will eventually increase in duration.[62]

A second method is meta-cognition: noting the specific contents and patterns of our mind games. A benefit of Buddhist insight meditation is its focus on these interior processes. We notice more closely our sensations (usually of pain or pleasure); our images; our feelings (especially shame, boredom, envy, fear, desire); and our thoughts (opinions, critiques, self-assessments).

I began to notice repetitive patterns in my reactions to situations, events, and other people. I started to relate clusters of thoughts and feelings to the triggers prompting them. I might notice, for example, that I often feel guilty or frustrated when I think of this person or that event. Then it gradually becomes easier to interrupt the game in the future and smile. "There goes the manuscript again... the kids again... The same old feelings about being fired a decade ago."

After noticing patterns like these more regularly and accepting them as just part of the game, the old tapes and stories become a little less insistent and compelling. Dull, actually. After all, we've watched these movies a thousand times before. This phenomenon

II THE IDEAL OF INNER PEACE (AND QUIETUDE)

of "flooding" is observed in many therapies and is one component in the treatment of post-traumatic stress patients. In those cases, it seems that after talking or writing about our pain, again and again, the energy and interest, and then the pain, eventually subside, in their own time.

Very occasionally, there's a third and more spontaneous way to access the present. Infrequently, we may be ejected from our private world of psychic mind games into the direct experience of the world beyond. These acute moments may be triggered by an intense emotion, a great loss, a religious conversion, or an awareness of great beauty. Other times, a novel set of circumstances—a change of scene or lifestyle—can help us disappear into the immediate, interactive well of life all round us.

A couple of weeks of volunteering and backpacking around Guatemala evolved into a kind of extended meditation for me. Lots of solitude, long walks, physical labor, stimulating reading... More important was what was missing: fewer thoughts, less writing, no electronic entertainment, no phone, no executive or familial roles to play, no worries to speak of. All contributed to an acceptance of my own impermanence and ordinariness, and to this poem.

Symphony

> By this muddy crossing
> settled by the Maya
> before the Dark Ages began,
> songbirds sanctify
> evening vespers
> and morning devotions.

Between times,
night after moonless night
I'm enraptured by madrigals,
sung by baying hounds
and crowing roosters,
sentinels reciting hourly vigils for a thousand years.
Rounds of annunciation ricochet from courtyard to courtyard, cascading to the lake, and return from the east to ignite the next nocturne, and the next.

These sacred carillons are
cradlesong for children
dreaming in households
four generations deep
of more grain in the morning
by every rural cross-
road of the world.

Foolish sojourner:
So this is why you've come.
To disappear, finally,
into the right question: not
who you are—but what life is.
To quiet your incessant mind,
and awake to the sound
all round— the sounds of
life itself.

II THE IDEAL OF INNER PEACE (AND QUIETUDE)

> Dear wayfarer, know
> now the glory revealed
> in this pitch night:
> that you might be
> one sixty-fourth note
> in this eternal symphony;
> a single drop in life's
> boundless stream,
> endlessly emptying
> to the sea
> beyond sounding.

Summary

<u>The Value of Quietude.</u> The fundamental need is to modulate our interior conversations, which are obsessive, compulsive, and distracting enough to make inner peace impossible.

<u>The Value of Mindfulness.</u> I mentioned three methods of mindfulness I've tried with some degree of success.

- Distinguishing between thoughts and experience and eventually widening the spaces between each thought.

- Meta-cognition: watching our thinking, feeling, and imagining. Then, learning from the recurring relationships between them until we begin to lose interest in the narratives they reveal.

- Spontaneous moments of peace and quiet. These occur for me only rarely and only when my routine is altered.

THE VALUE OF EQUANIMITY:

ACCEPTING THE WORLD AS IT IS

> In the end, the Buddha's enlightenment was to accept everything and everyone as they are; to sit down, as it were, for the full meal, and stop trying to eat around the broccoli.[63]

Less is More

A few years ago, just a couple of months apart, our dog and then our cat roamed far enough afield that they couldn't find their way home. Christina and I drove around the county each morning and evening in widening gyres. We nailed posters on phone poles at intersections for three miles in each direction. Twice a week we audited dog pounds and veterinarians' offices. In both cases, after three weeks, the animals were recovered when helpful strangers called after a sighting. Annie, the mixed breed, was found living in a deep wood with the usual Florida fauna of alligators and coyotes. She had crossed very heavily trafficked collector roads well beyond the radius of our search. During this whole ordeal, we were both depressed and certifiably nuts. Neither of us enjoyed a single moment of serenity for three weeks.

Wanting good stuff and dreading the bad interferes with our peace of mind. Peace requires that we be less upset, reactive, or distracted by (whether desirous or fearful of) the circumstances around us. Equanimity is the still point within life's cauldron of desire and aversion, hope and fear. It is especially challenging because equanimity is counter-intuitive and counter-cultural.

Non-Attachment

> Make a thousandth of an inch distinction,
> heaven and earth swing apart...
> cherish neither *for* nor *against*.
> To compare what you like with what you dislike...
> peace of mind is needlessly troubled. [64]

The far goal of non-attachment is to embrace all things equally—both misfortune and good fortune. The trick is avoid overreacting to the pleasant or the unpleasant, the pleasurable or the painful. Buddhists assure us that with a great deal of meditation practice, we can learn to override our hedonic drives altogether. But after events like our search for Annie and Kramer, non-attachment seemed *way* beyond my reach—and even my imagination.

<u>**Less Attachment.**</u> I decided that I'd better begin my pursuit of more equanimity by settling for a state of *less attachment*. I personally can't extinguish all (or even most) of my hedonic drives, but I can begin to moderate them. Becoming *less* attached to my desires for pleasure and my aversion to pain does reduce the volume and intensity of my responses to both of them. I'm making progress. . . slowly.

Opportunities to practice equanimity abound in the midst of life's inconveniences: a parking ticket, lines at the DMV, being put on hold *again*, missing a connecting flight... On both sides of a recent, normally routine medical operation, I lost a lot of blood. Before the docs could administer fluids or schedule transfusions, it got a little dicey. On the gurney in the emergency room in the first case, and in the ambulance returning to the hospital in the other, I realized I was no longer in control of virtually anything. During those last moments of consciousness, I was surprised by my full acceptance of all the clearly imagined outcomes.

While Christina and I were engrossed watching the seals at the Denver Zoo with a grandchild, a good friend left a message on my cell phone.

> You called for an update on the results of my tests. Inside the fog of neurosurgeon-speak about 'aggressive, invasive, inoperable,' I heard the final sentence pronounced: 'maybe six months.' Since that very evening, I've experienced long periods of bliss every night. Freedom has only taken sixty-three

years. Free of all need to control, or manage, or worry, or plan, or want something *else* to happen. Ever since my polio, more than anything in the world, I've always dreamed of flying. Each night now, I dream I'm flying with my brand new grandchild. See you soon, dear ones.

I'm reminded of a frequently cited passage by Tolbert McCarroll. "You always have the choice to take all things evenly, to hold onto nothing, to receive each irritation as if you had only 15 minutes to live." Why do we wait until our death sentence to make such a choice? Equanimity requires only a decision, which I, for one, find difficult. It calls for, and (paradoxically) promises, a profound and simple change in attitude.

CHAPTER TWELVE

DESIRE FOR "THE GOOD LIFE"

Dissatisfaction Inhibits Our Peace of Mind

[T]he Pali term *Dukkha* [means] 'dissatisfactoriness'... Even those who are wealthy and healthy nonetheless experience a basic dissatisfaction that usually festers... It is the very nature of the unawakened mind to be bothered about something..."[65]

The Buddha taught that the origin of *all* human suffering is our dissatisfaction. All our drives for pleasure and our aversion to pain arise from some unease or displeasure with our relationships, our circumstances, or ourselves. We can never eliminate all desire and aversion. Some dissatisfaction is beneficial. It encourages us to create novelty in our lives, reach for ideals and spiritual values, and work and play more skillfully. The only pertinent questions are the source, subject, frequency, and intensity of our dissatisfactions.

I recently attended two evening performances of Dissatisfaction Dramas. They provided a stage upon which to observe my life mirrored in slow motion. Each performance featured a different elderly, post-surgery patient who shared a double hospital room with me. They were medicated and not in much pain, but were very uncomfortable. Their discomfort consumed virtually all of their attention (until their needs were satisfied), an equilibrium which lasted no more than seven minutes, when the next discomfort arose to consume their full and immediate attention.

Their dissatisfactions were telegraphed by leaning on the nurses' station call buzzer, with requests for help: to turn from their left side to their right, and back again; for more covers on, a few more covers off; sitting up, lying down; for more pillows, fewer pillows; more pain meds, stronger sleeping pills; TV on, TV off; for more water, ice, and snacks, inbound and out. They were long nights for all of us, especially for the sainted night nurses.

My displeasures have endless media: my body, friends, marriage, boss, adolescent kids' work habits, an unreasonable client or contractor; my golf game, parents, career, or net worth; Congress, the restaurant's service, car alarms, loud cell phone users... One email humorist complains, "I can't hear the TV while I'm eating my crunchy snacks; my laptop is low on batteries but the charger is five feet away; I'm trying to text at a red light, but I keep making all the greens."

Dissatisfaction Creates Distractions

So, how do our dissatisfactions and consequent desires torpedo our prospects for greater peace? First, they distract us from the present. The time and energy to imagine, plan, and then change the things we wish to change, pulls us from the present. This is purposeful, since by definition, we're finding the present deficient and want it replaced by some more desirable future circumstance. These distractions are formidable for several reasons.

Our dissatisfactions are *constant*. Because they are matched pairs, they distract us *constantly*. For example, many of us desire more success, wealth, fun, or longevity. But each desire is only one side of a pair. In these examples, we also want to avoid (and therefore, fear) the possibility of future failure, poverty, boredom, or an untimely death. When preparing a speech, I toggle back and forth between a desire to look good and the fear of looking foolish. I want a new camera, but fear I'll pay too much (or too little, and buy a lemon). Our inner peace is compromised because *both* ends of this motivational seesaw of desire and aversion plague us.

Our dissatisfactions are *perennial*. My long-term plan was to eventually satisfy all my desires, one at a time, little by little. Then, I'd find peace. Well, not exactly. The Buddha's great teaching was that our normal end state is not equilibrium and satisfaction; but rather incessant dissatisfaction. As a kid living in New

York, I was frustrated with only six channels available on TV. Now, with hundreds of choices, Christina and I often can't find a show we want to watch on a Friday night.

Speaking of television, the prototype of dissatisfaction is a male with a remote control. He doesn't much care *what's* on TV; he wants only to know only *what else* is on TV. Dissatisfaction reminds me of a desert people. To the timeless question from the back seat of the caravan, "Are we almost there?" the father's response must always the same. "Kids, we're Bedouins; we're *never* almost there."

Our dissatisfactions *increase unceasingly.* Human beings do not merely want; they want *more*, which may be a part of our evolutionary biology. *Pleonexia*, a Greek noun, is the condition of having or wanting more and more. Abraham Maslow famously assumed that once our needs for security were satisfied, we'd slough them off and strive to fulfill higher needs, like self-actualization. In *Equality*, written at the end of the 19th century, Edward Bellamy imagined that the great wealth and physical comfort foreseeable by the year 2000 would diminish our needs and subsequent desires. By the millennium, he expected humankind would be in a position to say:

> We have now, for nearly a century, enjoyed economic welfare, which has left nothing to be wished for in the way of physical satisfactions… And thanks to a co-operation of the material with the moral evolution, the more we have, the less we need.[66]

Even a utopian could never have been able to imagine our actual economic abundance at the end of the second millennium. And he would've been appalled by its consequence: our desires have not abated; they've run amok. The more we have, the more we need, the more we want, the more we expect. With each passing year, the semi-custom homes we built for wealthy Floridians became more ostentatious. Eighteen-foot-high dining room ceilings, scores of faux columns, six-car garages, and walk-in closets larger than my first New York City apartment. Every few *months*, many of us need to upgrade their electronic devices to obtain the latest features, speed, and capacity.

As incomes rise, so do our minimal levels of satisfaction: better vacations and cars, for sure. And how can we do without the housekeeper, club dues, personal trainer, season tickets, and second home. All are reminders that the Latin source word for baggage is *impedimenta*. I've never met a multimillionaire who wasn't working overtime to acquire millions more—just for yuks, just in case, and just because he can. Also just because, even if he wanted to (and he doesn't), he *couldn't* stop. Seneca reminds us, "It is not the man who has too little who is poor, but the one who hankers after more."[67]

For years, I assumed that all these disadvantages of desire and aversion were unavoidable. Just the "costs of doing business" for the human being, to be stoically borne; the price of a good life. The good news is that they are not inevitable at all. The bad news is that these disadvantages get a lot worse.

Dissatisfactions Create Suffering

One of the Buddha's insights was that our dissatisfactions actually create a huge amount of gratuitous suffering for each of us.

For the balance of this discussion, we'll emphasize only one side of the hedonic equation: the painful consequences of desire for more pleasure. Personally, I was shocked to learn that my desires for more *pleasure* and good fortune—for more comfort, stuff, love, power, success, health—actually created more self-induced *suffering*.

Every single dissatisfaction creates five more painful emotions. Always. When a desire is satisfied, whether a great new relationship or the BB gun from Santa, our satisfaction results in much initial happiness. But following those pleasures is a very predictable and inevitable constellation of much less pleasant emotions. I've repeated this roller coaster scores of times, with new jobs, cars, friends, computers, lovers, business opportunities, homes ... Every desire cascades through these emotions:

- A desire arises from a current dissatisfaction.

- The pursuit of our object of desire ends in either *frustration* or gratification.

- Gratification results in either *disappointment* or satisfaction.

- Satisfaction is either diminishing (causing *grief*) or is constant.

- We *fear* that we may lose the source of our constant satisfaction.

- Because nothing lasts forever, eventually we will experience the *loss* of our object of desire. The *New York Times* technology columnist reminds us: "Forget about forever—nothing lasts a year. Of the thousands of products I've reviewed in 10 years, only a handful are still on the market."[68]

- And then a new desire appears, arising from a new *dissatisfaction*. And so it goes.

Let's more closely examine just one of these painful emotions: the fear of future loss. After a friend was partially paralyzed in a skiing accident, she sued the ski resort to recover damages. After years of *anxious* depositions and a half-dozen *disheartening* interim legal setbacks, the judge ruled in her favor and awarded her three million dollars. A great celebration followed. Ten years later on her deathbed, she acknowledged that her personal insecurity actually increased the day she deposited that check. For the rest of her days, she was plagued by an unrelenting (and, it turns out, unwarranted) *anxiety* about the possible diminishment of her family's only nest egg. Perhaps Seneca was right: "A great fortune is a great slavery."[69] The more we have, the more we have to lose; the more we have to lose, the more we'll fear losing it.

Our dissatisfactions often become *compulsive or addictive*. This last consequence of dissatisfaction is only a possible outcome, but the most harmful of all. Ivan Illich, an Austrian sociologist, wrote, "In a consumer society there are inevitably two kinds of slaves: the prisoners of addiction and the prisoners of envy."[70] *Addictions* are defined, in part, by their serious adverse effects on one's career, family life, or personal development. The National Institute of Health estimates that nearly one in ten Americans over age twelve (23 million people) is classified with substance abuse or dependence. And that figure doesn't include the tens of millions addicted to smoking, overeating, gambling, or sex.

Also uncounted are the millions more people who *compulsively* abuse pornography, shopping, exercise, hoarding, or the internet, each to the point where in one way or another, their lives, or the lives of others, are compromised. Even compulsive use of smart phones ("Crackberrys") falls in this category, particularly if used while driving.

Summary

The consequences of a lifestyle of recurring dissatisfaction adversely impact our spiritual ideal of inner peace in two ways:

First, we are *distracted* incessantly, since:

- We're never satisfied.

- Our dissatisfactions constantly increase.

Then, we *suffer*, since:

- A round of painful emotions trails each dissatisfaction.

- We may be entrapped by one of a dozen addictive or compulsive behaviors.

CHAPTER THIRTEEN

LESS DESIRE AND AVERSION: THE VALUE OF SATISFACTION (WITH THE PRESENT)

Let's turn to several spiritual values that can help to reduce our predisposition to desire. Reducing our desire lessens unnecessary distraction and suffering. Our dissatisfaction normally results in either a desire for something we expect to find pleasant or an aversion to something we anticipate as unpleasant. The only emancipation from a life spent on the Ferris wheel of endless desire and aversion is to consciously moderate our reactive responses to our present circumstances, whether positive or negative. We need to lower the volume and frequency of wanting this thing and hating that thing.

The Value of Self-Discipline

> Discipline. Tightness. Firmness. Crispness. Sternness. And Sternness in our lives. Life is tons of discipline.
>
> —Robert Frost[71]

Mother Teresa's Catholic Missionaries of Charity believe that the use of modern conveniences designed to increase our comfort violates their Order's vow of poverty. As a result, in cities like New York and San Francisco, the sisters refuse to live in buildings that include elevators, washing machines, clothes dryers, or dishwashers. A generous donor renovated a building in New York for their use. The day they moved in, the nuns disconnected the air conditioning system. They then rolled up the brand new carpeting and passed it all out the windows for the benefit of their grateful new neighbors.[72]

Discipline is an amalgam of the two Christian cardinal virtues of *temperance* and *fortitude*. St. Francis and Gandhi were exemplars of both virtues. Both were celibate, ate one meal a day, wore minimal clothing, and owned no personal possessions.

"Just Say No." Temperance is a way to deal with our desires for more pleasure, most usually our comfort and ease. Temperance combats self-indulgence through impulse control. The only way I can avoid wonderful sandwiches, artesian breads, morning toast, and Dunkin' Donuts pit stops, is to totally cut off my convenient access to *all* kinds of flour-based foods. A frequent clothes shopper and good friend of Christina's gave her some recent advice

LESS DESIRE AND AVERSION: THE VALUE OF SATISFACTION

while at *Chico's*. "Dearie, *please*. Shopping in the mall is not about buying what you need; it's about learning what you want." Temperance begins by governing our striving to scan the horizon to seek more of what else we might still want.

"Just Do It." Fortitude deals with our aversions to discomfort. In the face of unpleasant tasks, fortitude is the quality of perseverance. Exercise, cleaning the garage, weeding, or helping the kids with algebra, all come to mind. Churchill said, "Success is not final, failure not fatal: it is the courage to continue that counts." I've always been amazed at the fortitude of St. Francis. The night of his death, he asked the Brothers of his Order to lay him naked upon the stone floor of his beloved chapel, so that he might die alone. Buddhists and Hindu yogis free themselves from suffering through the physically demanding discipline of meditation.

I spent a month with an NGO on a U.S. Department of Agriculture program working in three East African Maasai villages. I was disappointed by the unwillingness of the other American volunteers to overcome their distaste for the more rustic aspects of rural life. They were too "grossed out": by chickens to crawl into coops to vaccinate them; by dirt, to dig garden beds three feet deep into hard soil; by unpasteurized milk, to drink chai with the village headman; by manure, to shovel and haul it for compost piles; by the lack of diapers, to carry babies; and by flies, to play with the kids. They couldn't muster the fortitude to endure some unpleasantness, and were therefore useless to the people they had traveled far to serve.

The policies of the Sisters of Charity illustrate both these aspects of self-discipline. They displayed temperance by resisting, as

Kahlil Gibran wrote, "...the lust for comfort, that stealthy thing that enters the house a guest, and then becomes a host, and then a master."[73] And they personified fortitude, to which anyone can attest who has ever spent just one humid August evening in a New York walk-up, without air conditioning.

Self-discipline is *an act of will*. It is hard work and alters *our behavior*. But discipline is a whole lot easier when paired with the spiritual value of satisfaction, which is *a decision* that alters *our perception and our attitude* about desire and aversion.

The Value of Satisfaction

> Those who are contented are happy even though they have to sleep on the ground. Those who are not contented would not be so though they lived in celestial mansions.[74]

Satisfaction begins with a decision to embrace the hand and circumstances we're dealt. Like most spiritual values, satisfaction initiates a new perspective and thereby, a new response to life. An admissions nurse tells of a legally blind ninety-two-year-old, enrolling in a nursing home after the recent death of his wife. He interrupted her canned sales pitch about the brand new facility to say this: "Miss, happiness is something you decide upon ahead of time. Whether I will like my new room here or not doesn't depend upon how the furniture is arranged. It's how I arrange my mind, and I've already decided to love it." The narrator of this story ends by urging her readers "to have a nice day, unless of course, you already have other plans."

LESS DESIRE AND AVERSION: THE VALUE OF SATISFACTION

In *The New Earth*, Eckhart Tolle writes of the famous theoretical physicist and cosmologist, Stephen Hawking, who has been paralyzed for forty years with a degenerative, immobilizing motor neuron disease. At seventy, he can communicate only by twitching his right cheek. Looking back upon his life, Hawking said to an interviewer: "Who could have wished for more?"[75] Three useful questions serve as trail markers for me while practicing the value of satisfaction.

Do I have a *need*? Are these wants or needs? Homeless people in a neighborhood soup kitchen dramatize my own confusion about needs and wants. Operating the dishwashing machine, I noticed that each day about two thirds of the two hundred and thirty diners discarded 20 to 25 percent of the total of all the buttered bread, desserts, fruit salads, meat, or vegetables they specifically requested to be added to their trays in the cafeteria line. Satisfying their *wants* requires more food than is *needed* to satisfy their hunger. Every day, the average American family wastes food scraps equivalent to five quarter-pound cheeseburgers, often because they bought or prepared more than they all could consume.[76]

I was distressed to learn that some of my "travel necessities" were unavailable in rural Guatemalan towns. These included a bank, between-meal snacks, an electric fan, *Imodium,* mosquito repellant, *Band-Aids,* malaria medication, aspirin, sunscreen, and *Raid...* These products had not yet risen to the level of need for the local inhabitants, including my host family. Who among us were more content, more serene, more free?

In an orphanage in Honduras, the boys sleep in one large room in long rows of bunk beds. Each kid's entire larder of clothes and possessions fits on one three-foot shelf. All their stuff consists of one toothbrush and comb, two pants and shirts (for school and for play), three pencils, four school notebooks, five marbles apiece, and no more. Between them, the fifteen preteen kids share nine teddy bears. As a group, these adolescents certainly seem to be every bit as happy as our own grandchildren, who occupy their own rooms piled high with toys and games with closets full of clothes.

Do I have *enough*? The value of satisfaction helps us recognize when we *already* have enough pleasure, control, and power. Lao Tsu wrote in the *Tao Te Ching*, "He who knows that enough is enough will always have enough."[77] My father didn't have a frugal bone in his body, but in the last decade of his life he refused to spend another dime for new clothes. Having decided that two pairs of trousers were more than enough, he simply had them repaired—six or eight times.

To be guaranteed a comfortable retirement with lots of travel, I'd assumed that Christina and I would have to save tons of money, just in case. It's a great relief to replace that goal with the constant reminder that, whatever our future brings, we'll have more than enough.

Más o menos

> Some parents are free
> to choose how much
> is enough.
> I stumble along
> half-blind, half the time,

> more often than not
> giving the kids
>
> much too much.
> Others are less free
> to choose how much
> is enough.
> Less work for him,
> too much for her,
> too little corn meal
> for the children,
> and not much choice
> in the matter—
> save one.
>
> The last freedom left,
> more bitter and holy
> than all the rest,
> is to choose to accept
> God's will or Fate
> or Whatever,
> for whatever little
> they're given—
> as more or less—
> enough.

The Value of Renunciation

Do I have *too much*? This is the third question I have to ask myself when I feel dissatisfied. This value counters the pervasive viral-like growth caused by our progressive dissatisfaction.

In *History and Spirit*, Joel Kovel cites the argument of Meister Eckhart who said that we can never become rich in all virtues "... until first one has become poor in all things. Whoever wants to receive everything must also renounce everything... We ought to have everything as if it were loaned to us and not given, without any possessiveness."[78]

Renunciation is the voluntary diminishment of pleasure, possessions, control, aggrandizement, and desire. St. Francis believed that renunciation was the highest form of religion. Francis and Gandhi continuously inspire me. They both relinquished attachments to results, to hate, to righteousness. Because they allowed themselves to be humiliated, beaten, and imprisoned, they also relinquished their safety and freedom. Ultimately, they renounced their lives: Gandhi was martyred in the sixth assassination attempt. St. Francis died in his mid-forties either from leprosy or because for two decades, he had so thoroughly mortified his body.

But what about the rest of us, the unsainted ones? Every addict in recovery voluntarily relinquishes the objects of his strongest desire. Giving donations of blood (and certainly a kidney) is a relinquishment *and* an offering. As I age, I note an easy relinquishment of high-end automobiles, fine restaurants, and destination resorts. Fancy hotels are fun, especially for the pillow chocolates and terrycloth robes, but if you've seen one... I suppose we gradually minimize our stuff as we get older, because we're preparing to take our leave.

Summary

<u>The Value of Self-discipline</u> is a recurring act of will.

> <u>The Value of Temperance</u>: Just say no.

> <u>The Value of Fortitude:</u> Just do it.

<u>The Value of Satisfaction</u> is a recurring decision, aided by questions:

> Do I have a need or a want?

> Do I already have enough?

<u>The Value of Renunciation</u> entails letting go:

> Do I have *more* than enough?

CHAPTER FOURTEEN

OUR FEAR OF SUFFERING

> Must we fear fear itself? How much of our creative and vital power is tied up—sometimes even paralyzed—by our fear of fear, our unwillingness to feel it and know it for what it is? It would be difficult to overestimate the potential power of fear to control our lives.
>
> —Joseph Goldstein, *Insight Meditation*[79]

In the previous two chapters we described ways to promote inner peace by reducing dissatisfaction with our *present* circumstances. We focused our discussion mostly upon desire (rather than aversion). In the next two chapters, we'll explore ways to reduce our overreaction to concerns about our *future* circumstances. Although either fear or hope will surely contaminate our peace of mind, space again dictates that our discussion be limited to only one side of our hedonic continuum: coping with our fear of (rather than our hopes for) our futures.

Anxiety

I mentioned my surprise when I first learned that my desire for more pleasure paradoxically caused me more suffering. But it was no surprise to learn that fear of emotional pain is also a form of suffering.

Anxiety about my work has always been a huge impediment to peace of mind. For years, before blessed sleep arrived, and again at four in the morning, I'd obsess about potential business problems, large and small. I finally reviewed my notes pertaining to the prior business quarter. Turned out, I'd worried about forty-one things that could have gone wrong, of which three eventually manifested as legitimate (and manageable) problems. Talk about over-prepared. What a stupid and painful amount of lost sleep, motion, energy, and peace of mind. As Mark Twain said, "I've been through some terrible things in my life, some of which actually happened."

One night, years later, I actually had good reason to worry about an unsolvable problem. The next morning the newspaper would accurately report that my large custom homebuilding business was failing. The next day, I'd scheduled to meet with affected subcontractors, suppliers, customers, employees, and bankers. My apprehension of the stakeholders' displeasure and my public shame was so pronounced that I assured God it would be perfectly fine on my end, if I didn't wake up the next morning, or for that matter, ever again.

From these events I learned a couple of valuable lessons about my obsessive anxiety. First, although the following day was even more awful than expected, none of it was as painful as the previous night of terror. Second, the succeeding eighteen months were also very difficult. With the help of two remarkable friends, I managed to complete a couple dozen homes for customers and banks; negotiated with suppliers and subs to complete their work (so they could receive the money already due them); and attended forty-odd depositions with claimants. Even so, when the dust had settled, I had to admit that all the cumulative days and nights of anxiety about the possibility of failure were immeasurably more painful than the experience of failure itself.

―――

Montaigne wrote, "A man who fears suffering is already suffering from what he fears."[80] But for me, the fear of suffering was even *worse* than the dreaded suffering itself. How is this possible? Four reasons help explain this mystery. The most important reason is that sooner or later, all suffering passes. On the other hand, our fear of suffering can last forever. In addition, our fear, unlike our actual suffering, is subject to three multiplier effects.

The imagination multiplier is caused by our ability to imagine possible threats many times more numerous and unlikely than even Job had to endure. The poem *Afraid So* by Jeanne Marie Beaumont begins with: "Is it starting to rain?/ Did the check bounce/ Are we out of coffee?"... and concludes thirty-two fears later with… "Is the wound infected/ Are we lost/ Will it get any worse?"[81]

The ritual multiplier. I must have decided (quite unconsciously and irrationally) that obsessive worry was indispensable and might actually increase my peace of mind. My evening thought processes had apparently become wrapped around the axle of ritualized anxiety. It went like this: If I thought long and hard enough each night about the business, I could probably imagine and anticipate almost every possible event that might go wrong. The next day, I could begin working to prevent it, solve it, or mitigate it. The avoidance of surprise, of being unprepared, and of feeling out of control were apparently more important than a good night's sleep.

I wonder if even ritualized prayers of hoped-for petitions can actually *increase* our anxiety. Believing we are rewarded for prayerful intercessions, the petitioner repeatedly, prayerfully revisits the subject of concern, which fuels the obsessive cycle.

The family multiplier. This is the most current reason my own anxiety usually exceeds my actual future suffering. Francis Bacon's aphorism resonates: "He that hath wife and children hath given hostages to fortune."[82] With large extended families, I can manufacture an endless supply of real or imagined threats in the very routine lives of my siblings, children, their spouses, and grandchildren.

Real or Imagined Concerns?

Personal or global, rational or irrational, conscious or unconscious, our fears can run us ragged. Anxiety and anxiety-induced insomnia comprise more than 30% of the patient complaints of primary care physicians. Many of us have a bevy of specific and idiosyncratic fears that verge on the phobic. For instance, I have surprisingly little fear of handling poisonous snakes or skydiving, which could kill me; but large insects scare me. Go figure.

A lot of our anxieties seem pretty unnecessary. Of forty-eight largely middle-class members of a recent juror pool for a murder case in our hometown, twelve people acknowledged to the court that they are permitted to carry concealed weapons. Eighteen others owned guns (often semi-automatic assault rifles) kept for protection in their master bedrooms at home. Michael Crichton, in his novel *State of Fear*, describes a contemporary sociological phenomenon:

> Industrialized nations provide their citizens with unprecedented safety, health, and comfort. Average life spans increased fifty percent in the last century. Yet modern people live in abject fear. They are afraid of strangers, of disease, of crime, of the environment. They are in a particular panic about the things they can't even see—germs, chemicals, additives, pollutants. They are timid, nervous, fretful, and depressed.[83]

Anxiety Management: Peace at Any Price?

I know of three ways to try to manage anxiety about the future. I've tried them all, and none work very well. In fact, if any of the three become obsessive or compulsive, our lives actually become far less peaceful, rather than more.

1. (Total) Risk Avoidance.

>...The person who risks nothing, does nothing, has nothing, is nothing.
>He may avoid suffering and sorrow,
>But he cannot learn, feel, change, grow, or live....
>Only a person who risks is free.
>—*To Risk*, William Arthur Ward (1921-1994)

For years, I assumed far too much financial risk in business and the stock market for my tolerance for anxiety and my level of competence. On the other hand, I avoided other kinds of risks I should have borne, which unnecessarily constrained my lifestyle and happiness. While traveling abroad, for example, more confident backpackers often strike out alone to uncharted territories. They have more interesting travels in non-English-speaking countries than I. When giving a speech, to minimize the possibility of looking foolish, I'd write the entire text and even memorize chunks of it. The presentations were informative and articulate enough. But they were also inanimate, because I avoided spontaneous interaction with the audience, which felt too unpredictable and frightening.

To avoid anxiety, some of us try to engineer a risk-free lifestyle by eliminating all novelty. The fear of emotional pain caused by possible failure or rejection can sometimes feel like a great risk: a new blind date, hobby, job interview, group activity. Agoraphobia, in sheep's clothing. All to feel safe. But a minimal life is half a life. A Buddhist teacher asked once whether we were all breathing just a little and calling it a life. And eliminating the pain of anxiety increases the risk of boredom, another kind of suffering. Inmates and combat soldiers spend the vast percentage of their time living with the impossible concoction of boredom *and* fear.

OUR FEAR OF SUFFERING

The Butterfly Effect

At dusk, a butterfly hurtles
through my open door
seeking refuge from a storm.
Losing altitude, she crash lands
on my starched white sleeve.

Two fragile souls freeze,
lest blink or breath
break the spell
cast by iridescent wings—
kaleidoscopes of violets,
umbers, and taupe.

Angel, muse, and messenger
delivering but one dispatch:
"Come. The full moon
and flood tide call."
In midlife now,
in two weeks, she'll be dead.

Refreshed at rain's end,
unfurling her mizzen sails
she tacks at my portal,
reaches into sable night
and runs free before the wind.

I've long preferred misty
histories or five-year plans,
all eggshell ornaments
of memories and dreams.
Now, after her flight tonight,
trusting all round her
on both sides of my door,
I'm not so sure
I'm right anymore.

For she sails on
ocean streams
more wild and free
than the shallow tides
in the lee shore
where I still ride
at anchor.

2. **(Over) Control.** This strategy to minimize anxiety is my personal favorite. The idea is to exercise as much control over our environs as possible. Prudence demands that we exert some

control over our immediate space, and certainly over the lives of our young children or the performance of our employees. And in the short run, through skillful control, we can often achieve the outcomes we want.

But for a long time I've known that control, even over the little stuff, is always somewhat illusory. As an avowed birder, my father decided to squirrel-proof our backyard bird-feeding stations. The rest of us were discretely rooting for the enemy, although the ingenious squirrels did well on their own. Each time they cracked the code to access a new cache of bird seed (never more thirty-six hours), Dad would order a more expensive squirrel-resistant bird feeder, custom designed by a craftsman from Wilton, Connecticut. My dear father spent a small fortune on state-of-the-art feeders, until at summer's end, he surrendered all vestiges of control over his air space to the triumphant squirrels.

Over the long term, sooner or later, we learn that we also have limited control over the larger events of our lives. Abe Lincoln acknowledged, "I claim not to have controlled events, but confess plainly that events have controlled me."[84] Life is a sea crossing. We can control the skill of our seamanship, the sturdiness of the vessel, and the adequacy of the provisions. But the weather can kill us. I've watched the lives of our children twice shattered after young and healthy mothers died, without warning.

As with all these pain management tools, using the illusion of control to manage our fear has a downside. First, the consequences of our control are often unintended. A friend arranged for a tutor to help one of his kids score above his natural ability on the SATs. He was accepted at an Ivy League school but struggled to keep up. When the lad took control of his own life and enrolled in a

Masters program in Fine Arts in a far less prestigious and less demanding place, his grades and his happiness soared.

A second problem with control is our tendency to over-control. Some of us (some parents and bosses come to mind) *do* tend to become control freaks. Control sometimes makes us feel committed, occupied, indispensable, even heroic (and also victimized by our voluntary managerial responsibilities). But the predominant message to the people around us is that children or associates are not trustworthy, which breeds dependency and resentment. This is a high price to ask *others* to pay for attempts to manage *our* anxiety.

3. (Illusory) Hope. When based upon reasonable expectations or possibilities, hope encourages the exploration of new horizons. But if hope is a response to our fear, it is probably illusory—and a narcotic of sorts. It is helpful to remind myself of the obvious: that all my unrealistic hopes (like my unreasonable fears) are of course absolutely *useless* to anyone. My hopes or fears for a grandchild's new tutor, a friend's chemo, or the prospects for my stock options have virtually no effect on the eventual turn of events.

I love a diminutive psychology professor who has good-naturedly conducted a "lifetime linear research study" to see if he could grow taller by simply focusing the power of his intention to do so. I saw him on his eightieth birthday. Preliminarily, I regret to state that the results of his experiment are not yet worthy of publication. Many actually do imbue their hope, by and of itself, with power enough to achieve their desired outcomes (like prosperity or longevity), as in "sending positive energy into the universe." Egads.

Others argue that, at the very least, our hopes are useful to make us feel better. I think the reverse is actually true; illusory hope can make us completely crazy. Jungian psychologist James Hillman writes, "No hope, no despair. That message of hope only makes hopelessness darker. It's the biggest instigator of the pharma industry ever!"[85] Because they feed one another, fear and hope are Siamese twins. The intensity of our anxiety generates equal and opposite doses of hope. And the more we hope for, the more we fear that our hopes will be unrealized. This spiral cycle of hope and fear is unrelenting. Seneca taught, "Cease to hope and you will cease to fear."[86]

On a Saturday night, we hope our child has a great time with her high school friends, but we worry about her safety. We hope she'll be home by curfew, but worry that she won't. We worry more when she isn't, but hope for a reassuring phone call to explain her tardiness. When the phone rings, we worry that this might be *the* call, and prayerfully hope that it isn't. But what are concerned parents of active high school kids to do? When their kids are out partying, the most serene parents I know turn *on* the bedside phone at 10:30 p.m., turn *off* the light, and sleep like babies.

In moderation, these three methods of dealing with our anxiety—risk avoidance, control, and hope—are prudent. But if we employ them obsessively or compulsively, these three strategies come with a high price. Risk avoidance detracts from a full life. Over-control consumes our attention, is ultimately frustrating, and is disempowering to others. And investing in unreasonable hope increases our investment in fear, in lockstep. Because none of these are very successful, they generate feelings of frustration and failure, as well. The least peaceful people I know are knee-deep in trying to manage their anxiety in one or more of these ways. All three methods are designed to studiously ignore the elephant in the living room: the fear itself.

I needed to find another way to decrease the anxiety about my future that had disturbed my peace of mind for so long. There is a better path to more peace of mind. Instead of trying to manage our fear, we might confront the fear; and examine how much of our fear, if any, is warranted and prudent.

CHAPTER FIFTEEN

LESS HOPE AND FEAR: THE VALUE OF TRUST (IN THE FUTURE)

Peace of mind depends upon our ability to accept our past, our present, and our future. The path from my desire for pleasure toward increased equanimity was through the value of *present satisfaction*. The path from my fear of suffering toward increased equanimity has been through the value of *future trust*. The following attitudes toward the future are encompassed in spiritual values that have helped to me trust more of the uncertain future outcomes.

The Value of Surrender: Acquiescence to the Inevitability of Suffering

> I should not have to suffer... My child should not have to suffer. That thought itself lies at the root of suffering.
>
> —Eckhart Tolle[87]

Trust in our futures calls us to accept our ultimate impotence to prevent, manage, or wriggle out of our eventual personal suffering. For me, the decision to try to embrace *all* of creation and destruction, and pleasure *and* pain, is a kind of faith: an offering of myself to life and death; an assent to all of it, with patience and amusement. For believers and nonbelievers, *total* acceptance is necessary to begin to free ourselves from our dissatisfaction with *half of it*. Ultimately, my fear of suffering can only be lessened by my willingness to embrace my future's ambiguity, chaos, and arbitrariness—and the consequent encounter with my own particular brand of suffering.

Poet Jane Kenyon reminds us in *Twilight: After Haying*, "The soul's bliss and suffering are bound together like the grasses..." [88] They "go with" one another. Limiting our tennis game to the forecourt or refusing to enjoy very hot summers or cold winters *demonizes* the half we deem less desirable or comfortable. Dana Jennings, a reporter for the *New York Times*, writes of her struggle: "Strangely enough, although cancer threatened my life, it also exalted it, brought with it a bright and terrible clarity. So, no, cancer isn't a battle, a fight. It's simply life—life raised to a higher power."

Two years after one of our children died, we were standing by Hilary's gravesite looking over the beautiful Maryland countryside. Christina acknowledged a feeling I often share: that the early death of this young woman just seemed so terribly—*wrong*. But we also both knew that during our brief visit with Hilary at the cemetery, five hundred more of this world's babies had died of malnutrition. Millions of children are always, everywhere dying. This acceptance of the inevitability of personal loss is not meant to sound facile. But "bearing up" seems easier when we can acknowledge the universality of suffering for each of us—and everyone else.

My trust in the future has three other facets.

The Value Of Suffering

It's easier to accept the inevitability of suffering after we appreciate suffering's possible use to us. After we stop trying to change or avoid the pain, pain can change us, if we'll let it.

Soul-making. Suffering humanizes and deepens us. All primitive initiatory rites into adulthood have a component of endurance of pain. Religions are right to address the necessity of sacrifice, surrender, service, and suffering. We *need* suffering. Too much or too little pleasure shrivels the soul and denies much wisdom; so also does too much or too little pain. I believe that soul- making requires moderate amounts of both good fortune and bad, which is a good thing, because sooner or later, that's what we're most likely to get.

Compassion. The experience of our own pain increases our capacity to be empathetic to the suffering of others. St. Thomas Aquinas declared, "No one becomes compassionate unless he suffers."[89] Among groups of people in therapy and recovery from addiction, the major gift each person offers to others in the group is her or his compassionate understanding.

Wisdom. I've very reluctantly (as in, kicking and screaming) learned a great deal from the most painful occasions in my life. Even my professional failures have been beneficial. After learning something about how to anticipate and avoid the kinds of business mistakes I'd made years ago, I was more useful to my clients as a management consultant. My experiences in therapy were always triggered by emotional pain; and *always* resulted in insight, growth, and healing. Hilary was ten when Mary died. In a college essay about the death of her mother, Hilary recalled:

> Several good things resulted from such a tragedy early in my life. I became more familiar with my own emotions, as well more sensitive to my father and brothers. I began to idealize my dead mother and take on some of her behaviors and interests. The loss of my mother was the leaven that produced an independent, determined, assertive leader. I witnessed the swiftness and finality of death at an early age and decided I didn't want to die with regrets or things left undone.

Self-confidence. Setbacks, traumas, and failures create growth and strengths of character, often unavailable in a life of comfort. Jonathan Haidt, in *The Happiness Hypothesis,* points out that our resilience in situations of severe adversity yields subsequent benefits to the survivor. Specifically, survival reveals hidden abilities to prevail that increases our confidence in the face of future stress. To pass through suffering relatively intact reassures us that we can stand it. Thereafter, we feel less anxious about its future prospect.[90]

Inspiration. MaryAnn took fourteen medications a day and struggled with acutely painful joints and muscles from post-polio syndrome. Mostly bedridden, she slept infrequently and fitfully. Because she was possessed of the most extraordinary and abiding good nature, she enriched our lives during the years she lived with us. Her courage was a daily source of inspiration.

Another friend died after a long and painful bout with cancer. Ten days before her death, she joined a dozen friends for a rare outing at a nearby restaurant. Carol regaled us with funny stories about her recent crazy months with doctors, nurses, medicines, hospitals, nursing homes, and insurance companies. Her light-heartedness was a testament to her courage and grace; and her eightieth birthday celebration a legacy to all of us she left behind.

The Value of Prudence

Others' Faith. My Honduran friend, Rosaria, tried in vain to teach me to speak in her native language and to share in her faith-based trust in the future. When she was twenty-seven, during her only visit to the States, she learned that she'd became pregnant by her first and only boyfriend. He abandoned her in Denver, broke, alone, ashamed, clinically depressed, and quite sick. Rosie lost sixty-seven pounds in three months and was hospitalized with an intestinal bug that even the CDC couldn't diagnose. A priest administered the last rites of the church. She longed only to return to Honduras to die among her family at home. She wrote to me:

I felt so alone. In my Catholic country, an unwed pregnancy brings shame to the entire family. Our evangelical church community was (and still is) evenly split between those who support—and those who refuse to speak to me. My mother had to borrow the money for the plane ticket home and we couldn't afford an obstetrician or special dietary food for me and the baby. I couldn't gain weight and didn't know what to do about my pregnancy. Then, in my fifth month, after lying fallow for years, the pineapple plants and the orange, banana, and grapefruit trees in our yard all began to bear fruit. I finally began to regain weight. The abundance of that fruit felt like a sign that I was being encouraged to live—and to give life to this child. My minister introduced me to a doctor who refused to charge us, but welcomed our weekly gifts of fruit for his other poor mothers.

Rosaria's daughter, Maria, is now six and their tiny household in the country is full of laughter. Rosie's faithful form of trust, inspired and nourished by her garden, reminds me of Gladys Taber, who wrote, "A garden is evidence of faith. It links us with all of the misty figures of the past who also planted gardens and were nourished by the fruits of their planting."[91] I loved Rosie's trust in God's and in life's beneficence, but my trust in the future is very different from hers.

My Reliance Upon Reason. Rather than faith, my future trust is based upon a more down-to-earth quality: a pragmatic kind of prudence. In *The Responsible Self,* Richard Neibuhr speaks of three ways of "seeing the whole" and the response to life generated by each perspective. One can see life as hostile or threatening; or one sees life as life-giving, nourishing, and gracious, the way a religious person like Rosie sees it; or one may see life as largely indifferent to human endeavor. I fall into the third category. Christians, like Rosie, might trust that God's providence will protect them. Many New Age friends (with or without faith in a personal God) believe, like Rosie, that life is trustworthy because they see it as primarily beneficent.

Whatever the grounds for your own trust, I believe there is value in making conscious the reasons underlying your belief that your future is, or is not, worthy of trust. The following three are foundation stones of my pragmatic approach to trust in an indifferent world.

- **A Trust based upon Risk Assessment (rather than faith).** Trust for me is based upon a prudent forecast of the probabilities of bad fortune and a guesstimate of my ability to endure the consequent suffering. I assess my life's circumstances: nestled in a wealthy country, in good health, and with health insurance. I would feel very different about my trust in the future if I were to become severely disabled or if I were one of the desperately poor of this world. Forget *trust*. I can't even imagine mustering the *courage to endure* the suffering shared by hundreds of millions of the world's poorest families.

- **A Trust based upon Awareness (rather than denial).** Through defenses like denial and illusion, many people prefer to shut out from awareness any threats they find fearful. But in my case, the danger I see is less frightening than the danger I can't see. This is not a courageous stance; it's just easier for me to confront the threat rather than studiously ignore it. While scuba diving for the first time in Key West, swimmers pointed out a barracuda hovering about ten feet behind me. I was comfortable as long as I could see this toothy predator. But I noticed a sharp increase in my heart rate when he was positioned where I couldn't see him. I had the same reaction to the tarantula with whom I shared an outhouse in Guatemala. When she was visible, I was comfortable enough to chitchat mindlessly with her, like I do with our dogs and cats. But I was fearful and vigilant when I couldn't find her in her favorite hiding places, including the warm cardboard cocoon inside the roll of toilet paper we also shared.

I recently spent a full afternoon in Countryside Hospital. At one o'clock, I learned from one surgeon I didn't have colon cancer. Good to go. At three o'clock, second surgeon called with biopsy results to announce that I did have prostate cancer. Not good. But knowing both facts, the good and bad, actually increased my peace of mind. They allowed me the chance to schedule the operation as soon as possible, and *then* to work on trusting the medical process.

- **A Trust based upon Past Experience (rather than future hope).** My trust in the future is based upon my past, which leads me to think that I could probably manage to deal with most emotional ill fortune that may befall me. My experience with past familial losses taught me that most *psychological* suffering is endurable, and eventually diminishes. On the other hand, I have no reason to trust that I could gracefully tolerate chronic *physical* suffering, which I intuit would be much more difficult for me. I'm amazed by the inspiring stories Borges and James Joyce tell about their blindness. I can't imagine enduring the loss of my sight with such grace.

The Value of Letting Go

> Nothing is more creative than death since it is the whole secret of life. It means that the past must be abandoned, that the unknown cannot be avoided, that I cannot continue, and that nothing can be ultimately fixed. When a man knows this, he lives for the first time in his life. By holding his breath he loses it; by letting go he finds it.
>
> —Alan Watts [92]

Letting go . . . of what? Letting go of the attempt to edit future possibilities *my* way. Letting go means nonresistance and surrender. One metaphor for the alternating exercise of control and letting go is kayaking on a stream, sometimes with, and sometimes against, the current. The question is always: what's possible and what's necessary. Letting go is an opportunity to increase peace of mind. "To let it go is like releasing a snake you have been clutching in your hand…"[93] A Thai monk said, a long time ago, "There's nothing to be, nothing to do, and nothing to have." Spontaneity, laughter, intimacy, joy, creativity, and perhaps God, are to be found in this place of non-striving; in the spaciousness, at rest.

Even though his health was declining, my father's mental outlook was positive, so my brother was surprised when Dad called to say: "Paul, I hate to mess up your family's plans to go to the lake, but I'm expecting to take my leave of you all and check out next weekend. I thought you might want to alert the other kids and [his sister] Joanie." Paul was confused and skeptical, but the following Saturday, most of the family had assembled in Dad's room at the assisted living facility. As his visitors were heading out the door to eat dinner at a nearby restaurant, he asked, and was told, what day and time it was. "Wow! I'd better get a move on. Anne, dear, could you turn me to my left side?" Sometime within the next hour, right on schedule, dear old Dad let go and just left.

Mary

I explored our reefs and jungles
to behold once more,
the fish, birds, and butterflies—
the quicksilver keepsakes
of our Caribbean honeymoon.

I fought to freeze
each flickering moment
with these radiant sprites.
But now, just weeks
since my rapture there,
I can't clearly recall
all the gossamer glory
of the fairie creatures
we once saw in Guatemala.

After vigils with respirators
and petitions to absent gods,
you'd think I'd have learned
to relinquish my desperate

After a decade, I felt
I'd dishonored you
when your scent and touch
and the timbre of your voice
began to fade like Polaroids,
'til finally, you slipped away
through my cramped hands,
like tiny grains of sand.

Maybe failed memories
are blessings. Had I well
remembered all I'd lost
how could I have turned away
to make room for each
new perishable encounter,
as inexorable
as the rising and falling
of the waves that break apart
only to vanish
on the shores

grasp of each moment
always wanting, "Doc,
just a few minutes more"
than the time allotted for
our great love affair.

of our cerulean sea.

Summary

<u>The Value of Trust</u> has several components, themselves values, that both serve to define what trust means to me and to guide my efforts towards greater peace of mind. These include:

<u>The Value of Surrender: Acquiescence to (the inevitability of) Suffering</u>

<u>The Value of Suffering (and its Gifts)</u>

    Soul-making
    Compassion
    Wisdom
    Confidence
    Inspiration for others

<u>The Value of Prudence</u> (in my case, based upon):

    Risk Assessment (vs. faith)
    Awareness (vs. denial)
    Past Experience (vs. naïve hope))

<u>The Value of Letting Go</u>

THE VALUE OF HEALING OUR WOUNDS:

ACCEPTING OURSELVES AS WE ARE

From Wisdom To Peace

[A] soulful personality is shaped by both pain and pleasure, success and failure. Life lived soulfully is not without its moments of darkness and periods of foolishness.
—Thomas Moore, *Care of The Soul*[94]

We've looked at ways to lessen the desire and fear prompted by our *exterior*, objective environment that impact our peace of mind. Here, and in the following three chapters, we'll discuss two concerns dealing with our *interior*, subjective psyche also threatening our peace of mind: our grief and shame.

As previously mentioned, knowledge of ourselves is indispensable in our spiritual pursuit of greater wisdom and peace. If I could have done so without consequence, I would have kept much of my personal unconscious forever unexplored. For a long time, I preferred to think I was too innocent to feel shame and too strong to feel loss. Eventually, I realized I needed to understand the ways in which my unacknowledged shame and my losses had made peace of mind unavailable. I'll share my labyrinthine path to become more attentive to my psychological life in order to help you better attend to yours. And, more personally, I'll share this because, as Rilke wrote:

> I don't want to stay folded anywhere,
> because where I am folded, there I am a lie.[95]

Healing

I should mention some sobering thoughts about this healing business. Healing our woundedness is restorative, but not magical. We get through—not over—the events that have triggered shame and grief. Anne Lamott writes about the limits of one form of healing:

> If you haven't already, you will lose someone you can't live without and your heart will be badly broken, and you never completely get over the loss of

> a deeply beloved person. And you come through, and you learn to dance with the banged-up heart.[96]

I've been meeting with a handful of wonderful guys for years. We've long ago come clean about our countless individual struggles, like depression, addiction, anxiety, risk avoidance, frustration, procrastination, fear of intimacy, irritability ... We've each worked hard on our own stuff, often with each others' help, and have made lots of headway. We lead happier, more fulfilled lives today than when we first began meeting thirty years ago. But my guess is that none of these issues will ever totally disappear for any of us. A recovering alcoholic is always recovering—and always alcoholic. I've been shy and self-conscious and always will be. The psyche successfully resists attempts at mastery. We can't control our personal growth; we can just work on it. Sometimes progression and other times regression.

So, what *can* we expect of this nonlinear healing process on the road to greater equanimity? Eugene O'Neil said, "Man is born broken. He lives by mending..." Healing and mending are gerunds, ongoing conditions, not verbs in the past tense, as in, "Alleluia, we're healed!" It's all a lot better now, but I suspect the old bruises will always ache a little on cold, damp mornings.

CHAPTER SIXTEEN

THE WOUND OF SHAME

> The blessing is next to the wound.
> –African Proverb

Inner peace is a phenomenon that occurs only in the present. But we noticed that our present experience can be contaminated by a fear of, or desire for, *future* events. In the balance of this section, we'll note that our experience of the present is also contaminated by *past* events. In my own my case, these were my unhealed shame and unresolved losses. My shame has come in two principal flavors.

Toxic Shame: "Feeling Unworthy"

In my late thirties, my employer conducted formal group exercises with all their division presidents to assess our leadership skills and promotability. I scored poorly, which was a new experience for me. Upset, I arranged for feedback from the psychologist who had supervised the exercises. In exchange for a ride to his predawn flight, he reluctantly agreed to see me for a few minutes at his hotel at 5:45 the next morning.

Al wanted to understand why I seemed to lack the self-confidence to lead my peers more forcefully. He began our interview with a half-dozen slow-pitch questions about my early childhood, starting with my favorite subjects in school. (This was gonna be a piece of cake.) Another innocuous question followed: "Tell me about your very first memories." Unbidden, a little boy's deep sadness washed over me. I was having a teensy bit of trouble breathing, and then this hotshot executive began to sob. I hadn't cried since I was a child, and for eight or ten minutes I couldn't stop.

Since my tears had soiled two large Hilton bath towels, Al was left without the linens or the time to shower before heading to the airport for his speech in Chicago. While I was losing it, he was trying to brush his teeth and pack. I don't know which of us was more flummoxed. He had became a management consultant precisely to avoid emotional outbursts like this. For my part, I'd already gathered that this performance in front of the company shrink was unlikely to be a career highlight. The good news was that, at long last, I was alerted that my repressed feelings of malaise were not exactly within the range of normal. For the first time, I understood I couldn't continue to outrun my past psychological dragons, now hauled into the light of day.

"Toxic shame is experienced as the pervasive sense that I'm flawed and defective as a human being."[97] Toxic shame manifests in childhood, when I began to feel deficient, unimportant, and just not enough. My parents had been raised in opposite financial circumstances, but their childhoods were otherwise similar. My mother was the youngest of many kids in a poor farming family. Her folks had little extra time for much of anything, including caring for the children. All five of her brothers became alcoholics. Mom wept each time we asked about her childhood on the farm, so we learned to stop asking.

At twenty-nine, my father's father became the very busy editor-in-chief of the *Cleveland Plain Dealer* and unavailable to his family. Dad's mom was also unavailable, suffering from severe chronic depression. Under duress, Dad stuttered badly. My parents shared childhoods devoid of much attention and nurturance, so each stumbled into parenthood themselves ill-equipped and shame-based.

Their early love letters clearly indicate the first seven years of their marriage were happy ones. They socialized together several nights a week with friends and colleagues in Milwaukee. After we moved to a suburb of New York, a long commute on the New Haven Railroad and the fast-paced advertising business conspired to separate them. On most weeknights, Mom felt Dad had abandoned her to raise their five kids alone, in favor of drinking with associates and clients in Manhattan. He was guilty as charged and Mom could never forgive him. Their mutual alcoholism consumed increasing amounts of the family's time and space. In the midst of their emotional conflict and confusion, the five of us fended for ourselves.

We were especially unarmored to cope with a melodrama performed a couple of nights a week for twenty-five years. The two people we loved most in the world, both drunk, one feeling scorned, verbally cannibalized each other before their frightened kids. The result was a kind of PTSD for some of us, each lying vigilantly awake in our beds. As the volume of the arguments rose, we all tumbled downstairs to negotiate a temporary and fragile truce.

As in all matters alcoholic, this scenario got progressively worse. Then, in her sixtieth year, with the help of neighborhood AA friends, Mom became sober. After her death from emphysema, seven years later, Dad entered an alcohol treatment center. He emerged, nearly seventy, a very different guy. Both parents' transformations to sobriety struck all five of us as near miraculous.

I had always hoped that through achievement in the world, I'd be able to earn the approval and admiration I had vainly sought at home. I dreaded feeling as unnoticed and anonymous as I did as a kid. The motivation to "become somebody" prompted some successes over the next couple of decades. After my graduate work at NYU, I'd become the president of a new homebuilding business at twenty-nine. I liked being one of the youngest and well-prepared executives in the room—far too much. So far, so good.

THE WOUND OF SHAME

In spite of some very happy familial and professional circumstances, I was not a very happy guy. I was aware of a general malaise—a shadow of insecurity and loneliness, of social unease and alienation. I was just a little off; anxious, short-tempered, and flat of affect. A lot of my energy was spent negotiating the conflict between unlimited ambition and more limited talent; a drive for success matched only by a fear of failure.

I was perfectly content to let sleeping dogs lie and forever repress my early memories and feelings of shame. As an Irish Catholic lad, I felt well bred for longsuffering. A little shame from a marginally painful childhood? No sweat. "What's the big deal? Millions of people have a much harder time. Suck it up." I'd managed to successfully suppress my family-of-origin wounds below my level of awareness until my late thirties, when Al and I had our early morning chitchat.

Self-Created Shame: "Feeling Ashamed"

> Out of the right speaker in your inner ear will come an endless stream of self- aggrandizement… of how much more open and gifted and brilliant and knowing and misunderstood and humble one is. Out of the left speaker will be the rap songs of self loathing… of all the mistakes one has made over an entire lifetime, the doubt, the assertion that everything that one touches turns to shit… and on and on. —Anne Lamott[98]

Toxic shame is inherited and familial. The second kind of shame I've experienced is more common and universal, and consists of later, self-inflicted wounds. I'm referring to stuff like failing at work, school, or sports; feeling rejected or humiliated or looking foolish. In the fifth grade, one afternoon along my paper route, I rehearsed my introduction to the school play. That evening, backstage, on my way to part the curtains, Sister Ambrose confiscated my one-paragraph note of introduction written in large letters. Onstage, before a full auditorium, I drew a blank and completely forgot every word of my *three* lines.

I was always particularly aware of comparing myself unfavorably to others. A dozen old school classmates have become prime ministers, presidential candidates, distinguished jurists, CEOs. The first shaming thought is always a question: "What's the matter with me?" The second is a feeling of diminishment in the face of others' good fortune. Such shame-laden states of mind are not conducive to spiritual growth *or* to inner peace.

Addiction

> If you are shame based, you're going to be an addict—no way around it... The mood alterers we use to take away our toxic shame become our addictions.
> —John Bradshaw, *Healing the Shame that Binds* [99]

The greatest source of my self-created shame as an adult was my bevy of addictions, all begun quite unawares in my early twenties. In spite of my grandiose claims of courageous longsuffering, I really dealt with my childhood toxic shame by medicating those painful feelings—with too much alcohol, food, and work. I was enmeshed in the iron[ic] maiden imprisoning all addicts:

that which begins as a way to mask old shame, becomes itself a further cause of shame. We become powerless to stop the old pain *and* our new dependency. Just like my childhood shame, I managed skillfully to minimize, and thereby deny, this trio of addictive behaviors for twenty years.

Booze neutralized my social insecurities in gatherings of people I didn't know well. When partying, after several drinks, I was a fun drunk. More insidious were the two or three drinks most nights at home that served to replace my anxiety, not with relaxation, but with relief. But that short relief was often followed by an edginess. Not much fun for anybody, especially for Christina.

I worked about seventy hours a week for thirty years. Even when I was with the family, I was absent, thinking about the business. Like all addictive behaviors, my work served to structure my time, provide a steady adrenaline drip, avoid unpleasant feelings (like anxiety and loneliness), and screw up my life. I was burned out and growing ever more distant from Christina and the kids.

I'd been addicted to food for years and was usually thirty to forty pounds overweight. I looked forward to the next snack or meal, justified as a nurturing reward for working so hard. This tripartite addictive pattern was self-reinforcing. Whether in town or on the road, a working dinner with colleagues over a few drinks was a perfect way to end the workday. It was nuts.

Healing: The Beginning

I'd never imagined that my ability to repress all this shame could ever be overcome by the insistent demand of my psyche to heal itself. But after the "come to Jesus" meeting with the company psychologist, I finally went to work. After all, I *was* a work addict. I addressed three fronts, each of which eventually became a powerful catalyst for my psychological and spiritual growth. I immersed myself in the human potential movement of the late seventies and eighties through scores of books, workshops and trainings. Off and on, for a few months at a time, I also attended individual and group therapy, which was a godsend.

Finally, I became a part of the recovery community. Christina, a psychotherapist whose specialty was dealing with addictions, was central to my recovery. The alcohol fell away after a week-long bareboat charter in the Bahamas, during which I had been drinking and smoking dope. From nowhere, came the realization (finally) that it just wasn't as much fun at it used to be. Duh... Work lost some of its compulsive appeal more slowly, as my youthful energy decreased. Sobriety from the compulsive comfort of food has come in several steps and has taken the longest of all.

I worked at healing this shame for a long time. I'll describe the process in the following chapter because it also works for other kinds of wounds. I want to speak about this healing process because it's so much more powerful and rich than the general culture's misunderstanding and ironic portrayal of a remarkable psychological and spiritual experience.

CHAPTER SEVENTEEN

HEALING OUR SHAME: THE VALUE OF SELF-FORGIVENESS

In the midst of the lengthy process of healing, I was too involved to reflect upon what was taking place. Looking back, the healing seemed to progress through four stages, beginning with self-awareness, through authenticity, to self-acceptance, and finally, to self-forgiveness.

The Value of Shame: Acknowledging Our Imperfections

Many in the 21st century maintain there is no place for the notion of sin; that dwelling on our destructive past behaviors is unhealthy. They prefer to call sin by different, less critical names: perhaps an error, mistake, regret, misstep, bad judgment. But I think that shame is helpful to dispel our illusions of innocence and independence. Acknowledging my scars—inherited and self-induced—was an indispensable first step towards eventual healing. And facing my responsibility for my self-induced shame was especially necessary for my integrity, self-respect, and humility. I agree with John Bradshaw's view: "Our healthy shame is essential as the ground of our spirituality. By signaling to us our essential limitations, our healthy shame lets us know that we are not God ... Our healthy shame is the psychological ground of our humility."[100]

Self-Awareness and the Value of Regression

To learn more about the causes and effects of my shame, I needed to stop looking away, and look backward instead. Regression is an initiatory rite of passage, about which the mythologist Mircea Eliade has written:

> Even specifically modern techniques, such as psychoanalysis, still preserve the initiatory pattern... The patient is asked to descend deeply into himself, to make his past live, to confront his traumatic experiences again; and this dangerous operation resembles initiatory descents into hell, the realm of ghosts, and combats with monsters.[101]

This process of regression begins by accessing the forgotten or repressed memories buried in the comforting oblivion of amnesia. All parents are so powerful, and the spells they cast so binding, that progress through my toxic shame was futile, until I began to unravel past events. Therapy was helpful in this work. I began to recall events at three and four years old, like being caught playing doctor in the garage with my next door friend Sally; and accidentally stepping upon (and fatally squushing) my pet turtle on the front stoop.

I remembered feeling lonely and thought I was a little funny looking early in grammar school. In the fourth grade, during recess, I was the only kid excluded from a huge game of Cowboys and Indians organized by the big kids. They said I had a baby face. (I did.) Retreating to the far corner of the playground behind the big stump to hide my tears, I recall deciding that I'd better get used to being alone. So I did. We lived a long way from school, and I often played by myself by pitching a hardball or hitting a tennis ball against a wall. I've always waited "behind the big stump in the far corner" to be chosen. It was often a long wait. I still can't bear to visit the dogs in the Humane Society: all those critters just waiting, some for years, to be chosen.

Some old memories were quite sweet: eating raw string beans in the victory garden and the Victory Day celebrations in the street in Milwaukee. I was also reminded of the good stuff long forgotten about grammar school: one of the best athletes in a class of fifty-four in the eighth grade and a class salutarian… But most of the recollections carried with them the old painful feelings; a movement, not away, but *into* the pain.

Why on earth would anyone want to dredge up and exhume the shameful moments buried in our interior shadows? Actually, recalling the painful events was not nearly as bad as I feared. Unearthing the past in therapy was like looking at an un-bandaged wound, less horrible seen, than imagined. "So *that's* the stump of a leg shattered by shrapnel… or, a radical mastectomy looks like that. Got it. It had to be awful. I'm so sorry you had to go through that." In a nanosecond, however, what next comes to mind feels more important than my reaction to the original trauma: "Does it still hurt; how does it affect your life now?"

The payoff, of course, was not just understanding the causes of all this, but its effects. Facing my old shame seemed to release a lot of energy that had been consumed by trying to stuff my memories out of sight and out of mind. Free of much of the old emotional charge of those memories, I began to slowly heal. This day feels more complete after incorporating these past fragments. I learned how my early childhood decisions affected my subsequent relationships with Mary and Christina and others; how they contributed to my anxiety, alcoholism, compulsions about work, my need to control, difficulties in finding my writing voice.

———

Group therapy was most helpful in my own process of regression because I could piggyback on the unearthed memories and insights of others. Many others are able to examine their past without any help from a therapeutic process. Long-term prison inmates often achieve the same results through reading, introspection, or religion. After years in the foggy adrenalin of rage, pain, or drugs, many "on the inside" were driven by their shame to figure out how and why they wrecked so many lives, including their own. A few even report that " the time served has become a blessing."

The ability and willingness of long-term, once-violent, prisoners to regress to better understand themselves struck me as quite remarkable. During an Alternatives to Violence weekend workshop, I asked about twenty of the men to recall their favorite hiding places when they were kids. In less than one minute, *all* volunteered to share the spots they found to escape their often chaotic homes. The urban guys went to the project rooftops or a favorite street corner; the rural guys ran to the woods or hid under their home's crawl space to hang with adopted snakes or feral cats. A thirty-something Miami gang leader found Jesus in prison. "I hid and slept many nights in the trunk of my mom's car, so she couldn't leave us all again to get high with some new dude." He smiled sheepishly and intentionally slipped into social worker, psychobabble-speak. "I've been told I have a few abandonment issues to resolve. I suppose I do."

Mircea Eliade, in the context of rituals celebrating the old myths, explains *why* this process of regression works:

> One frees oneself from the work of Time by recollection… This technique, then… is the importance of knowing the origin and history of a thing in order to obtain mastery over it. By reliving these memories, we free ourselves from their power by "burning them up."[102]

The Value of Authenticity

A good friend and another associate professor addressed a full lecture hall of one hundred and fifty undergraduates at Rollins College. Their subject was anorexia and bulimia, problematic for many college-age women. Midway through their lectures, the two speakers acknowledged their own recovery from the abuse of food begun when *they* were college kids twenty years earlier. This public acknowledgement of bulimia to one's students was an act of inspiring bravery. The new stillness of the audience in mid-lecture reflected the students' appreciation of this rare gift of candor. It signaled an unmistakable shift from a lecture to a testament; from academia to a sacred space and time.

Novelist Harry Crews felt humiliated by his hardscrabble South Georgia childhood in a family of impoverished tenant farmers. His abject poverty carried with it such profound shame that he said he couldn't stand to think, much less write, about it. He much preferred his identity as a respected author and professor of English Literature at the University of Florida. But his writing had languished and he'd come to understand the importance of all that early pain in that difficult place and time. "It was all I know about… it shapes the way I see out, it is what made me me… and it's what makes me unique," as a writer and a man. He decided he needed to tell the whole truth about those early years. His compelling memoir, *A Childhood: The Biography of a Place*, unleashed a more authentic and very powerful narrator.[103]

Telling the truth can be empowering for the speaker and inspiring to the rest of us. Speaking honestly about our self-inflicted wounds to another can embolden others to speak their truths, at least privately to themselves. In the silence that followed a discussion of the violence and drugs in their homes and neighborhoods, one inmate, serving a life sentence, had this to say:

> This whole conversation reminds me to warn my kids about the dangers that literally surround

them. But it also reminds me that I was the only one loading that gun. I was free to walk away and didn't. No one else's fault. Mine. Not my family, my homies, the hood, poverty, discrimination; none of that. In this place, we know now what we all knew then: "You play, you pay."

In a room full of very tough guys—now tougher on themselves than anyone else had ever been— everyone, without exception, nodded their assent.

Support Groups

I relied upon support groups to help me navigate through all four steps of regression, authenticity, self-acceptance, and forgiveness. Support groups are gatherings of like-minded people joined by a common interest. With the help of the internet, they're everywhere. In a Tanzanian slum, I spent a half- hour with a woman dying of AIDS in her one-room hovel. Her daughter and husband, also infected, had recently pre-deceased her. In pain, she managed to smile only once, when she told us of the one community that would not abandon her to die alone. Seventy other impoverished, infected sisters in her neighborhood had formed a mutual support group to counteract the isolating stigma of HIV/AIDS sufferers. In African slums today, the recovery slogan, "We're only as sick as our secrets" takes on new meaning.

Notices in our local Florida paper included these announcements for just health related meetings this week, among others: a group for anxiety and depression; a brain injury support group; a breast cancer orientation program; an Awake-sleep disorder group for apnea; one early-stage Alzheimer's support group for patients, and another for caretakers of people with dementia. Each of these meetings offers opportunities to share with a roomful of other people available to listen, understand, encourage, and teach each other.

Many kinds of support groups helped me heal from my shame and grow. Centering prayer groups, couples' and men's support groups, Marriage Encounters, psychodrama workshops, rebirthings, Life Spring weekends, The Forum, Landmark Education, group therapy, spiritual conversation groups, recovery groups, mandala circles… They ranged from five to two hundred people, meeting together for one evening a week, for one long weekend, or for years.

These communities offered safe opportunities to practice behaviors and values initially very new to me: humility, integrity, courage, attentiveness, trust, listening, empathy, truth telling, and especially, asking for help. The circumstances, mutual needs, and ground rules empowered people to speak spontaneously from their hearts, often "lean of expression." These gatherings were frequently sacred rituals to me: solemn, respectful, compassionate, egalitarian, insightful, focused, inclusive, emotionally charged, and transformative. In the mutual safety of the weekend workshops I've co-facilitated in prison, many guys reported that they played, laughed, cried, trusted, and spoken their truth—for first time *in decades*.

Most people in these various support meetings have been attentive, respectful, trustworthy, and present for each other—in and out of the rooms. Our intimacy was uncontaminated by the complications of longer-term relationships: we carried no accumulated judgments or resentments, nor any requirement to refashion intimate futures together. We felt safe to speak the most damning truths about ourselves and to welcome difficult feedback from others. Relinquishing long-held secrets to trustworthy confidants was remarkably freeing. What a relief; what a leveler. With everyone's cat out of the bag, there was no more need to pretend or work to "be looking good." No more feelings of one up, or one down; just a room full of imperfection—and courage.

Life Support

> New rituals have been born
> after centuries of silent response
> from cloistered Gods
> to countless requests for
> more detailed instructions
> about exactly how to become
> "more perfect, as our
> heavenly father is perfect."
>
> New sacraments
> are sung in minor keys
> by storytellers round
> circles of intimate strangers,
> seeing eye-to-eye each
> week or month or so.
>
> Tales of shared circumstance
> and imperfect perseverance are burnt
> offerings to revive

the communion of souls through
heart-to-heart resuscitation.
Their stories spin
adhesive threads
suturing patient-healers
back together again.

As only a converted agnostic can,
I wonder what—or whose—mystery
indwells at the still point
of these living mandalas,
ceaselessly spinning
these sacred circles?

The Value of Self-Acceptance

Many of the shared stories I heard in these various support groups were a lot more shameful than my own—some, because of the hurt the narrator caused others; others, because of the pain endured by the speaker. I was surprised by my mild reaction to even the most horrible of stories told by authentic people in these sacred spaces. My old need for understanding and approval was slowly replaced by a wish to merely understand.

Consequently, when I felt *their* acceptance of all my shameful stuff, in return, I trusted it to be as genuine as my own. I believed that they understood; they "got me". We all accepted that we caused suffering and have suffered. In those rooms, the most important shared subtext was that none of that mattered any more. Just people screwing up and recalibrating their bearings, to begin anew. Only that. Eventually, the groups' unconditional and compassionate acceptance evolved into my own self-acceptance. Poet Derek Walcott writes:

> You will greet yourself arriving
> at your own door in your own mirror,
> You will love again the stranger who loved you all
> of your life
> Who you abandoned for another, who knows you
> by heart.
> You will love again the stranger who was yourself. [104]

The Value of Self-Forgiveness

In the same way, my compassion and forgiveness of others led me to trust in *their* forgiveness, as well as their acceptance of me. This opened the door to the possibility of forgiving myself. Some inmates speak of the long process of finding forgiveness for their violent crimes committed decades earlier. Some felt the forgiveness of God. Others couldn't forgive themselves until a person they had harmed spoke aloud to them of their forgiveness: a child, lover, parent, or sibling; occasionally, even a victim. Jack Kornfield, a Buddhist teacher, writes, "Forgiveness is the necessary ground for any healing. We must learn how we may forgive both ourselves and others."[105]

Sometimes in therapy I've asked for the forgiveness of those no longer available to hear my request. Long after her death, I expressed my regrets to Mary. I asked forgiveness for the times I received more from her than I gave; and for my preoccupation, anxiety, addictive behaviors, and short temper. And I told her how sorry I was that I'd been unable to keep her memory as vital and alive as I wished for the benefit of her children. All this contributed to my ability to forgive myself, which felt like the last step in my healing process.

Healing

Healing my shame advanced all four of the spiritual ideals I'd adopted. *Wisdom*, as self-awareness, replaced the denial that had kept my toxic shame and my addictions under the radar for two decades. Healing allowed me to finally live in greater *peace*, less plagued by insecurity and loneliness. Recovery programs benefited my extended families, a belated act of *love*. Essayist Scott Russell Sanders explains why he writes about his alcoholic father: "... to drag into the light what eats at me—the fear, the guilt, the shame—so that my own children might be spared."[106] Finally, when exposed to the hundreds of others in support groups who suffer, as most of us do, it's almost impossible to avoid feelings of deep *compassion*.

Summary

Healing from my versions of toxic and self-administered shame was accomplished through the help of people in very different kinds of support groups. I spoke of:

The Value of Shame, (once acknowledged) as a prompt for humility.

The Value of Regression, fostering self-awareness and reintegrating our past.

The Value of Authenticity to further our integrity and connection with others.

The Value of Self-acceptance, the result of observing our acceptance of others.

The Value of Self-forgiveness, after noticing the ease with which we forgive others.

CHAPTER EIGHTEEN

HEALING OUR LOSSES: THE VALUE OF GRIEF

Losses and Life's Impermanence

We can't seem to hold onto a lot of important stuff. We lose our faith, illusions, youth, money, jobs, privacy, hearing, control, sight, agility, and friendships. We lose our bearings, memories, opportunities, self-respect, dignity, innocence, trust, and independence. And we lose most of our dreams: of how our life, or those of our children, were to have turned out, derailed by failed marriages, debilitating illnesses, lack of meaningful work… Because my father lived so long, he'd lost more than most: his wife, a grandchild, countless friends, and then most of his physical powers—his potency, balance, mobility, speech, dexterity, continence, and intermittently, his mental acuity. I wonder if the emotional impact of our losses are cumulative. In this chapter I'll focus upon only the losses incurred through the deaths of loved ones.

Hilary was our middle child. To get back in shape after the birth of her second baby, at thirty-five, she enrolled in the annual Marine Corps Marathon in D.C. In spite of her five hundred mile pre-marathon training program, she began to have trouble early in the race. At mile marker twenty-one, she collapsed in the arms of her family. Her brother, Galen, consoled her two little ones while Keith held his wife until the ambulance arrived an hour later. She died of hyponeutremic encephalopathy, caused by her body's inability to absorb the sodium intake of too much water in her system, a particular risk to "charity runners," on the course for more than four hours.

Avoidance and Repression of Our Losses

It's hardly surprising that we put off the emotional work of grieving our losses. Anne Lamott nailed it: "Grief sucks. It really does."[107] In a college essay written a decade after her mother died, Hilary recalled how difficult her own grieving had been:

> After experiencing such a great loss at such a young age, tree forts did not seem so much fun; and my best friends provided little relief. Bereavement is

definitely an individual sport. In the beginning, I awoke each morning surprised that grief had not strangled me in my sleep.

Some people I know have avoided grief work for a long time, because they felt too vulnerable to endure any more deeply felt pain. A friend's son died alone from a drug overdose, half a world away. She worried that if she allowed herself to really break down, she might never be able to stop weeping. Perhaps she feared that completing her grief would break her last connection with what she'd lost. She was right about one thing. If she never started to grieve deeply, she *would* never stop.

Men like me, on the other hand, employ an opposite rationale. To avoid grieving, we construct an illusion of responsibility and invulnerability. "A man *should* and *can be* strong enough" to contain and manage feelings of sadness. The implication, of course, is that deep feelings are for less self-reliant and more self-indulgent souls.

My reactions to the idea of actually taking time to grieve my loss after Mary died were not unlike those of our then four-year-old. Galen was not reluctant to share his dim view of this grieving business. After taking his turn offering the grace before our evening meal, he once added this postscript: "God, help me not to miss Mommy too much. And *please* God; make everyone at this table stop crying. My spaghetti is already cold." I've personally used any number of grief avoidance mechanisms "to stop crying," but my signature specialties are versions of the defense mechanism of substitution.

Instead of feelings of grief, I substituted something, anything, else that would distract me: travel, moving, new relationships, more work, harder play, a busier schedule—all effective short term methods to keep the wolf of grief at bay. On evenings and weekends, I was happy to keep my mind (and emotions) occupied by driving the four kids and friends thither and yon: to schools, the mall, baseball, soccer, softball, swimming, football, diving, horseback riding, gymnastics, tennis, piano, cheerleading, friends' sleepovers, the movies...

To avoid feeling, I even substituted the children's grief for my own. If any kid was having an especially hard time, my tears were for *their* pain—not mine. Years later, after Hilary died, I did it again. At the time of her death, she was weaning her ten-month-old, and nursing him only once each day, at eight in the evening. Without his mother, Walker was inconsolable. As all parents have done with hungry or ailing babies forever, Christina and I took turns swaddling him, holding him close, pacing, rocking, singing to him. He screamed for three hours every night for a week, until he finally fell asleep in our arms. We three were shattered by our loss of his mother, but only one of us felt free enough to express the anguish of all.

From Repression to The Value of Grief

Like most everything else on the spiritual journey, I learned about grief the hard way. I'd been blessed with a great teacher. When Mary died, my grief counselor was a ten-year-old. Hilary had done the heavy lifting of grief for her mother in our family, which her three brothers and I diligently worked to postpone. After her brothers went to sleep, Hilary climbed out of bed and tearfully crept into my lap in the family room. She spoke of her great sadness and loneliness and cried herself to sleep. Night after night, for months.

The rest of us couldn't face then what we know now—how much we all missed and needed Mary. But Hilary knew. God, she was brave. I finally put Hilary's lessons to use in my own therapy a decade or so later to say long-postponed goodbyes to Mary. And because of Hilary's example as a child, I was a little better prepared, twenty-five years later, to grieve Hil's own early death. I guessed that I should've been able to endure as an adult what she had at ten.

Grief

Grieving is allowing ourselves to feel deeply—to mourn—our losses. Referring to the deaths of her father, and years later, her best friend, Anne Lamott describes her own healing this way:

> ... It is only by experiencing that ocean of sadness in a naked and immediate way that we come to be healed—which is to say, that we come to experience life with a real sense of presence and spaciousness and peace.[108]

Like our shame work, the first work of grieving is regression. Much of the experience of the above-mentioned "ocean of sadness" is actually "re-experiencing" it. Our son, Ted, served on the board of a nonprofit in Denver that helps kids of deceased parents to heal, usually through helping them express their emotions.

The children are guided though experiential exercises like sand painting, theater performances, and individual and group counseling. My favorite is a padded room where the kids can let off steam together by roughhousing and pillow fighting.

The healing process consists of re-experiencing, recollecting, and re-telling our stories to ourselves and to others. These are stories about the deceased, their parting, our relationship, our regrets—told again and again. Finally we begin to tire of these, and then the stories lose their power over us. It takes time to relinquish the old attachment—and accept the new reality. An hour after getting news of Hilary's impending death, while dashing through the Cleveland airport on the way to Georgetown Medical, I kept trying to imagine how our family could ever live without her. The recurring images were twofold: an explosion that had torn a hole in the nexus of the family; and, of all things, a sock. The only way to close this hole in our hearts and this family would be as a sock is darned, threading one stitch at a time. Grief is not a seamless repair of course, and we're all still darning. The hole is much smaller, but nine years later, it's still apparent. Grief is not complicated; nor is it brief.

Good Grief—But Why Bother?

What's the point? Why is it important to feel all this pain and grieve our losses?

- "Our bodies hold the tears our eyes refuse to shed." Emotional pain seems to follow a natural life cycle that demands completion in due course. When I avoid feelings of shame, anger, sadness, or grief, it takes a lot of energy to repress them below the level of awareness.

- Grief and relief go together. Grief is bittersweet. At nineteen, Hilary wrote of the end of her first love affair: "I'm feeling pretty low now, but tomorrow I'll probably be elated. I'm not depressed; I'm just a little empty. I'm feeling strong and all mixed up at the same time. Do you understand? My heart is aching and healing at the same time." Yes, Hil, I think I understand now.

- We are anchored to the past until we release it. In the meantime, we're unavailable and absent from the present. "Avoiding grief robs us of life, of the now, of a sense of the living spirit."[109]

- Grief for the loss of loved ones is almost always complicated by anger or regret, followed by guilt. "If I'd... only reached out... not let her drive ... noticed the symptoms ... apologized... been more persuasive ... told him how much he meant..." Guilt may be the most difficult to resolve, because we have to forgive ourselves, whether or not our guilt is deserved or unjustified, rational or irrational. These powerful feelings can run us ragged. Feelings of guilt make it doubly difficult to cope with loss and therefore, doubly important to resolve through grief. Instead of repressing these feelings, we need to forgive ourselves, so we can begin to grieve.

Hilary had told us all that completing a marathon had been her dream since college, when she watched the racers sail past Wellesley College. I'd been an enthusiastic supporter of her marathon plans, and had I been there, I would have probably encouraged her to push through her discomfort to finish her race. Seven long years after she died, I spent a couple of months feeling overwhelming regret that I hadn't spent enough time with her. After she left Florida, Hil lived the last half of her life in the Northeast. We visited her each year and spoke a couple of times each month by phone. I know this sounds odd, but had I guessed she'd have so little time, I'd have never let that young woman out of my sight.

- The only consolation I've ever found for the loss of people I've loved is my memories of them nestled deep in my soul. If I haven't been able to finish my grief because the memories hurt too much, I'll suppress *all* the memories. Then, what have I left? If I listen carefully, I can still hear Mary's and Hilary's laughter. "Some folk say a person… is not dead until they are forgotten."[110] The value of remembrance is epitomized in this wonderful poem Christina found, by St. John Chrysostom:

> She whom we love
> and lose
> is no longer
> where she was before.
> She is now
> wherever we are.

- Suppressing our memories of them dishonors loved ones who are most deserving of our fond recollection and our celebration. How else do we keep the legacy of their gifts alive? Judith Anderson writes: "Re-member us, / You who are living, / Restore us, renew us. / Speak for our silence."[111]

- Our grief increases our compassion for the losses of others. Even after grieving runs its course, our heart never quite closes tightly again; it's therefore more open and available, as needed, for us and for others. After his kitten died, a dear friend wept every day for months. Each night, he still thanks her for opening his heart. He says he's never been the same. He hasn't. He was a wonderful friend to start with, and today he's more available, patient, kind, and open.

- In public, at least, wartime leaders are stoic. As always, Lincoln was the notable exception. Sandburg writes that the President wept often and openly for the terrible suffering he witnessed in the hospital tents (before anesthesia). And his heart opened in the scores of private audiences he granted to grieving widows begging for personal favors to relieve their families' poverty (before the welfare state). The capacity for such compassion must have been partially a consequence of grieving his own personal losses: the deaths of his mother when he was nine; of his closest sister; of Ann Rutledge, his only love; and of two of his four boys. Willie died at age twelve during the war years of his presidency.

- For me, the greatest benefit of our grief work is that it opens us to the spiritual value of gratitude.

Through Grief to The Value of Gratitude

> Bless what there is for being,
> Which has to be obeyed, for
> What else am I made for,
> Agreeing or disagreeing?
> —W. H. Auden[112]

Grief and gratitude go together. To appreciate the true value of what we've lost, it's necessary for us to grieve deeply and free ourselves to feel something else: gratitude for all that we once so enjoyed. I earlier defined equanimity, the nexus of our inner peace, as the satisfaction with, and acceptance of, life's good fortune and bad. Even greater than the value of acceptance is the value of gratitude. Ultimately, serenity is found in our ability to hold *all* our experience with an attitude of gratefulness. Freedom is being able to enjoy and embrace all things and lose them, again and again. The more easily I can toggle between grief and gratitude, the more peaceful I shall be.

Brother David Steindl-Rast writes: "… everything is gratuitous, everything is gift… And gratefulness is the measure of our aliveness. Are we not dead to whatever we take for granted?"[113] For the thousandth time, I see an eight-by-twelve-inch four color newspaper photo magnetized to our refrigerator door. I'm in awe of Samera Kadhim, a lovely thirty-something woman, dressed colorfully in layered rags, standing in the midst of her bleak, permanent homestead, the Taji trash dump outside Baghdad. She is laughing and her countenance is absolutely radiant. "It is not easy living here. But whenever I can, I smile and laugh."

―――

Sometimes I feel gratitude for my blessings in the full bloom of my *present good fortune*. Typically, Hilary once wrote, "Hi folks, things are ten on a scale of one to ten—as usual." She sent another letter during her first week in Kenya:

> The people are fantastic and the professors and the ranch are an incredible resource. My hut mates are

great. Kenya is amazing. Monkeys come freely into camp, and on a walk this morning I saw a calf being born. P.S. There are three beautiful men here. I'll keep you posted.

I'm ashamed how infrequently I express appreciation aloud. I sigh in our yard when I detect the fragrance of gardenia blooms, grapefruit blossoms, or rosemary. My breath catches in a wood when I see, just for an instant, a Baltimore oriole, bluebird, indigo bunting, or cedar waxwing. And I'm often grateful at the end of the day, when Christina and I talk of the children and their families, admire the beauty and sweetness of the animals curled round our feet, and delight in our warm, dry bed. But not nearly often enough.

Other times, we may feel gratitude *in the midst of our losses*. In spite of all my father's losses—perhaps *because* of them—he was always grateful for all of it. "At ninety-three, I should complain? I've been one of the lucky ones. I am immensely grateful for such a full, rich life." Christina and I are both companion animal folk. Four dogs mark each corner of the home site where we've lived for three decades. And between the north, east, south, and west burial sites lay our cats, fish, guinea pigs, rabbits, gerbils, and parakeets, all enriching Christina's gardens. Each burial is a blessing. As we dig, we savor the time to say goodbye, and thank each critter for all the magical moments of delight, touch, beauty, conversation, and wonder.

At Mary's funeral Mass, I spoke of gratitude *following our losses*:

> We're the lucky ones. Think of the joy she brought each of you intermittently; and how fortunate the

five of us were to return every day to her kind of support, counsel, and love… And Mary has left to all of us these dear ones. Teddy's equilibrium and warmth; Hilary's energy and competence; D'Arcy's clarity and sensitivity; Galen's sense of discovery and wonder.

Joseph Goldstein, a Buddhist teacher, writes of a hermit monk in eighteenth-century Japan. A thief stole his few possessions from his little hut. When Ryokan returned and saw what had happened, he wrote this haiku:

> The thief left it behind—
> the moon
> At the window.[114]

For months, the only sound I heard was the funereal silence at Hilary's graveside when the bagpipes stopped in mid-measure. How am I to finish that refrain, when the joyful possibilities of young women everywhere make me weep? After a year, I could finally reread a note Hil wrote when she was thirteen. "All the qualities you give to me is your gift to me. What I have become is my gift to you. On this Father's Day, I give you my happiness." How could one not be grateful for the gift of thirty-five wonderful years with such a being? Thanks, for all of it, kiddo.

Summary

The Value of Grief reduces the pain of our heartbreak after our inevitable losses. This spaciousness fosters our inner peace. Healing offers these eight gifts:

Grief relieves our heart of the tears we'd refused to shed.
Grief releases the energy needed to suppress our feelings.
Grief helps to dissolve our guilt and regret.
Grief immolates painful memories.
Grief makes room for sweet memories
Grief increases our empathy.
Grief unlocks the Value of Gratitude for all we once so enjoyed.

PART FOUR
FROM SELF-INTEREST TO THE IDEALS OF LOVE & COMPASSION

CHAPTER NINETEEN

FROM SELF-INTEREST TO SELF-FORGETFULNESS

> Love and compassion are the essence of all religion... It is important to understand that between you and others, others are far more important, because others are far more numerous.
> —the Dalai Lama[115]

The Primacy of Self

Thus far, we've addressed only the first of our two spiritual tasks. The personal challenge is to free ourselves from our instinctive *hedonism,* our predisposition to favor comfort and ease. The objective has been to increase our own wisdom and peacefulness through the practice of spiritual values. But of course, spirituality is not merely a quest for one's own happiness. In the remainder of the book we'll address our second spiritual quest, the interpersonal one: the increase of our love and compassion for others. The initial challenge is to free ourselves from our instinctive *self-interestedness*, which has a couple of origins.

Instinct. In *Behold the Spirit*, Alan Watts reminds us, "Our nature is selfish and we can no more change this nature than we can lift ourselves up by our own belts… This entire state of inescapable selfishness, blended of pride and consequent fear… is what the church terms the fallen state of man…"[116] Two different instincts manifest self-interestedness. To be *self-centered* is to be confined inside a *cul de sac* of our own making. The ego that serves our self-preservation so well, creates boundaries that protect and define—but also constrain us. Our self-absorption and self-consciousness consume enormous amounts of our attention. Our *selfishness* is different. It arises from competition for limited resources: food, mates, territories, attention, and status, all based upon the underlying assumption of scarcity, both imagined and real. In some circumstances now and in many circumstances in our past, there has *not* been enough for all.

A Culture of Neglect. In the West, our instinctive self-centeredness and selfishness are culturally reinforced. Ideas like secularism, democracy, capitalism, existentialism, and post-modernism all emphasize the primacy of the individual. One result of our individualism is an increased level of mutual neglect. We neglect our families, which are more geographically dispersed than ever. Since we moved fifteen hundred miles to Florida, we're less and less frequently in touch with Mary's extended New York- based family. The clearest measure of increased familial neglect is, of course, our divorce rates. Barbara DeFoe Whitehead writes:

> The American family has weakened because, quite simply, many Americans have changed their minds: about staying together for the sake of the children, about the necessity of putting children's needs before their own, about marriage as a life-long commitment, and about what it means to be unmarried and pregnant. This is not a political and economic conversation; it's about cultural values.[117]

We've also been neglecting our community organizations. In *Bowling Alone*, Robert Putnam noted a sharp decline of active participation in clubs and community volunteering. Even our governments are more neglectful. In economic downturns, domestic welfare programs and national foreign aid commitments are subject to chronic budget cuts, which eventually amount to permanent levels of aggregate under-funding.

This combination of our instinctive *and* cultural preferences for individualism stacks the deck against efforts to increase our love or compassion for others. I'm aware of only a couple of ways to offset this strong bias of self-interest and selfishness. The Eastern contemplative traditions insist that through disciplined training in meditation, we can expect to achieve a fairly recurring state of egolessness. After several years of practice, I'm embarrassed to admit that I don't expect be capable of a sustained sense of selflessness any time soon. On the one hand, as a Westerner, my ego is culturally too self-reliant to dissolve without a fight. Paradoxically, my ego is also much too fragile to voluntarily relinquish the field. I've found the following option to be more feasible for me than meditation.

From Self-Interest to The Value of Self-Forgetfulness

I think Nietzsche and St. Paul were *both* right. *Both* self-interest *and* selflessness are necessary to enjoy a full life. They both give me great satisfaction. For me, self-absorption and self-forgetfulness are alternately predominant, moment-to-moment. It may be futile for me to try to extinguish my self-centeredness and selfishness. But I *can* develop spiritual countermeasures to *coexist* with my self-absorption. Although my instinctive behaviors lunge forth, unbidden by thought, my self-forgetful behaviors require conscious intention. By forgetting myself from time to time, I *can* bridge the gap between another and myself. These self-forgetful moments occur through three conscious acts intended for the benefit of others: subordination, attention, and sacrifice.

Subordination to Others: an Antidote to Self-Importance. Self-forgetfulness occurs when I defer (and then submit) to something beyond myself. Anything I acknowledge to be more important than I am, at least for now, will do: a child, a friend, a stranger, the community, a program, a principle, the law, God. What are the higher causes to which we can choose to subject ourselves?

Attentiveness to Others: an Antidote to Self-Absorption. Self-forgetfulness occurs through absorption in *others'* lives. I'm able to disappear from my own sight most completely when responding to a need of a kid or a friend, particularly if they're hurting. The challenge for me is to broaden the circle of those to whom I respond. My full attention is engaged while arranging to repair a wheelchair for a homebound friend or finding a crib for a migrant family's newborn. My disappearance is also complete when focusing on the two or three most withdrawn and invisible pre-K kids to whom I occasionally read in a Migrant Head Start program. In those moments, nothing else matters than eliciting *their* engagement and pleasure.

Sacrifice for Others: an Antidote to Selfishness. Familial love and compassionate action can be best measured by our willingness to devote substantial portions of our lives for the sake of another. Oriah Mountain Dreamer has written: "It doesn't interest me to know where you live or how much money you have. I want to know if you can get up, after the night of grief and despair, weary and bruised to the bone, and do what needs to be done to feed the children."[118] When three of the kids were under five and the flu was making its nursery school rounds, Mary and I took turns on weekends high-fiving each other passing in the hall on the way back to bed for much-needed sack time. On countless winter Saturdays and Sundays we were nurturing the children *and* each other.

Sacrifice, of course, is in the eye of the beholder. Preparing fruits and vegetables for salads and soups for five hours in a homeless-shelter kitchen actually feels more like fun than sacrifice. But getting out of bed at four a.m. to do so is another thing entirely. It feels like a huge sacrifice and an enormous pain in the ass. You'd have thought that sleeping for a total of twenty-two years, (so far), would have been more than enough rest to satisfy me. I'm shamed by Kabir's exhortation:

Wake up, wake up!
You have slept millions and millions of years.
Why not wake up this morning?[119]

The Ideals of Love and Compassion

Both love and compassion require action. Because they are, by definition, acts on behalf of others, these spiritual values are also beneficent gifts to them. I'll use values and gifts as synonymous to describe our practice of love and compassion.

Spiritual ideals serve as inspirations to re-imagine what our love and compassion might look like on some days, in some ways. The following chapters in Part Four are designed to help remind us, as Stephen Covey urges, "to keep the end in mind." For example, focusing on love as a spiritual ideal helps me recall the far goals that inspired me to marry and have children in the first place. In the chaotic cauldron of families and communities, these two ideals of love and compassion can inspire us to more routinely praise, serve, appreciate, admire, celebrate, encourage, and bless each other.

In Section III, we'll turn to the subject of compassion, which I'll define briefly here as financial generosity and service for the benefit of strangers. But in the several chapters immediately following, we'll examine the spiritual ideal of love. As a matter of personal focus, I've arbitrarily limited my own ideal to love in families: of parents for children and between long-term partners.

FROM SELF-INTEREST TO SELF-FORGETFULNESS

Strangers and Families

To organize my ideals and this discussion, I've arbitrarily distinguished between my love of family and my compassion for strangers. This distinction between families and strangers may be convenient, but it is an arbitrary and flawed demarcation. Anne Lamott reminds us that, after all, what it "means to be saved—if we are to believe Jesus or Gandhi—is to see everyone on earth as family."[120] One challenge, for sure, is to imagine strangers as family. But another is to treat all my family members, day in and day out, with the civility, patience, curiosity, warmth, and deference with which I greet strangers for the first time. My experience with families in Tanzania has reinforced the idea that our love for members of our family is sometimes bound up with, and indistinguishable from, our love for strangers.

I dined with a Catholic priest at a youth hostel in Arusha, whose twelve siblings were murdered in the Rwandan genocide. A Tutsi, he survived only because he was enrolled in a Kenyan seminary at the time. He still doesn't consider it safe enough to return, and his "thirteen nieces and nephews wouldn't recognize me if we passed on the street." This stranger nevertheless sends almost all of his modest monthly stipend to help support his extended family.

Most of the fully employed Tanzanians I met contribute a fifth of their income to sponsor at least one, and often two, AIDS orphans. The money is used to send them to government-run rural boarding schools. They had never met these kids until a friend of a friend or a church lady asked for their help. I stayed for a month with Lydia, a fifty-five-year-old with four adult children. The Sunday morning before I left, two fifteen-year-olds appeared at the breakfast table. Lydia introduced the beaming boy and girl as her own. Her church had found a bevy of children foraging for roots in the countryside, dying of malnutrition after the death of the last adult in their rural hamlet. Because they're still underfed, these two skinny, delightful kids "come home" on vacations, to be stuffed with more nutritious food. These former strangers do chores around the house, attend church, and are encouraged, coached, and loved by their new families.

The Spirituality of Familial Love

One could argue that the family is too prosaic to warrant description as a "spiritual" container. After all, neither Jesus' call to love one another nor the Buddha's call to loving-kindness said much about families. To pursue his own enlightenment, the Buddha forsook his wife and child, whom he named "Fetter," translated as "Ball and Chain." Jesus warned us of using our familial ties to distract us from the need to, "Come, follow Me." The real issue that our religious founders left unaddressed is not *whether*, but rather *how* to love one another, in the context of the family.

One could argue that our founders didn't teach us about familial love because it's instinctive and therefore easy and natural to do. But my own experience is that love within our families is often more challenging—than easy. Hans Kung, in *On Being A Christian,* agrees: "It is easier to plead for peace in the Far East than for peace in one's own family. The more distant our fellow men, the easier it is to profess our love in words."[121]

In households, our physical proximity, unequal authority, mutual dependence, and lack of consciousness all challenge our consistent ability to love well. Add the chaos and emotions and the banal comings and goings of families: "Amy took my favorite skirt without asking *again*." Or, "Not two *more* C's?" For sixteen years, our family of nine was both wonderful *and* challenging. To the reasons already discussed, I now add these two, with several more to come, in support of the idea that marriage and parenting are indeed the most spiritual of tasks.

- Many religions consider marriage and the birth of offspring to be sacred events, deserving sacramental celebration. The reason they are such special occasions is evident: the survival of the kinship, the tribe, and the race depends upon them.

- "When Jesus challenged us to 'love one another,' he defined our neighbor as anyone who needs me here and now."[122] He was presumably not excluding a spouse who needs a hug or help doing the laundry; or kids who need vaccinations or help with geometry. Who is more worthy of our love than each member of our families?

Summary

The Value of Self-Forgetfulness helps me coexist with my more instinctive and culturally reinforced secular value of self-interest. Forgetting myself is both a means to, and a result of, love and compassion. I can minimize my self-interest by subordination, attentiveness, and sacrifice.

I – LOVE IN THE FAMILY

MARRIAGE AND THE GIFTS OF NURTURANCE

A Crucible of Spiritual Transformation

Why do we marry in the first place? Perhaps because we are in love; are expected to; can live cheaper than one; will double our joys and halve our sorrows; are lonely; want security; wish to share the responsibilities of raising children; or maybe because we anticipate needing help with the challenges of growing old. Or, all of the above reasons. But having adopted familial love as a *spiritual* ideal, I believe we need to add one more critical goal to our long-term partnerships: to further each other's growth: secular, psychological, and spiritual.

1) *Nurturing The Growth of Each Other*

In *The Road Less Traveled,* Scott Peck argued that the ultimate purpose of marriage is to encourage each other *to grow* to lead fuller lives, even if it threatens one or both parties' sense of security. Resistance to promoting one another's growth manifests in several ways. In a marriage counseling session, the wife of a friend announced that only her husband was in need of therapy since *he* was the one who had changed. It was a matter of considerable pride that she had remained steadfastly the same woman with whom he had fallen in love half a lifetime ago. But long-term stasis is not a feasible (or desirable) option for individuals or relationships. These two are divorced now.

Another friend married after high school and raised four kids. At forty, she decided to audit two college courses. Her husband vetoed this initiative by burning her college brochures in the fire place. He couldn't fathom why she left him the following year to pursue her bachelor's and master's degrees, both earned with honors.

Christina and I have both been pretty good at encouraging each other's growth. And the kids inspire us. Galen and his fiancé worked and lived together in D.C. Sara was offered a scholarship to attend Stanford, one of the country's three great law schools. Rather than have Sara willingly attend a good Virginia law school nearby, Galen left a great job in Washington for a good job in San Francisco—all just to encourage Sara's professional growth.

Our Differences: A Challenge And an Opportunity

I wish to avoid "lovey-dovey" platitudes about committed relationships. For most of us, such partnerships involve work as well as lovely satisfactions. There are good reasons that forty-three percent of new marriages don't make it. I want to acknowledge the reality of differences between partners that offer the potential for conflict. Our two binary stars may share the same gravitational field, but we occupy different orbits.

Different Genders. Like all caricatures, many of the hackneyed differences between men and women have bases in fact. Our complementary biological roles regarding children help explain different neurological wiring. For example, compared to me, most women I know are less tolerant of risk, more interested in matters of health, and more communicative.

Different Personalities. Jung isolated sixteen different types of people, depending upon the way they use their psychological faculties. Therefore, *very* roughly, on average we have a pretty slim (6%) chance of marrying someone who sees the world, feels, and judges in the same way; and attends to the same interests, as we ourselves do.

Different Life Experiences. Christina and I have different schooling, professions, religious backgrounds, interests, senses of humor, hobbies, values, social histories, friends… Of course we'll prefer different styles of relationship, parenting, and home management. In our case, our differences are exacerbated because for two decades we refined our divergent styles in two previous marriages.

2) *Nurturing A Growing Relationship*

Christina and I can serve as a catalyst for each other's growth only if we choose to use our differences in an intentional and conscious way. Marriage is a hybrid. Synergism combines the best qualities of two very different partners. But synergy requires each partner to willingly surrender some of themselves in order to enrich the relationship and each other.

The Value of Feedback. A primary responsibility of each is to hold up a mirror to help the other learn who we and they really are. This includes conveying and listening to information that may be deliriously unconscious to one of us, but painfully obvious or troublesome to the other. Partners help ferret out what is crooked or needy about ourselves, which we always prefer not to know. Here, both are teachers and both students. John Wellwood explains the "sacred combat" of personal relationships:

> Viewing one's partner as a sort of live-in guru may take some getting used to. But we should not romanticize this kind of connection, imagining that it will only bring sweetness and light. It is more like finding a worthy opponent.[123]

I mentioned to Christina recently that someone had found my participation in a meeting "too controlling." I was stung and feeling a little put-upon. She said (tactfully of course), "Ned, you orchestrate all the time, most recently last weekend with our friends over dinner. Much of the time it's stimulating and fun. Sometimes, for some people, including me, it's overbearing and feels controlling. Enough already. So, get over it."

The Value of Mediation. A dozen married friends recently talked about the countless issues about which they disagree: household order, maintenance, cleanliness, recycling, and chores; saving and spending; the hoarding or disposal of stuff; the *only* proper way to do the dishes, fold the laundry, drive the car, feed the cat, and discipline the children. Oh, we also disagree about risk, vacation destinations, future plans, aesthetics, libido, movies, sociability, food preferences…

Every couple acknowledged their numberless differences and incompatibilities taught them the usefulness of negotiation, cooperation, and generosity. Their differences also leavened their own preferences and points of view.

Many issues require a couple to agree upon only one solution. In those matters, I found I needed to be more willing to sacrifice a fair share of my own collection of opinions and habits to accommodate many of Christina's values and beliefs. For example, I wanted us to join the Peace Corps in retirement. Christina's objection to living in the underdeveloped world was stronger than my preference to do so, so we stayed put. Instead, I traveled on my own to Central America and Africa for a couple months of service work at a time. I would like to move to the mountains of western North Carolina; Christina prefers to remain in Tampa near old friends. We agreed to spend portions of some summers in the mountains.

In addition to the seven with whom we began our journey, I'd looked forward to having a couple of children together. After one month of living in the chaos of hers and mine, Christina was aghast at the mere thought. At Our Lady of Lourdes Elementary School, Galen announced to his first grade class during "Show and Tell" that "today my mom is having an operation so she won't have any more babies." The good Catholic nun asked the children to bow their heads and pray for the immortal soul of Galen's new mom. I was very disappointed that we wouldn't be having our own kids together, but Christina's wishes trumped my fantasies, and seven turned out to be just the right number.

The Value of Constancy. Perhaps our most important task to promote the growth of the relationship is to remain on the playing field to hang around and sort out our differences. Christina and I have had more than our share of disagreements, never much fun. But we've stayed together long after others might have walked away because quitting didn't feel like an option. We were once concerned about the dislocation of the kids. But then and now we also knew we'd drag our unresolved issues around behind us like dead cats.

Our conflicts dramatized how much we each needed to heal ourselves. Like the friction between sand and oyster, the end result of staying in the midst of our differences has been slow but discernable growth, for which we're both grateful. Our friend Howard wrote on our thirtieth anniversary, "You guys are an inspiration in the arena of marital survival, then success, and finally grace."

MARRIAGE AND THE GIFTS OF NURTURANCE

Summary

Marriage tests our willingness to accept necessary limitations to our autonomy.

<u>The Value of Nurturance</u> of mutual growth is axial for long-term lovers. This involves for me the practice of three subsidiary values:

<u>The Value of Feedback</u>
<u>The Value of Mediation</u>
<u>The Value of Constancy</u>

———

Because I'm aware of them in my own marriage, in the next two chapters I'll continue to emphasize the challenges caused by differences between two strong people in love. The spiritual values of *magnanimity* and *intimacy* are ways to compensate for those differences. They have each helped us to reduce the volume and frequency of conflict between two lovers in it for the long run.

CHAPTER TWENTY

THE VALUE OF MAGNANIMITY

> To be related to any other human being is to be *both* healed and hurt, *both* wounded and made whole. Our choice... is to which of those always present realities we shall attend.[124]
> —*The Spirituality of Imperfection*

In our discussion of desire, we listed a palette of painful emotions triggered by our *dissatisfaction*. Our dissatisfaction may manifest as a disappointment with our marriage or with our partner.

Magnanimity

Following is a snippet from a Prayer for a Magnanimous Heart, recited by a friend before every family meal for years.

> Keep us, O God, from all pettiness;
> … Let us be done with fault-finding and leave off all self-seeking.
> Grant that we may realize that it is the little things in life that create differences;
> that in the big things in life, we are as one…

Aristotle coined the word *magnanimity*, meaning large-heartedness. He also invented the opposite word—*pusillanimity*, or pettiness. Pettiness or small-mindedness, however, doesn't adequately describe me at my least magnanimous. Then, "petty" is too small a word. At my worst, more apt adjectives might be, "annoyed, frustrated, pissed, fault-finding, self-righteous, passive-aggressive, preoccupied, withdrawn…"

But in my least admirable married moments, mostly I feel resentment, a result of my perception that I'm being discounted or denied. I come by resentment honestly. The Big Book of AA says: "We decided that resentment is the number one common manifestation of our self-absorption that destroys more alcoholics than anything else. From it stems all forms of spiritual disease."[125] I know that when I feel resentment towards another, my heart has slammed shut.

My antidote to resentment is magnanimity. For me, this is the most axial of marital gifts. At a child's wedding a few years ago, I referred to the couple's professional expertise as litigators. "Your considerable intellects and willpower are valued assets in the law, but great liabilities in this new venue, where all cases are settled out of court, heart-to-heart." I define, and try to practice, magnanimity through the values of *generosity, acceptance, blessing, forgiveness, and renewal.*

The Value of Generosity

Magnanimity is the generous expenditure of time, energy, and attention for the benefit of another. It usually shows up in little ways. Once or twice in the middle of the night while their infants are being nursed, a few young fathers in our family also awaken, just to change diapers and keep their wives company, even if they have to catch a dawn flight.

Thirty-three members of our extended, inter-generational family spent a few July days under one roof to attend my father's funeral in Ohio. The spirit of generosity was palpable. There were insufficient beds, bathrooms, and circulating fans to go around. But there was a graceful, unspoken willingness of all to equally share a moderate amount of discomfort. It felt like a sacred space and a time of healing, especially since we were staying across the street from our parents' former home, about which there were some conflicted memories.

The Value of Acceptance

A broadcast e-mail message I received last month reads, "True love is an acceptance of all that is, has been, will be, *and will not be*." (Italics added.) Acceptance was a central theme in my discussion of the values of satisfaction and trust to increase our sense of peace. Acceptance is also a central value in loving relationships. We need to come to terms with the limits of our relationship in general, and with the limitations and idiosyncrasies of our partners, in particular.

Accepting The Relationship. Compared to the enchanting illusions with which most marriages begin, the everyday reality of the married state can be disappointing. To embrace and accept the possible, I had to release some impossible expectations, which of course are resentments waiting to happen. I'd thought that my primary relationship would provide:

- *Perfectibility*. As in "the perfect couple." In response to the question, "How do you create a happy marriage?" Iris Krasnow wrote in *Surrendering to Marriage*, "Lower your expectations... Most people, including myself, have imperfect marriages..."[126]

- *Meaning*. The love affair with our partner, like raising the children, is an important source of meaning for many of us. But for the duration of one's *entire* life, neither of these undertakings can possibly meet *all* our needs for meaning.

- *Stability*. We've spoken of the impossibility of static partnerships. All life is perishable, including last year's relationship with our partner. Renewable, but perishable.

- *Gratification*. Before I married, I had wired it roughly like so: Since she loved me, my partner was going to want (or at least be willing) to meet most of my needs, including all my sexual, support, *and* privacy needs. Right?

Accepting Our Partner. Once we've adjusted our expectations of the marriage contract, we begin to accept the limitations of our partner. Don't misunderstand. If I *could* have changed Christina, I'd have done so. But I've noticed that Christina doesn't seem to want to change that much; probably can't; and adamantly resists all requests to change, especially requests from me.

I tried passive resignation for a while, but that was only accompanied by more smoldering resentment. My strategy of staying, complaining, whining, and trying to either control or change us (read "Christina") had never worked. It was tedious, counterproductive, upsetting to people who loved us, and made us both crazy. I realized finally that rather than trying to change Christina, it might be a lot easier to change myself, most specifically my feelings of dissatisfaction. All I had to do was accept Christina as she was. Interesting concept. "A rock is hard, water is wet, Christina is Christina." A musicians' favorite proverb was helpful: "You get to choose the room you work; but you've got to work the room you're in." Adaptations like the following helped to change *me*:

- I can laugh aloud with Christina about the mutual disappointments we've *both* felt, for different reasons, during our marriage. It's more fun to laugh than pout.

- I can choose to ignore my disappointments. A friend acknowledged that his wife's automobile driving makes him half-crazed, alternating between frustration and terror. His most recurring spiritual practice is to avoid expressing his feelings aloud about her driving skills. Ever again. For the two of us, arguing has finally reached the point of terminal boredom.

- I can choose to attend to my own (very brief) list of shortcomings. For some odd reason, these negative qualities seem to be as resistant to change as Christina's own. I *suppose I could* start with my inconsiderateness, my sloppiness, my...

The Value of Blessing

> The practice of loving-kindness develops the habit of well-wishing. By celebrating positive qualities in other people, cultivating forgiveness, and manifesting kindness, I can make blessing my habit.
> —Sylvia Boorstein, Buddhist teacher and writer[127]

In Latin, magnanimity means "benediction." It is the generous bestowal of blessings on another's behalf. A generous spirit conveys blessings by praising others and wishing them well. Magnanimity involves the progression from passive acceptance to the active celebration and cherishing of all the qualities of my partner that attracted me in the first place, and still give me enormous pleasure.

Life with Christina has always been interesting. I love her steadfast values, leadership, articulateness, growth, curiosity, candor. Christina is energetic and enthusiastic about so many disparate parts of life: ministering to newborn grandchildren, hospice patients, and prison inmates; canoeing in the Canadian Boundary waters or the floodwaters of the Amazon; mothering, step mothering, and grand mothering; singing *a capella* medieval rounds or pop tunes with her sister; talking about spirituality or using profanity that would land grandkids in time-out for months; reading *Martha Stewart, Fast Company,* or *Organic*

Gardening; playing on the trampoline, in right field, or in her organic gardens for nearly fifty years. Christina is a character, whose very uniqueness is her gift to all of us, including me. I'm blessed.

The Value of Forgiveness

If we could all accept one another's shortcomings more frequently, there'd be no need for this fourth aspect of magnanimity. About 97 percent of the time now, mutual acceptance of each other's preferences works well enough for Christina and me. Peter asked Jesus: "Lord, how often shall my brother sin against me, and I forgive him? Until seven times?" Jesus said to Peter, "I don't tell you until seven times, but, until seventy times seven." (Matthew 18:21-22.) Four hundred and ninety occasions of forgiveness amounts to about once every three weeks in our thirty-odd years together. Sounds about right. The challenge to forgive is perhaps greatest in one's own family. In his interviews with Joseph Campbell, Bill Moyers said, "In marriage, every day you love, and every day you forgive. It is an ongoing sacrament—love and forgiveness."[128]

I know a man who has not spoken to, much less forgiven, his wife since their divorce forty years ago, even though he was, by most accounts, an absent, indifferent, and unhappy partner. I'm reluctant to admit that I can certainly imagine that degree of resentment, providing fuel for such a long-term grudge. My mother died in 1978. I realized only ten years ago that I hadn't fully grieved her death. One spring, during a family retreat on the shores of Lake Superior, I had some lovely and painful conversations with my father and my sister, Anne. I finally understood that I'd been unwilling to forgive my mom for behaviors occurring half a century earlier. Good Lord. I was profoundly ashamed by my self-righteousness and petty refusal to forgive anybody, much less than a person I so loved. Mom's photo is much better displayed on our wall than in the box in Dad's apartment.

A couple of friends have written, "Forgiveness is something you do for yourself to release your own anger and fear..."[129] The beauty of forgiveness is that one partner, alone, can begin to heal a relationship. After a crossed transaction in a talk with a friend, Christina and I noticed that our judgment was constricting our hearts to roughly the size of peach pits. It was so much easier to remind ourselves that we have, and will always, love him. Period.

As in so many areas of my spiritual life, once again Lincoln has been my greatest mentor. In a letter to his Assistant Secretary of the Navy, he wrote, "You have more of that feeling of personal resentment than I... Perhaps I have too little of it, but I never thought it paid. A man has no time to spend half his life in quarrels. If any man ceases to attack me, I never remembered the past against him."[130]

The Value of Renewal

Renewal is the restoration of normalcy if the relationship is damaged or breached, and our more normal routines of mutual acceptance fail. Renewal is the willingness to recharge, reconcile, and heal a relationship that is not working. It could be the result of diverging lifestyles, decreased interest, boredom, infidelity, or incessant conflict. Renewal is much more difficult than it looks. A married friend who has not been intimate with his wife for a very long while asks, "Why is it so hard for me to break the frozen sea that keeps us from venturing one foot across the bed, or across the kitchen, to begin to touch again?"

There are some issues or transgressions that a partner cannot accept or forgive until the other acknowledges fault and asks for forgiveness. Contrition begins with self-reproach, remorse, regret—and ends with saying out loud, "I'm really sorry." This particular concession has always been outlandishly difficult for me—in my relationships with friends, at work, and with Christina. Lately, I've noticed that my admissions of wrongdoing don't increase my self-reproach one whit; they actually help dissolve it.

Renewal rests upon our previously negotiated commitment about the longevity of our relationship. It may be as long as both still want to stay; or until a period of negotiation has passed; or after attempts at reconciliation have failed; or perhaps, forever. About fifteen years ago, Christina and I agreed that if, and when, either one of us changes our mind and no longer wishes to stay, we'd each feel free to terminate the relationship, without recrimination or guilt on either side. Granting each other that freedom, each day at a time, was liberating. Paradoxically, the subject of leaving doesn't come up much.

Summary

The attitude of big-heartedness is a necessary antidote to my tendency to harbor resentments about not getting my way.

It seems to me that the Value of Magnanimity has at least five different manifestations requiring continuous practice:

- The Value of Generosity.

- The Value of Acceptance of the limitations of marriage and of my partner.

- The Value of Blessing. The end game. It requires that I shift the focus from flaws to endearing traits.

- The Value of Forgiveness, for those times when we are unable to accept another's behavior.

- The Value of Renewal. The willingness to restart or heal the friendship after a hurtful fracture.

CHAPTER TWENTY-ONE

THE VALUE OF INTIMACY

Enchantment

By the time we're married, most of us figure we have a pretty good handle on who our life partner is. My guess is we probably don't. Our beliefs about one another are usually contaminated by some or all of these four delusions.

Through transference, we see lovers as our parents. We unconsciously choose a mate with the characteristics (positive and negative) of our parents. Some of the traits I view as negative in Christina are the same ones that bothered me as a child about my mother. I selected a partner with many of my father's characteristics: fun, critical, progressive, curious, reserved, energetic. Periodically, Christina and I have to remind each other that we are not one another's mothers or fathers.

Through romance, we see lovers as princes or princesses. This delusion is fostered by both parties' enthusiastic role-playing in the domesticated myths we call fairy tales. We want to be wedded to perfect princes or princesses, because if perfectly matched, we'll live happily ever after. As befits actors in a play, we both work hard at "looking good," dressed in our best courtship costumes. Christina pointed out that during our romantic period, I never smoked smelly cigars and rarely even wore my glasses. In the beginning, I was more trim, more solicitous, and more patient.

During the romantic phase our relationships, I suspect we're every bit as reluctant to really know the other as we are to be known. We'd rather pretend. We overlook a lot, because we want to. But acting is hard work, and when we de-role and see each other more realistically, we resent the deception, mutual though it was.

Through projection, we see lovers as gods or demons. Carl Jung noticed that initially, men unconsciously project the image of a Siren onto women. The woman's romantic projection on men is that of a Savior. I was drawn to Christina's striking physical beauty, and she to my articulateness and attentiveness. Fair enough. But then we up the ante.

Through increased familiarity, our illusory gods and goddesses become something very different. Before our positive projections morph into a realistic picture of the other, however, they become every bit as negative as they were once positive. From siren to witch; from savior to devil. Many relationships don't survive this about-face from vast overvaluation to vast undervaluation. But once we become aware that *we* are responsible for creating both the heroic and the villainous polar projections, we can begin anew with a partner who is, sadly and blessedly, just an ordinary mortal.

Through myopia, we see lovers as ourselves. We often believe that we both *do* see the world in the same way; that, at least, we *should* see the world in the same way; oh yes… and that my way of seeing the world is a smidgeon superior to yours.

———

Enmeshed in these delusions and feeling misled and trapped in long-term commitments, we tumble from surprise to disappointment to blame. Untangling these misunderstandings often takes some time, honesty, and painful disillusionment.

The Value of Transparency

> [W]e need relationships of the profoundest kind through which we can realize ourselves, where self-revelation is possible—whether in analysis, in marriage and family, or between lovers and friends… We are working at transparency.
> —James Hillman[131]

How do our long-term partnerships possibly overcome these biases caused by transference, projection, myth, and myopia? By working to become more transparent and uncover the authentic partner in each of us. When we marry, we yearn to love and be loved, to be close and connected. But this proximity comes with a non-negotiable price: our willingness to abandon our hiding places, to break cover, and become visible, as the wonderful, flawed person we are.

Because the conversational exchanges in all of the following stages of transparency are so emotionally charged, I found them difficult to navigate. These talks can easily veer from furthering transparency towards very different, disguised agendas, and thence to incivility. Instead of increasing our mutual transparency, Christina and I would be tempted to debate, rescue, disagree, assume, criticize, advise, mediate, disapprove, or object to something we thought the other had said. This contamination would invariably torpedo any attempt at transparency. The three parts of transparency I have in mind are revelation, listening, and intimacy.

The Value of Revelation: Sending

To reveal ourselves is to invite another inside our boundaries, which is a risky proposition. Sharing inside information is ammunition for an intimate partner to use against us in the heat of an argument or through a breach of confidentiality. And men, especially, harbor an additional concern about appearing vulnerable:

> [F]ewer than 10% of men fully disclose their feelings to their wives. Men see being standoffish, being imperious, as the right way. 'If I tell you about my problems, then that's weakness.' Yet that

attitude keeps them from an intimacy that leads to true understanding of self and a richer life.[132]

———

I avoid self-revelation in two ways. First, *I conceal myself* behind the persona I present to you in order to disguise my true identity. I may hold back thoughts and feelings about which I feel shame. Since I think *you* are an important arbiter of who I am, I hide my vices, insecurities, failures, self-doubt, humiliations, grief, guilt, regret. I hide myself. Second, *I embellish myself* and make believe. I pretend a little; (OK, a lot). Specifically, I want you to believe that I'm innocent, in control, beneficent, improving, righteous, and right.

To reduce my need to camouflage my defects and embellish my virtues, I practiced self-revelation with Mary and Christina, a little at a time. I found I could also prudently practice this kind of authenticity with our adolescent kids. They benefited from hearing about my foibles and disappointments and even some rules I broke as a kid—and the consequences I incurred. Sharing some of my own adolescence was a lesson in honesty and humility. It helped the kids to trust, from time to time, that they could safely be more forthcoming with us.

I also began to practice "copping to" my destructiveness, confusion, and pretense with other people also learning to tell more of the truth about themselves. One friend feels safe enough among a half-dozen buddies to speak about his own pettiness, dishonesty, selfishness, or cowardice. In so doing, he *always* mirrors something equally true about me. His straightforwardness is an inspiration to the rest of us. While spending a month in an addictions treatment program, eighteen men practiced the most rigorous honesty with each other. During the subsequent family weekend (during a very difficult time in everyone's marriage), we found that it had become easier to reveal more of ourselves to our spouses.

The Value of Listening: Receiving

Empathy is an emotional resonance with the speaker's experience, including his or her feelings. Empathy is "getting it." In *Out of the Dust*, Karen Hesse writes of Billie Jo's future stepmother, a woman who clearly gets it.

> And what I like best about her,
> Is Louise doesn't say what I should do.
> She just nods.
> And I know she's heard everything I said,
> And some things I didn't say too.[133]

I've learned empathy from two extraordinary teachers. At her funeral, Mary's brief life was summarized by her cousin, Paul, in three words: "Mary paid attention." She listened so well to her children, friends, and strangers because she was genuinely curious about their lives. And as a psychotherapist, Christina spent thousands of days with clients learning to listen attentively to hear everything they said, and some things they didn't say too.

I practice empathy by just trying to get the hell out of the way; becoming an empty space, free of my own interference. Empathy calls the listener to openness and silence, smoothing all the jagged edges that might catch and tear the delicate fabric of the speaker's vulnerability. Sustaining the openness to hear the intent, meaning, need, and message of the other creates a sacred space. Like a butterfly at rest on our hand, even the space itself feels fragile; the slightest disturbance causes flight.

This value of just listening has taken me forever to learn. I repeatedly stepped on landmines during my own empathy training. One obstacle to empathetic listening was my disagreement or disapproval, expressed or implied, about some aspect of the story or of the narrator. Instead of opening a window of trust for our partner, the slightest signal of judgment closes him or her down and leaves a bitter taste. Empathy is acceptance: nonjudgmental, non-critical, and non-assumptive.

Besides telegraphing disapproval, the other cause for my failures of empathy was my management consultant's interest in resolution. I've probably heard the speaker's specific issue several times before. I'm bored and frustrated by the person's need to process it aloud, again. I'm tempted to intervene to resolve the problem or the speaker's feelings. It's taken a long time to be able to just shut up. Empathy is dialectally opposed to my need, and dubious qualifications, to repair anything or anybody, especially friends, kids, siblings, Christina...

The Value of Intimacy

> The opus of the soul needs intimate connection, not only to individuate but to simply to live.
> —James Hillman[134]

If we reveal ourselves and listen to each other, we can expect moments of intimacy. Intimacy is being close. With the ideals of love and compassion, we ask: "*How* should we be closer to one another?" In this discussion of intimacy, we add a second question, which is "How close *should we be*?

Two Misunderstandings. Some of my initial problems stemmed from misunderstanding what married intimacy should look like. My first and most familiar expressions of intimacy were romance and sex. I recently visited the college campus in Canada where Mary and I fell in love more than fifty years ago. The sweetest memories of those college years were the thousands of hours we walked, hand in hand, around the campus and the city of Toronto. Too broke to hang in restaurants, we wandered about, huddled against the buffeting winds of Lake Ontario.

The first misunderstanding I refer to is that during the early stages of a new relationship, many of us imagine that our romantic and sexual passion should endure indefinitely, with similar intensity. They can't, of course. Their intense chemistry and emotions are too fleeting, charged, and inconstant for passion to support the heavy weight of ordinary days. When three good friends in their fifties married younger women, they considered their active sex lives as barometers of the health of their partnerships. That Hollywood standard of intimacy sounded like a harbinger of some future disappointment, and it was.

A second misunderstanding about intimacy shared by many men I know is very different. Instead of the concern that romance and sex might not endure, they fear that intimacy will. They worry that they will lose themselves and be suffocated by the other. But I've found that intimacy is so focused and intense it's necessarily brief and momentary. Intimacy is passing, almost fleeting, and followed, not by suffocation, but by withdrawal. In *Living the Questions*, Sam Keen said intimacy was like "hawks loving in mid-air."[135]

At a recent workshop, a dozen men and women participated in a brief exercise during the opening moments of the second day. Standing in pairs, we each shared a minute and a half about our first day's experience. We spoke and listened, entirely focused upon the other, exchanged a brief hug, moved to the next participant, and shared the same experience. A couple of opinions were memorable; most were not. But each meeting was sweet and… intimate. This experience raises this question. In intimacy, just what *are* we sharing with each other?

Two Gifts. First, I think we share our hearts. Transparent intimacy is open-heartedness. Father Di Cicco, the former poet laureate of the City of Toronto, writes of sharing our hearts in another intimate setting in his poem, *In the Confessional*: "… You hear the heart; the words drone, halt, put on hats,/ it is the heart you want…"[136]

Second, we're sharing the present moment. In the workshop I mentioned, most of us had no shared histories or shared futures that complicated our shared present moment. On the other hand, intimacy is a challenge for us in long-term relationships *precisely* because the experience of arriving and staying in intimate *present* moments is so easily compromised and contaminated by a couples' *past* disappointments or *future* concerns.

But the good news for long-term partners is a compensatory feature unavailable to other relationships. After years of self-revelation and empathetic listening, long-term lovers can feel at ease.

Each is in the care of another who knows and *accepts* their complicated past and problematic future. In a longer-term partnership, this ease, knowledge, and acceptance is an opening to something lovelier, deeper, and more meaningful than momentary intimacy, about which poet Bill Holm writes in his closing stanza in *A Wedding Poem*:

> ...But the dark secret of the ones long married,
> A pleasure never mentioned to the young,
> Is the sweet heat made from two bodies in a bed
> Curled together on a winter night
> The smell of the other always in the quilt,
> The hand set quietly on the other's flank
> That carries news from another world
> Light years away from the one inside
> That you always thought you inhabited alone.
> The heat in that hand could melt a stone.[137]

Summary

To achieve intimacy, we need to overcome the misinformation and unfounded expectations that cloud many new committed relationships. Becoming closer to each other requires the willingness of both to become more transparent.

This <u>Value of Transparency</u> requires a degree and skill of communication I have found challenging.

- The <u>Value of Revelation</u> requires the courage to openly share our unembellished selves.

- <u>The Value of Listening</u> is a limitation of our role to that of a mirror, to better understand and to encourage our partner to "think out loud."

- <u>The Value of Intimacy</u> promotes the exchange and sharing of our hearts in the present moment. For long term lovers, the present moment incorporates mutual acceptance of shared pasts and shared futures.

II LOVE IN THE FAMILY

PARENTING AND THE GIFT OF GENERATIVITY

I had guessed that raising kids would be a little like nurturing a garden: a lot of work for the first three years; close observation of what works and doesn't; and the need for balance, patience, and luck. A large responsibility for sure, but not a spiritual one. I came to see the spiritual aspects of all this much later. I've argued earlier that the family is a spiritual container. Following are three more reasons I view parenting, specifically, as a spiritual project.

1) *Parenting: Renewal*

Psychologist Eric Erikson coined the word "generativity" to describe the seventh stage of life, the creation of a new generation of offspring. All the members of our extended family experienced this generative relay when Mary, and twenty-five years later her daughter, Hilary, lay on their deathbeds. Both women were in intensive care units, comatose, on life support, and approaching brain death. Over a couple of days, each of their parents and siblings had time to visit with them alone. Later, we shared that we had each assured both women (then in their mid-thirties) that their babies would be cherished by all of us. Forever. In whispered tones, we had each encouraged them to release the dear ones into our care and freely take their leave. The day before Hilary died, her siblings flew thousands of miles with all their kids to join her one and three-year-olds to "celebrate the very, very best Halloween ever!" Foremost, families are keepers of the children.

Parents are the generational axis, the linchpin, of a spiritual relay race, and so, our best opportunity to renew the world. In the *Saviors of God*, Nikos Kazantzakis writes:

> Your first duty in completing your service to your race, is to feel within you all your ancestors. Your second duty is to throw light on their onrush and to continue their work. Your third duty is to pass on to your son the great mandate to surpass you.[138]

Kazantzakis's final sentence helps to account for our compelling and primitive responses to the presence of the newborn among us. Children represent our continuance and our topmost fruit. Through genetic insistence, the long-term survival of the race depends upon their promise to exceed us. Each new child is our furthest offering to our race and to each other.

Magician

At her first party,
the magician's
translucent fingers
perform a deft shell game:
walnut fists with parchment nails
hide Cheerios and string cheese
queued to soon disappear
in cauldron cheeks.
Then juicy sausage arms
are raised in triumphal
benediction.

This infant broke the spell
I'd cast over my office citadel,
and lured me to the kingdom
where babies dwell—
of strollers and baths and
naps of milky dreamings.

A potlatch gives to each,
all we have.
Our legacy to you, Greta
is the gift of life
at the farthest point
of our tribal lance.
Your gift to us,
abracadabra child,
is the ransom of our
lost hope and innocence,
now come round again.

Dear, sweet child,
Wave one last time
to the grandfather reborn
through your magic today
before you disappear
and go on your way.

2) Parenting: A Source of Meaning, Purpose, and Identity

Parenting is spiritual work because parenting, for many of us, is the source of our greatest meaning, purpose, and identity—the existential grounds of spiritual endeavors. Because families of origin have the influence to either expand or constrict the souls of its members, parents can do great good or great harm.

Because we know so little of the private life of Jesus preceding (or during) his public ministry, we are left to imagine that *his* family life was not particularly decisive for the quality of his later life and work. But for most of the rest of us, our families of origin are *very* formative, and often determinative, of our later happiness. And what else is a spirituality for? Hosting memorable dinner parties; or growing the business fifty percent; or creating albums of exotic vacations?

3) Parenting: The Need & Value of Spiritual Teaching

We need to civilize and prepare our kids for the secular world. But some of our parental training is spiritual in nature. Our "home schooling" is especially influential because the family is so ubiquitous. I've lived my entire life among families: with six others in my family of origin; among eight future in-laws while in law school; with Mary and Christina and all our kids; and now, with Christina, as empty-nesters. The family initially provides protection; later, a support network; and later still, perhaps a source of seed capital or a boarding house.

Living the values we espouse is certainly our most effective pedagogic tool. But in addition, as teaching moments occur, our mentoring will involve more explicit conversations with the children. Following are two courses in the "Home Schooling" syllabus, which the kids can't easily glean elsewhere.

The Basic Course in Love and Compassion. Parenting is spiritual because it is our most effective training ground for the spiritual ideals of love and compassion. These lessons will be indispensable to our kids much later, when they're faced with the challenge Rilke wrote about. "For one human being to love another: that is perhaps the most difficult of all our tasks, the ultimate, the last test and proof, the work for which all other work is but preparation."[139]

Training our kids to be more loving and compassionate adults can create ripples that extend forward into future generations. Our child becomes a self-aware, empowered, self-regarding parent, well trained to enlighten and love *her* children. They, in their turn, will more likely become good parents. I said once to Hilary and Keith: "This wedding ceremony is the still point between your grandparents' dreamings and the songs of all your unborn descendants, to the aftertime."

The Advanced Course in Character Formation. Sometimes we don't pass on very adequate spiritual advice to our kids. Most of us warn the kids about the dangers of strangers and drugs and premarital sex. But these "just say no" concerns are often presented to warn them of the *physical* consequences of imprudence. They're heard as dire threats to be obeyed rather than as issues of personal choice. Further, these discussions (especially about sexual restraint) are often proxies replacing weightier ethical issues.

Peter Singer thinks that teaching children to responsibly drive a car is a much more important moral lessen than weighing in on sexual issues. Beyond the "family values" of chastity and obedience, what *other* values are important in the creation of their characters?

Once the kids leave home, the subject of character is unlikely to be revisited beyond the church walls. But why *do* so many parents, certainly including this one, often avoid speaking directly with their kids about matters of character? These next reasons may contribute to our tendency to water down our effective spiritual interventions with our children.

Parental Impotence. Emboldened by the expiration of the unofficial ten-year "statute of limitations," our seven kids felt free to share more of their old high school high jinks. For parents who thought we were pretty hip to our kids' lives, Christina and I were embarrassed by the extent of our delusions about the kids' safety, prudence, and innocence. We apparently didn't want to know about the drinking, sex, and drug experimentation of some of them, partially because we felt impotent to do much about it.

Pedagogic Ambiguity. The question is *how* to teach the kids. Our challenge has been to invite our children to consider our points of view without triggering their resistance to "forcing it down their throats." Easier said than done. I've had better results with open discussions about values *they* espouse instead of lessons about my beliefs or moral standards. Some of the more useful ethical conversations we've had at home concerned discussions about issues confronting our friends or theirs. These talks provided a context in which to share, a little at a time, the values we wished to encourage them to at least consider including in their repertoire.

Parental Confusion. A lack of parental clarity about *what* to teach the children may be due to parental ambiguity or disagreement about *their own* current beliefs and values. Since I hadn't given them much thought myself at the time, I felt I was in no position to teach them about spiritual principles. Parents with one foot in the religion of their youth and the other in post-modern pluralism are in an especially awkward position. Books like this may stimulate parents' thoughts about their own beliefs and values as a platform for broader discussions with the kids.

Summary

The Value of Generativity. Parenting is a spiritual responsibility because it fulfills our genetic duty to raise children who will contribute to the progress of the race. The creation of strong, healthy, compassionate offspring is a clear contribution to spiritual and secular progress.

The Value of Teaching. Parenting is a spiritual task because it's a unique opportunity and obligation to teach lessons rarely discussed elsewhere about character, compassion, and love.

CHAPTER TWENTY-TWO

THE VALUE OF LIBERATION: SETTING THE CHILDREN FREE

...Visiting the inequity of fathers on the children and the children's children to the third and fourth generation.

—Exodus 34:7

Parental Hand-Me-Downs

Upon their graduations from college, we informed each child that we considered our financial responsibilities complete, with only two exceptions. If we could afford it, we'd pay *some* of the costs of their post-graduate work, should they ever want it. And, whether or not we could afford it, we'd pay *all* the costs of their psychotherapy, should they ever need it. Both offers still stand.

Our natural impulse as parents is to bestow fulfilling lives upon our children. We all want to honor the Hippocratic oath to "First, do no harm," but I'm pretty sure we *all* bequeath the kids emotional scars. A professor of philosophy reminds his students, "It is ontologically true that, by virtue of being a human being, every last one of you was hurt as a child." These hurts are especially harmful because they're unconsciously embedded early in a child's life.

The aspiration to raise happy and healthy kids is often mitigated by parents' economic constraints, genetic legacies, or emotional challenges. Many parents are burdened with mental disorders difficult to treat or heal. Here, I wish to address more common and less severe parental dysfunctions that *do* respond to consciousness-raising interventions, including reading, coaching, therapy, recovery, or workshops. But this was always slow work for me. Facing my destructiveness in the first place took a while; shedding the habitual negative behaviors took even longer.

Many of our own parenting flaws are inherited from our original family. Some may impact our children's development and even bloom in full force in their subsequent families. The term "liberation" is meant to describe the intentional work of setting the kids free from intergenerational contaminants. Following are my own parental hand-me-downs that, to one degree or another, have surely impacted our kids. By the time I could significantly repair most of them, the children had already begun families of

THE VALUE OF LIBERATION: SETTING THE CHILDREN FREE

their own. I hope some of these personal discoveries may be useful to others and to them in raising *their* children.

1) *Parental Spells*

A life script is a message, usually from parents, designed to influence a child's adult behavior. A script is an expectation, expressed or implied, about the course of a child's future. Scripting is harmful because it is predicated upon the parent's unconscious personal preference rather than the child's choice. In *Scripts People Live*, Claude Steiner writes:

> A person with a script is invariably disadvantaged in terms of his own autonomy or life potentials… [A] man whose script was to become famous, became the most successful surgeon of his city, at the expense of a satisfying family life and happiness. On the other hand, a person with a script such as alcoholism has no socially redeeming features… Banal scripts, such as 'Woman Behind The Man' or 'Big Daddy' are the rule, and script-free lives the exception.[140]

These intergenerational influences are powerful and often pronounced. I've no doubt that my social reformer great-grandfather was the influence for the idealist script embedded in this book. Some scripts are easier to discern from a distance, like the scripting (and coaching) of adolescent athletes by overbearing parents. Most scripts are less obvious, particularly for the participants.

Scripts are also very hard to reverse, even by adult children. I was a management consultant for a real estate developer whose founder had endured a very public and messy bankruptcy twenty years earlier. He was succeeded by his very competent eldest son. Because he was impatient to restore his lost fortune and his reputation, the father urged his child to grow the business at an obviously imprudent rate. His son didn't feel free to break the father's spell and reject the legacy of his bankruptcy script. The business continued to grow apace, failed, and was foreclosed by the same banks that had participated in the tragic drama two decades before.

Sometimes of course, children rewrite their own scripts, with or without others' help. Terry Hershey tells a story of two parents concerned about their ten-year-old daughter's inattention, inability to sit still in class, and lackluster grades. The three of them met in the office of the Middle School's student counselor, who was listening to classical music when they arrived. He asked the parents to join him outside. The three adults wandered around to his office window. Inside, they watched the child respond to the music by pirouetting in graceful spirals around his office. He looked at them both and said quietly and firmly: "This child is *not* learning challenged. She's a *dancer*." The young woman grew to became a distinguished Broadway choreographer today.

Hopefully, parents can help avoid passing heavy scripting along to the next generation. Adverse life scripts have plagued several of my ancestors. Depression, anxiety, and addiction were often secreted from the view of the extended family. Separately, my parents acknowledged that a primary motivation for their own recovery from addiction late in their lives was the probability that their kids were four times more likely to become alcoholics than were children of non-alcoholics. We've worked hard in the last twenty years to interdict these threads and alter that script. Our seven kids have been encouraged to be vigilant about the risk of contamination they bear, and if ever need be, to ask for help.

2) *Parental Curses*

All marriages include some anger, but excessive conflict is pervasive and damaging. The curse of conflict can be insidious. In the first year or two after Christina and I merged our two families, our children were often the victims of our unconscious passive-aggressiveness. To avoid expressing our displeasure with each other, we'd share our disapproval about the behavior of one of the other's kids. Until we began marital therapy, Christina and I weren't even aware of this crazy triangulation, which caused such painful confusion and recrimination. We've tried to make amends for catching these kids three decades ago in the crosshairs of our own emotional chaos.

Paradoxically, even divorce, the ultimate parental conflict, can serve as an opportunity for conscious parents to model a more civil, negotiated conflict. I've always admired Christina. For fifteen years, when her children were especially impressionable, she never said a negative or critical word about their father in their presence, even to defend herself from his frequent criticisms of her. Not once.

The trick in this process of parental conflict resolution seems to be to view conflict as arguments to negotiate rather than as battles to win. We are called to sheath our weaponry and agree upon a set of ground rules. The most difficult ground rules for the two of us to honor are these two: acknowledging our own mistakes; and acknowledging each other's point of view. We work to enjoin and shelve blaming, shaming, shouting, pouting, withdrawing, accusing, insulting, interrupting, and exaggerating. Most importantly, we struggle to distinguish, again and again, between nine different positions: *mine, yours, and (hopefully) our blended* views—of the way it was once; is now; and the way we wish it to be in the future.

3) *Stereotypical Abuses*

The source of all parental abuse arises from the inescapable disparity of power between parents and children. All kinds of physical abuse are terrible. But abuse has many, less violent faces. These two harmful stereotypical behaviors seem fairly common.

Household Rules. A common abuse of parental authority is their often unconscious, but deeply etched, "family rules." These rules are toxic because the parent's love is conditioned upon the children's compliance. These instructions to kids may consist of a few attributions, like these: Be Nice, Be Quiet, Be Careful, Be Perfect, Be Strong, Be Quick. As important, are parental injunctions, that might include: Don't Be Yourself, Don't Think for Yourself, Don't Show Off, Don't Talk Back, Don't Cry, Don't Feel, Don't Be Conceited.

Parenting Styles. Another form of subtle abuse is gender-specific parenting biases, that may look something like these:

Toward a child of <u>the same Gender</u>, a parent may be:	Toward a child <u>of the opposite Gender,</u> a parent may be:
Competitive	Supportive
Judgmental	Conspiratorial
Persecuting	Rescuing

Some Typical Parental Behaviors:	Some Fathers' Behaviors:	Some Mothers' Behaviors:
Irritability, seen as:	Preoccupation	Nagging
The default feeling:	Anger	Moodiness
Control is through:	Criticism	Guilt

These stereotypical behaviors are hardly indictable offenses, but they take their toll. The most effective interventions were conducted by the kids themselves. Eric resolved that he would never imitate my ill-temper or his mom's nagging when he came to parent his own kids, and I think he rarely does. Eric is one of the best-natured fathers I know.

4) *Over & Under-Parenting: The Value of Balance*

Kids' future happiness is impacted by the degree of parental involvement in their lives. While the children are younger and still at home, parental involvement might take the form of more or less *control*. The question then is the appropriate length of the parental tether.

Below, we'll address another kind of parental involvement. This is the question of the most appropriate amount of *support* for the kids, both before and after they leave the nest. Regarding the ideal amount parental support, I imagine parents fall on a continuum on either side of "Just Right." On the less supportive side, a parent might move from disengaged, to distant, to absent on the extreme end. On the more supportive side, the positions might move from co-dependent, to enmeshed, to helicoptering, to smothering at the opposite extreme. Rather than the specific needs of each child at different stages of her or his life, many parents' location on this continuum seems to be more determined by the emotional disposition of the *parent*. I have erred on both sides of this equation.

Over-Involvement. In relation to my children, at various times, I've wanted to feel needed; to make their passage risk-free for them; or to make their passage worry-free for me. These biases induced me to err on the side of over-involvement. For many months after their mother died, the four kids and I slept together on wall-to-wall mattresses spread across half the master bedroom floor. Sleeping in a big pile together was fun and comforting for all of us then. One by one, as they began to heal, the children would end, and then begin, their night's sleep in their own rooms. I was a little disappointed when Galen finally withdrew, teddy bears in tow, to sleep in his own bed.

I still feel pretty tangential and a little lost when all the kids and their families gather during the summers for a week together. I much preferred my old role as the leader of the band. Now in those gatherings, I often have to repeat myself just to be heard. I remind myself that feeling like an outsider is just a new version of my old stuff. My new supporting role is just as it should be.

Under-Involvement. I spent a weekend in Mexico scuba-diving with a father and his fourteen-year-old. Anxious to display his readiness to share adult responsibilities, the young man frequently asked his dad if he could help with the boat, the fishing, and the diving. It was painful to witness his father's preoccupation and inability to even hear the boy's petitions to work and play together. On that day, in the confines of that small boat, his father was absent, and his son, invisible. I wince at the thought of the times that, preoccupied with my own work, I was equally unavailable to my kids. I neglected to spend enough time teaching them and just hanging out.

In Tanzania, I spent time with two Americans, both obsessed by their absent fathers who they believed had abandoned them and their mothers years before, in favor of their divorced fathers' new wives and families. One was a lovely fifty-year-old former Peace Corp volunteer, scraping by on the minimal wages paid by NGOs. The other was a twenty-something college student, having a hard time finishing his undergraduate course of study. Ellen Goodman writes about the more extreme cases of lack of support, but these two adults were also certainly *feeling* abandoned:

> One third of American children, nineteen million, live away from their father. Every year forty-percent of them don't see their father and one in five haven't seen their father in five years. The thought of a deserted child is simply: 'Why are you unwanted?' That is the only question. Or, 'Why were you unwanted?'[141]

Whether parents have been excessively over- or under-involved in their kids' lives, some of the resulting long-term problems for the children are quite similar. They originate from their shared self-portrayal as victims.

- *Dependence.* Both absent *and* indulgent parents promote the child's continued dependence. The overindulged child will feel diminished and incompetent, especially if she continues to accept advice or financial help upon which she has long been trained to rely. At the opposite pole, the two American expatriates still desperately need their fathers' approval decades after their fathers had left. As long as they wait for this (increasingly unlikely) eventuality, their growth and independence are stunted.

- *Undervaluation.* Both sets of kids (under *and* over- parented) want acceptance and admiration. Instead, they feel they get only advice and judgment. This disrespect has predictable long-term implications for their self-esteem and self-confidence.

- *Blame.* If the kids continue to blame their parents for much of anything, they're relieved from responsibility for all the decisions and consequences of the rest of their lives.

Both the under- and over-indulged child will have to learn to separate from their parents (and from the need for their approval) before they can commit to a mature spousal relationship of their own. Until then, the temptation to find another dependent relationship is pretty irresistible. If not fully separated from their own parents, they may remain children to their spouses and children parenting their children.

Our passage from blame, to independence, and then to forgiveness, set me and some of my siblings free. During the twenty-five years between my mother's and father's deaths, their five children, with each other's insight and support, were able to heal many of the childhood wounds. At the time of Dad's death, the rancor so numbing when Mom died was replaced by empathy and gratitude for *both* parents' gifts of life and their lasting contributions to each of us.

Summary

The Value of Liberation refers to our opportunity to shed our dysfunctional parental legacies so that our kids, and their kids, will be spared. The baggage I carried into my parenting role, both inherited and self-created, impeded our children's growth.

The Value of Balance. The right balance between too much and too little parental control—and later, too much or too little parental support—seems to require travel along a razor's edge. The problems created by erring on either extreme of parental overindulgence or absence are quite similar.

CHAPTER TWENTY-THREE

THE VALUE OF ENCOURAGEMENT

The Gift of Self-Confidence

As a co-parent of seven and grandparent of eleven, I learned to measure young children's self-confidence by the length of the tether they maintain between themselves and their mothers' sides. For those under eighteen months, this distance is usually measured in meters. One afternoon, a few months after Hilary died, I introduced her sixteen-month-old to our neighborhood park. After a quick turn on the swing, he waved bye-bye, turned on his sneakered heel, and did what Walker does best. He walked. And walked. Vectoring through scores of older kids and adults, he navigated empty ball fields and a playground teeming with kids, to the far side of a huge recreation building. *Way* out of sight of his point of origin, he pushed open the gym door and bee-lined for a basketball being used at the time by ten members of the senior high school basketball team. I finally intervened to scoop him out of harm's way.

So the kid can walk. But on Walker's journey of a sixth of a mile, this toddler *never* looked back to see where I was. Not once. He busted the curve on my "mother's skirt" theory for children several times his age. His self-confidence seems boundless. My reactions to Meriwether Walker's inaugural journey are mixed: apprehension for his untutored fearlessness and celebration of his confidence. Walker is the sum of my fears and hopes for all the children. I'm inspired by this little boy's boldness and a self-reliance (imprudent or not) that I've never known. Go, Walker, go. For all of us. Where are you taking us, little one?

———

In the last chapter, we spoke of the goal of reducing the unhappiness parents unintentionally cause their children. Now, we'll address our great opportunity to increase their happiness. I believe the primary influence on children's longer-term well-being is their self-confidence. This attribute determines the size of their comfort zone as well as the store of courage necessary for them to set sail beyond it. We can help prepare our kids to face the world with more confidence through our encouragement.

THE VALUE OF ENCOURAGEMENT

Inexorable Cycles

In rural Guatemala, I spent a few weeks with a large extended family. One of the senora's grandsons was a nine-year-old orphan. His father had been executed two months earlier, murdered by vigilantes in the town plaza for cattle rustling. Ramon, who was sad and shy and diminutive, was always invited last to the family table and granted the smallest portion (often just tortillas). After I realized he was not just skinny, but malnourished, each evening we drew upon my emergency stash to discretely savor a couple of Snickers bars on a short walk together. This family's dynamic mirrored the pecking order of the flock of chickens in the yard and five watchdogs tethered around the property.

We've all witnessed uneven distributions of *psychological* nourishment for children in households, classrooms, and playgrounds. Parents, siblings, teachers, and other kids seem to make largely unconscious assessments of children, based upon some combination of their energy, appearance, physique, intelligence, aptitude, friends, personalities... We might describe a kid, for example, "as not very well coordinated," or " nice," or "bright." It also seems to me that each child intuits the consensus of opinions of others about herself; that is, whether she is more or less appreciated, noticed, heard—valued—by others.

Thus begins a cumulative, self-fulfilling, helical process. Based upon the confidence gained through favorable recognition by others, the confident child becomes more secure. She telegraphs her self-assurance, and because self-confidence usually creates a positive response, her self-assurance is reinforced. The reverse is true for the insecure child; he takes fewer risks based upon his discouragement about others' inattention or disapproval. Around his peers, the child lacking confidence avoids eye contact, hangs back, and is therefore left to himself. Left out, he feels rejected and invisible, retreats a little, is overlooked even more… and on and on.

This unrelenting cycle is a draconian psychological determinism that can last forever. When the kids are younger, parents and teachers have some degree of influence over a child's initial accumulation of self-confidence. We can provide reassurance in a steady, reliable stream. We can manage the level of challenge at home to assure each child more successes than failures. We can reinforce the less dominant children in the family and continuously recalibrate the volume of encouragement distributed *between* our kids. I watched several middle-aged Latina teachers in a Migrant Head Start program. They each devoted extra attention to the least articulate of their charges. They knew that the following year, the busy kindergarten teachers in public school will have to leave the limited English students to their own devices.

But our ability to influence our kids' self-confidence diminishes as they get older. A college professor categorizes his senior psychology students thusly: he calls the self-confident few "players." They're the ones who more freely participate, and are more enthusiastic, engaged, and enlivened. The more numerous, passive, and less interested students are "spectators." He urges them to practice participation in the safety of his classroom. "It will be harder to learn to participate in the larger world. My concern for you is that if you don't play, you can't win."

"Fathering and Mothering"

> ... One parent may be more supportive, the source of emotional security that all children require... The other parent may be more achievement-oriented, pushing children to extend themselves beyond the comfortable cradle of love... In some contemporary families children are cuddled by their fathers and disciplined by their mothers.
> —Amitai Etzioni, *The Spirit of Community*[142]

To encourage self-confidence in our kids, we offer them two gifts of great price: assurance about their lovability (learned through parental comforting); and assurance about their competence (earned through parental challenges). Marilyn Ferguson writes in *The Aquarian Conspiracy*, "The child develops self-esteem in an atmosphere of unconditional caring, (and) mastery in an atmosphere of appropriate challenge."[143]

Instilling Self-Confidence in the Child Through Two Kinds of Parental Encouragement

	The Masculine	The Feminine
The Goal is the Child's:	Competence	Self-esteem
The Parenting Gifts are:	Discipline	Support
The Parenting Process is:	Challenging	Comforting
The Predominant Style is:	Demanding	Accepting
The Objective is the child's:	Self-mastery	Self-satisfaction
Parental Approval is:	Conditioned	Unconditioned

- The good news is that these two sets of training tasks are *not* gender specific. For instance, my father, raised and spoiled by a houseful of servants, was more accepting and less demanding of his own children. I inherited more masculine lessons from my mother, who had learned how to work hard on a the farm. Thank goodness she insisted her children learn "the value of hard work." In South Africa, while studying animal tracking, I shared a campsite for a week with a forty-something couple from Hamburg. She was a pediatrician who pissed ice water. He taught fifth graders and was the most nurturing soul I've ever met, before or since.

- Each parent needs to provide *both* comfort and challenge. The problem is that these two tasks call for opposite skill sets, often distasteful to one or another parent. Although we naturally gravitate to one style or the other, dual parents need to develop *both* their masculine and feminine aspects. To become more fully developed human beings, the work of individuation calls for fathers and mothers to be androgynous; to become *both* mother and father, in more equal measure. One role is not enough—for their or their children's best interests.

- As with all parenting tasks, this exercise is easier (and easier to avoid) in two-parent households. But most single parents don't have the option to split up their two parenting roles. Forget individuation; the more urgent goal is the *sanity* of the single parent, who has to learn to toggle back and forth between "the more supportive and more achievement-oriented modes of parenting."[144] A few weeks after his mother died, when Galen was still four, he asked a question that accelerated the development of my own mothering role: "Dad, I still don't understand one thing; if you're going to be the new mom, who's going to be the new dad?" Although both of us justifiably questioned my ability to adequately play both parts, learning to better do so became indispensable for all of us.

- Parents need to clearly distinguish between the encouragement of self-esteem *versus* the encouragement of self-discipline. Parents and children sometimes confuse our efforts to instill unconditioned self-esteem, with our conditional admiration for their competencies. Our frustration about the boys' shoddy homework and household chores contaminated our expressions of love and appreciation for them, which should have always been kept an entirely separate subject.

- Sometimes the contamination of these two objectives is more subtle. A neighbor's family in Ohio included two kids who were outstanding student leaders and athletes. Their parents unconsciously (but I thought, obviously) held these two in greater esteem *because* they were more successful in school. Esteem for all five of their girls was confused with, and conditioned upon, their performance. I think the three other children accurately intuited that they were less valued as a result.

- Without any help from parents, the two objectives of support and challenge can be confused by the kids themselves. Some high school teachers are dismayed by students who have received large doses of self-esteem training in earlier grades. Many of these kids still believe that their self-worth (never in doubt) insulates them from criticism for non-performance. The wrong answer on a math test? "Hey, no problem, Mrs. Johnson. See, I was just thinking about it differently." Of course, in the real world, self-esteem and competence are not fungible assets. A wrong answer is always just a wrong answer.

The Value & Gift of Self-Esteem

The Feminine is conveyed through Support and Comfort. Abraham Maslow clarified two kinds of motivation. To feel loveable is to feel sufficient; to feel the need for love is to feel deficient, which might be expressed through a hydraulic metaphor. A person operating with a sufficiency motivation is like a freshwater spring; a deficiency motivation is a drain without a stopper.

Deficiency Motivation	Sufficiency Motivation
My *need* for more love is paramount.	Once my needs are satisfied, my love is available to *give* to others.
I draw others' love into myself like a black hole.	Life flows from me in abundance. There is enough love to give away.

Self-esteem is the acceptance of ourselves as unconditionally worthy of love. Self-esteem is also the foundation of our ability to genuinely love another. The basis for children's self-esteem seems closely related to the degree to which they feel valued, which partially depends upon their parents' *availability* and *warmth*. If a parent is unavailable, the child feels abandoned. If parental warmth is lacking, the child feels rejected.

Parental Availability. The greatest measure of how much our children feel valued is surely the amount of time we spend with them. Because she had been a first grade teacher for thirty years, my kids' maternal grandparent knew how important it was to make herself available to her seventeen grandchildren. She stopped whatever she was doing to sit down to pay close attention to each child's stories. All those kids knew they were cherished. While sheltered from an afternoon's squall under the canopy of our grapefruit tree bursting with fruit, I think again of Memom.

Scott Peck writes, "If you can only play patty-cake halfheartedly, you are running the risk of having a halfhearted child."[145] Last weekend, for three hours, I had fun playing with Lego blocks with an eight-year-old. We built part of a Super Space Station with 2,000 pieces the size of memory chips. But playing dolls with a two-year-old for more than ten minutes is numbingly boring to me, inducing a listless trance. In those moments, Scott Peck's admonition haunts me.

Parental Warmth. The most obvious indicator of warmth is a parent's willingness to be close—to touch. My favorite times with my kids were rough-housing and pillow fighting on our king size bed. Touch is easy for most of us when the children are infants. For several weeks, Christina and I cared for two grandchildren still in diapers. Our bodies were exhausted; but in constant touch with the babies, our hearts were full. Recently, Christina and I walked with two grandchildren for hours and miles around Sea World. I loved it. Weeks later, I can still imagine the grip of a seven-year-old girl's sticky fingers in mine.

The Value & Gift of Competence

The Masculine is conveyed through Challenge and Self-Discipline.

Challenge. Our more feminine qualities, like enthusiasm, mutual support, and trust are developed for safer environments. These contrast with qualities of fathering, which include training children to meet challenges. The masculine parent teaches boys and girls to solve problems and deal with adversity—and adversaries. Theodore Roosevelt personally epitomized and promoted this aspect of the masculine:

> ... I wish to preach not the doctrine of ignoble ease, but the doctrine of the strenuous life; the life of toil and effort; of labor and strife; to preach that highest form of success which comes not to the man who desires mere easy peace, but to the man who does not shrink from danger, from hardship, or from bitter toil, and who out of these wins splendid, ultimate triumph.[146]

I recently spoke to a pair of sixty-five-year-old friends making very divergent strategic life decisions. One, a former college history professor, was planning to return to graduate school to become a therapist. The other mentioned that he had known for years that he needed to see a therapist, but "now it's way too late in life to do anything about it." A partial explanation of the contrast between these two is the quality of self-discipline needed to perform a challenging or unpleasant task. For one, spending less than an hour a week in therapy for two months was too challenging; for the other, spending more than two years in graduate school was not.

Training. Parental training makes a difference. My parents encouraged me to work part-time when I was twelve. I had a paper route of fifty-seven subscribers yielding a cash flow of eight bucks a week. I recall the satisfaction I felt when I periodically peeked at the savings passport book. Over the next decade I was proud to have earned over nineteen grand in summer jobs that paid for most of my college education. On the other hand, fathers of two friends had been absent most of their lives. Neither had a parent who modeled the satisfaction of surmounting difficult challenges. Even now, they avoid hard work and boast of successfully arranging their lives to be as *easy* as possible. They're at a loss to understand why anyone would ever *want* to work hard—at much of anything.

Failure. I'd long considered failure as personally shameful and to be avoided at all costs. But now I believe that part of competence training is learning how to deal with (and even encourage) failure. Winston Churchill defined leadership as "going from failure to failure without losing enthusiasm." A small group of engineering students in Tampa founded an intentional community of urban homesteaders. They're constantly experimenting with one sustainability initiative after another: erosion control, affordable irrigation, solar stoves, and urban gardens planted atop carpet remnants. We asked to see their new tilapia pond.

Unabashed, one of the students proudly fished out a mollusk the size of a dime. "The tilapia haven't exactly worked out yet," he cheerfully offered. "We're going to try a different approach in the spring. But in the meantime, I highly recommend one of these little critters, an unexpected by-product of our failed experiment." They embrace the permaculture ethic that 'failure is useful as long as we learn.' I'm inspired by their enthusiasm about their successes *and* their failures.

Discipline. A sense of competence for girls and boys stems from achievements acquired through the practice of self-discipline. During the few days preceding their transplantation, seedlings grown under ideal indoor conditions are denied water until they begin to wilt. The purpose is to harden the young plants to better prepare them for the trauma of relocation to the rigor of outdoor beds. Hardening the kids for the challenges of the real world sometimes feels as counter-intuitive as this gardening lesson was to me. (It certainly works well for the seedlings).

Today, young people feel especially conflicted about discipline, perhaps for the reason shared by sociologist Alan Wolfe:

> The capitalist society no longer posits a sharp dichotomy between self-discipline and self-indulgence… Capitalism requires self-restraint in order to produce its panoply of goods, but, then again, it also requires hedonism to encourage people to buy them. [Daniel] Bell called the resulting tensions the cultural contradictions of capitalism.[147]

For example, against the current headwind of the general culture, it is harder today for a parent to enforce rules about homework. From Monday to Friday, the average teenager spends twenty-one hours watching television or listening to music; and 3.7 hours doing homework (often concurrently). The old college standard of eight hours of homework for each class hour has been replaced by a new ratio of two to one.

THE VALUE OF ENCOURAGEMENT

I did a lousy job of teaching self-discipline to our children. On one hand, my work model was pretty unattractive to them. One child watched firsthand how much stress, obsession, and absence accompanied the professional lives of his father and stepfather. He decided the work lives of adults were pretty stupid.

But mostly, I failed to model the kind of self-discipline I preached. Consistent supervision was needed to effectively reinforce house rules, help with algebra, limit TV, monitor friends and evening activities, audit piano practice, follow-up on their chores, and teach money management. Between my long hours and travel and Christina's full time enrollment in college and grad school, we were often unavailable to enforce the rules. Persistent follow-up was consistently lacking. The truth is also that this kind of persistent follow-up bored the hell out of me. I have enormous respect for mothers who have the discipline to home-school their kids.

My lazy supervision of the kids, while insisting they honor their home work and household commitments, had a predictable outcome. In place of teaching and following-up with the kids on their projects, I substituted my frustration and criticized them for nonfeasance. Ted and I were at loggerheads about his mediocre grades some semester in high school. He said that my nagging felt designed to "intimidate me into getting good grades; and that isn't the right way to do it." Two decades later, Ted earned a Masters degree with straight A's, while running a very profitable business. Thank goodness the boys learned most of their work and saving disciplines *after* they left home.

Summary

<u>The Value of Encouragement</u> is designed for the intentional increase of children's' self-confidence. This is best accomplished through these two gifts to our children.

- <u>The Value of Self-Esteem</u> is the feminine contribution to more self-confidence. This comforting support is unconditional acceptance by available and warm parents.

- <u>The Value of Competence</u> is conveyed conditionally by parents who teach the kids to meet challenges, risk failure, and learn discipline.

III COMPASSION FOR STRANGERS

OUR RESPONSIBILITY FOR OTHERS AND THE VALUE OF ABUNDANCE

We've spoken of the two faces of spiritual transformation. The first is personal: gradually moving from our instinctive hedonism toward greater wisdom and peace. The second is communal: replacing our selfishness with acts of love and compassion. Zen Master Deshimaru was asked, "Isn't a personal quest for inner freedom selfish in comparison with the quest for freedom for all?" The master replied:

> *Both are necessary*. If I can't solve my own problems, I will not be able to help other people solve theirs. I have to free myself of my own problems before I

can help other people to free themselves. So both are necessary... You must know how to combine compassion with wisdom.[148]

The Value of More Abundant Life For Others

Mary and Hilary were both organ donors. On the first anniversary of her death, the Regional Transplant Consortium in Washington reported the specific ways Hilary's donations had helped others. Because of the medicines administered to her while on the respirator, Hilary's heart and corneas were suitable only for medical research. Her orthopedic tissues were implanted in thirteen patients. These were used to hasten the recovery of bone grafts used in reconstruction surgery, spinal fusions, and oral surgery. In addition:

- Hilary's liver was received by a fifty-seven-year-old woman in imminent danger of death.

- Hilary's left kidney and pancreas were received by a twenty-nine-year-old diabetes patient on the critical list.

- Hilary's right kidney was given to a man who had been on dialysis treatment for four years.

- Both Hilary's lungs were transplanted to a woman who had been confined to a wheelchair, and was now ambulatory.

My God. How awful. How wonderful. Harvesting the perfect gift. A life, a death, and more life. The ancient religions' sacred offerings and blood sacrifice were always one and the same event. I joined fifteen organ recipients in their fifties and sixties during a local support group meeting. They no longer celebrate their biological birthdays. They celebrate their "new birthdays," the anniversary of the day of the implantation of their new organs, reverently referred to as "the gift of life, given them."

In the last two centuries in the West, "more abundant life" has been manifest in several ways, including greater wealth; broader political freedoms; and progress in racial and gender equality. Albert Schweitzer wrote:

> ...The man who has become a thinking being... accepts as good preserving life, promoting life, developing all life that is capable of development to its highest possible value. He considers as evil destroying life, injuring life, repressing life that is capable of development. This is the absolute fundamental principle of ethics, and it is a fundamental postulate of thought.[149]

But More Abundant Life for Whom?

"Every day Americans waste enough food to fill the Rose Bowl... The average family of four throws out an estimated $1,350 annually. Cutting that food waste in half and giving the money to a food kitchen would provide 700 meals."[150] Issues like organ transplantation and food conservation are blessedly clear ethical courses. But most of the time, the enhancement of life is not clear cut at all. The tasks of preserving, improving, and extending life raise our most important and difficult ethical issues.

Does "more life" mean an increase in the quantity or the quality of life? Does it promote more life to divorce and disrupt one family to begin a second one, in which the adult may be a better lover or parent? Is peace at any price superior to more violence, even if it solidifies an oppressive peace for the vanquished? For one generation? For two hundred years? When does euthanasia detract from—or add to—life? Does the existence of the death penalty (and its possible deterrent effect) increase or diminish life? Should the West's very recent ecological concerns about coal-fired factories and generating stations trump China's long awaited economic growth?

A Numbers Game

Bear fewer children with more stuff, or more kids, with less? Sovereigns plan like we do, weighing the quantity against the quality of life for the clan.

In China, after five millennia of too little to eat, the Party planned for more food for all. But now, the sated villagers, on rations of one-quarter of a grandchild apiece, are haunted by ghosts in their midst.

They mourn for the few hundred million or so unborn, who cast their votes in absentia, each one adamantly opposed to The Plan.

A world apart, another small village celebrates Mass for one hundred and fifty poor families with four kids apiece, fidgeting in hand-me-down jackets, zipped-up and hooded like flippered baby seals against the cold, cobblestone church.

I fret for these pups, the pride of their family planners, the celibate, well-fed priests. This Mexican puebla will never support all these children bathed in Christmas candlelight, each radiant one a source of unspeakable joy tonight.

But this planner wonders now: how to identify exactly which three hundred of these smudged, cherubic ones should not have been allowed to eat our rationed food, mortgage the commonweal, and break apart this statistician's heart?

More Life for Other Sentient Beings?

This is not an ethics book designed to weigh the specific pros and cons of public policy—with two exceptions. I present these exceptions to illustrate the kinds of thorny issues prompted by the ideal of compassion, solutions we often delegate to others or to the state. The question in these ethical matters is always the same: more life for whom?

> Late on the third day, at the very moment when, at sunset, we were making our way through a herd of hippopotamuses, there flashed upon my mind, unforeseen and unsought, the phrase 'reverence for life.' (Albert Schweitzer)[151]

In what ways am I similar and connected to nonhuman life? Schweitzer feels a connection with hippos. Gandhi's identification was broader still: "I want to realize brotherhood or identity not merely with the beings called human, but I want to realize identity with all life, even with such beings as crawl upon earth."[152] It sounds like he would have identified with gnats and wood lice. But our discussion of non-human life here will be limited to only sentient beings, defined as those possessing sensation, feeling, and consciousness.

Most of us share a curious ambiguity about the lives of animals. With some, we identify very closely indeed. A 2002 survey for the American Veterinary Medical Association found that 47 percent of pet owners regard their pets as family members. And we've (finally) been galvanized to protect wild animals, the larger the better (see hippos, above), most especially carnivores like ourselves. I personally have an unfathomable, joyful response to interspecies cooperation: playing with our dogs and cats; watching swimmers soaring with killer whales or a choreographer on foot, whispering dance instructions and encouragement to eight mares and geldings in the equestrian show, *Cavallo*.

But we don't attach the same value to farm livestock. Every year, we slaughter 100 million cows and pigs and five *billion* chickens (not including the 160 million male chicks we grind up to feed to the more productive egg-laying females). Atop a long food chain of "life consuming itself," carnivorous behavior leaves little room for sentiment. We seem to work hard *not* to identify with the source of our next meals, although they're immeasurably beneficent to us. In exchange for three squares a day and protection from (other) predators, we get to consume delicious steaks, chops, sausage, and *Chicken McNuggets* pretty much when we please, thank you very much.

———

Married to a vegetarian of eight years, I've been consuming less meat and more vegetables. Like millions of others today, I'm in the throes of an ethical reassessment about my continued consumption of meat, cheese, and eggs. Some folks base their decision to become vegans, vegetarians, or pescatarians upon dietary or digestive rationales. Others have ethical concerns. They decry the exploitation of farm animals for our sustenance; some consider the slaughter of another animal to be barbarous. Many are concerned about the environmental costs (the disposal of animal waste) associated with growing large farm animals to maturity as economically as possible. Some object to the adverse impact on the third-world caused by devoting so much grain to grow livestock rather than to nourish hungry humans.

People like me protest on narrower grounds: I'm especially concerned about the lifelong and gratuitous suffering we impose upon many of the animals we husband, caused by acute overcrowding. Defended by producers as necessary to maintain competitive costs, overcrowding affects veal calves, hogs, milk cows, egg-laying hens, and broiler chickens. To conserve every valuable calorie, hogs and veal are never allowed to move about, even to turn around, for an entire lifetime. Five laying hens share a floor area equal to two pages of typing paper, requiring some to lie above or below one another. (Permaculturists allow twice that much space for *each* hen to forage). Because of the stress on the crowded animals, the weaker birds are mutilated and cannibalized. The poultry breeders' solution is to remove the animals' beaks. Not to provide more space, but more pain.

I confess to be particularly identified with the plight of poultry. To complement their drought-ravaged stock of cattle and goats, the Maasai are being encouraged to raise chickens in Tanzania. But unless vaccinated, New Castle disease kills 70 percent of the poultry stock every year. To help vaccinate all the flocks in the smallest villages before they're released from their coops, we set out at dawn. Our team of four still holds the World Record for The Maasai Morning Chicken Bowl. Vaccinating 229 birds all over town was a ball; feathers, dust, chickens, and roosters squawking and flying every which way. One of my most enduring images is a yellow handful of chirping, wiggly chicks. One drop of vaccine in each of five reddish eyes extended their lives another four months, 'til next time.

OUR RESPONSIBILITY FOR OTHERS AND THE VALUE OF ABUNDANCE

More or Less Similar?

To return to the question at hand. How closely can I really identify with a hog? In what ways are we connected with, and similar to the animals we eat? A surprising source, the philosopher Jeremy Bentham, wrote this about cruelty to animals: "The question is not, Can they *reason*? Nor, Can they *talk?*, but *Can they suffer?*"[153] Three centuries later, from Princeton, philosopher Peter Singer responds to those questions:

> Humans are not the only beings capable of feeling pain or of suffering. Most non-human animals, certainly all the mammals we habitually eat, can feel pain. Many of them can also experience other forms of suffering. For instance, the distress that a mother feels when separated from her child or the boredom that comes from being locked in a cage...[154]

A young man in his twenties, raised in a Western ranching family, rationalized the slaughter of livestock because they were after all, "dumb brutes." He spent a summer during college working at an animal rescue farm, where, to his surprise, he became attached to one particular heifer. Three years later, he stopped by to visit the farm staff. While he and the owner were catching up, a lone cow sauntered from the far corner of the field. She walked directly to him, placed the top of her head firmly against his chest, and nuzzled him. This dumb brute had recognized and remembered him fondly after all that time. He wept; and his life and vocation were changed.

A friend sent me a fresh lobster from Maine in a dry-iced container. For the two-day journey, the creature was trussed with claws banded, in his rectangular Styrofoam straitjacket. When I opened the top of his snug cage, he made the same distinctive, high-pitched squeak we hear when we boil live lobsters, while we sip a divine Chenin blanc. There's a question about whether a clam feels pain. But as his eyes followed my movements around the kitchen, I had no doubt that my lobster was a lot more like me than I'd ever before allowed myself to imagine.

We might ask whether we can justify the infliction of unnecessary suffering on other sentient beings. Matthew Scully, a well-known conservative, has written *Dominion: the Power of Man, the Suffering of Animals, and the Call to Mercy*. He believes that, at the very least, "We cannot just take from these creatures, we must give them something in return. We owe them a merciful death, and we owe them a merciful life."[155] Their death to satisfy our desire is one thing, and perhaps arguable. But causing gratuitous physical suffering for millions of lifetimes to save a few pennies a pound seems inexcusable.

CHAPTER TWENTY-FOUR

OBSTACLES TO GENEROSITY & THE VALUE OF RE-VISIONING

Compassionate intentions are one thing. But it's another to put our time and money where our mouth (and maybe even our heart) is. If the enhancement of life for all is so clearly beneficial and a clarion moral imperative of every religion, why do most of us avoid offering strangers very much of our time or wealth?

A third of a century later, I'm still ashamed to admit a Faustian bargain I made during a business junket in Mexico. Waiting for some companions to complete their business in a nearby brothel, I walked through a barrio stretching to the horizon. Building-paper walls enclosed dirt floors and corrugated roofs. Barking dogs, crying babies, and Tex-Mex music competed for sensory attention with cooking fires and swales of sewage. I remember deciding that I needed to earn lots of money so that, someday, I could afford to devote myself to serving the poor. Such grandiose horseshit. Of course there'd never be enough money, nor a better time, than right then. Like the rich man in the parable unwilling to give up "all he owned," I just wanted to buy more time.

Excuses, Excuses

I might well be a microcosm of the culture's procrastination, conflicted motives, and empty good intentions regarding compassion for strangers. Until my retirement, my generosity was manifested by token contributions and future aspirations. In an attempt to understand my lack of generosity for such a long time, I've recalled a dozen elaborate explanations, some of which may resonate with you. First, I noticed three preeminent *cultural* inhibitors to more generous acts of compassion.

Sacrifice is Counter-Cultural. Successful parenting and partnering call for a sacrifice of our instinctive *self-interest*. Compassionate generosity requires a different kind of sacrifice—the relinquishment of my consuming, instinctive *selfishness*. Sacrifice is a loss; and loss is always painful.

The more valuable to the giver, the greater the assumed value of the gift to the recipient Deity. No pain, no gain. For desert nomads, burnt offerings of lamb and oxen were gifts of enormous value. But today, amidst our great wealth, the very idea of sacrifice feels alien: not just counter-instinctive and counter-cultural, but even counterintuitive. In the West, many can manage to design their whole lives around the avoidance of any painful sacrifice. This phenomenon extends even to the middle class in the developing world, including, for example, the newest generation of educated Hindus in India. "The old path you took to God was through suffering and renunciation, the way of the *sanyasi*. That doesn't appeal to the young crowd... There is no sacrifice required with these new gurus."[156]

Individualism has run amok. Faust was the first prophet of the modernist myth. The Faustian ideals of individualism and aggrandizement run contrary to the very idea of generosity. Goethe's hero expressed virtually no interest in the nurturance of loving couples or children, and even less in the support of needy strangers.

Urbanization. In 1850, only four cities in the world had a population of a million. Today, fifty percent of the world's population live in cities. Because cities are so densely settled, their occupants require more privacy. Additionally, due to the accelerating rate of immigration into the world's cities, most new neighbors are strangers. With distant strangers for neighbors, our xenophobia trumps our neighborliness (and opportunities for compassion).

In addition to our cultural avoidance of sacrifice, the onslaught of individualism, and inexorable urbanization, I've personally employed several, more timeless rationales to avoid acts of generosity to strangers.

Denial. A Presbyterian prayer asks that God, "Forgive us… for pasting stained glass on our eyes and on our ears to shut out the cry of the hungry and the hurt of the world."[157] We can avoid seeing the poor by re-routing our commuting routes. After living in Tampa Bay for thirty years, I just recently learned that forty-five minutes to the east, in a single Catholic parish, there are *seventy* migrant labor camps, home to several thousand Mexican farm workers. Who knew?

Noble Sentimentality. Expressing our good intentions makes us *feel* good, often good enough to substitute for good actions. But in *On Being A Christian*, Hans Küng observes that there is "no easy out":

> In Jesus' way of speaking there is not even a hint of 'embracing millions,' of 'a kiss for the whole world,' as in the poem by Schiller… A kiss of that kind costs nothing: it is not like kissing this one sick, imprisoned, underprivileged, starving man. The more distant our fellow men, the easier it is to profess our love in words.[158]

Delegation to Others. "At least a billion other citizens of the world are surely closer to others' desperate needs than I am. I bet they have more time to help than I have. I'm kinda busy here."

Delegation to the State. "We paid taxes for that, didn't we?" For centuries, governments have assumed responsibility to relieve the most severe forms of suffering endured by destitute citizenry or disaster victims. Is it possible that spiritual generosity may require a higher standard and more personal attention than only bureaucratic generosity?

"I Gave at the Office, Serve on the Church Liturgy Committee…" This issue might be best reduced to this question:

Are my contributions to my church, the United Way, my university, or the Girl Scouts, adequate repayment for all I've been given?

The Primacy of Family. Generosity thins out as we move further from our immediate family or clan. Fair enough. But for many, one's family is the *full* extent of their love practice. Many have domesticated their compassion. Matthew Fox says:

> Family then becomes the nucleus of a rotten society… for it buttresses what is essentially an egocentric way of life. Such a way of life is narrow and parochial and bent on the idol named security, which is meant to keep at bay all suffering and celebration that is not in one's own family.[159]

"It's on My 'To Do List': See…Right There, Down Near the Bottom." This is a personal favorite. My present, visible, urgent, and proximate needs always seem to trump my generosity or service to strangers, who, by definition, are out of sight and out of mind. No matter how much money we have, there doesn't seem to be any leftover after paying the bills and setting aside some for a rainy day. And I never have free time. I *suppose I could* actually budget some money and time for these projects on a regular basis…

Pain Avoidance. "Look, I'm sorry, but if I allow myself to get involved in this suffering business, I know I'll experience some *very* uncomfortable feelings. I'd rather pass. Here, let me write a small check." Feelings like these:

- *Guilt.* Whether the service locale is overseas, in prisons, or in soup lines, sooner or later I'll return to my comfortable hotel or to my own home. And I'll feel both grateful and guilty about leaving.

- <u>Heartbreak</u>. If I get too close to it, I'll become infected by the suffering of others. How can I stand to open my heart to that much pain? To open our hearts to just one child of the thousands who are dying today would be unbearable—or would it? Probably not, but I imagine the sight and the sound of that one child's cries might change us forever.

Beneath all of those cultural influences and personal rationalizations that helped me avoid or delay giving away much of my treasure or time to needy strangers for so long, lies the following, the biggest excuse of all.

The Tyranny of Vast Numbers. If *you* can really comprehend the following data, perhaps you could help me wrap my mind around these facts: that the human body contains tens of trillions of cells; or that our four-billion-year-old sun is only one of four hundred billion gravitationally bound stars in our galaxy, of which there are *140 billion* other galaxies. Oh, and that every galaxy is *expanding*.[160]

Likewise, the amount of suffering in the world is so vast it is conceptually overwhelming. According to the United Nations' World Food program, nine hundred and twenty-five million people (one in seven of us) won't have enough to eat today. The tragic Japanese earthquake captivated us all when 20,000 people died. But that very same day and *every day since*, over nine thousand kids died of hunger-related diseases. That's 3,475,000 children a year, every year. These mind-boggling statistics have three numbing effects on my own motivations to help.

- *Disassociation.* My imagination is overwhelmed and shorted out. The arithmetic of suffering is not inspiring; it's emotionally stupefying. A statement attributed to Joseph Stalin resonates: "A million deaths is a statistic; a single death a tragedy." The more suffering, the less compassion. Advertising Agencies for nonprofits have learned that an appeal to help one child is more effective than an image with seven expectant faces.

- *Distancing.* Most of the world's suffering people are almost insignificant to us because they're so far away. Beyond our family and friends, who do we *really* care about? How much do we care for the children of strangers across town? Across the world? Our empathy for distant strangers seems *very* limited. Annie Dillard asks,

    > What were you doing April 30th, 1991, when a series of waves drowned 138,000 people in one day in Bangladesh? Where were you when you first heard the astounding, heartbreaking news?... Did your anguish last days, or weeks? What *will* move you to pity?... Can our prizing of each human life weaken with the square of the distance, as gravity does?[161]

- *Impotence.* The staggering extent of suffering in the world raises the question: "Why bother?" All our efforts will *feel* insignificant in comparison to the need; and they will be. But when we're overwhelmed by the size of the world's need, Mother Teresa taught us how we might overcome our discouragement. She reminded us that our contributions will be significant to the first person we help. And what should be more important to us than that one person? She writes:

> I picked up one person—maybe if I didn't pick up that one person I wouldn't have picked up forty-two thousand. I never look at the masses as my responsibility. I look at the individual. I can only love one person at a time. I can only feed one person at a time. Just one. Just one... so you begin— and I begin.[162]

The Value of Re-Visioning Our Relationship To Strangers

In light of all these rationalizations that reinforce our instinctive bias for selfishness, how can we overcome our indifference to helping strangers? I believe we'll be indisposed to act compassionately until we can re-imagine closer connections with—and similarities to—all The Others.

This is a challenging task for the imagination. After all, it's painfully *obvious* that our "skin-encapsulated" bodies are *not connected*, but separate. And it's just as obvious that we are *not equal*: look at our physiques, coloring, abilities. . . Our obvious separateness and inequality are underscored by our cultural heritage of individualism and meritocracy, the polar opposites of union and equality.

Adopting the two visions of Union and Equality directly contradict our culturally reinforced common sense. This is a tall order. But the imagination invites us to look again and discern what we've left in shadow, just out of sight. The challenge and opportunity of spirituality is precisely to examine the unseen and uncover its secrets and mystery. We've seen what the imagination is capable of. It can create ideals of future perfection; encourage empathy; prompt individuation; help us to regress to uncover long forgotten events; and inspire visions that contain philosophy, poetry, and prophesy. If we're willing to inform and engage our imaginations, we *can* alter and broaden our perspective to more closely identify with strangers. If we can re-imagine others as mirrors of ourselves, we may be more receptive to some compelling reasons to help them: reasons like equity, redemption, altruism, and even hedonism (since giving gives us great pleasure).

In emerging countries, the public conveyance of choice is most frequently a microbus, a seven seat van. The "daladalas" in Tanzania cost pennies per kilometer and are usually stuffed with three dozen commuters. As the only white foreigner aboard, the Africans in this space are clearly and obviously different and separate from me. And our mutual uniqueness certainly makes our interaction more interesting. But I'm also free to choose to feel largely identical and connected to these other commuters. I notice we share in common the same intertwined limbs, sweat, and laps full of bundles and babies; and the same smiles, eye contact, goodwill, fatigue, resignation, and irritation; and similar shopping lists and errands ahead of us. This experience and knowledge balances the more obvious separation and uniqueness that need not prevail as our exclusive or dominant vision of others. It is enough that our new visions of connection and equality lie alongside— and not necessarily replace—our more predominant cultural view of our separation and difference from others.

CHAPTER TWENTY-FIVE

THE VALUE OF INTERCONNECTION

> Human nature is a complex mix of... extreme selfishness and extreme altruism. When opponents of evolution object that human beings are not mere apes, they are correct. We are also part bee.[163]

New Connections

Sharon is a Korean-American who shared a flophouse with eight of us while working in rural Tanzania. Very accomplished, she'd been a hotshot copywriting executive for a prestigious San Francisco-based international ad agency. She was assigned to create a new ad campaign for a large cellular phone company in East Africa, the goal of which was to increase the company's annual revenues (and profits) by fifty million dollars. She was told in her first meeting with the client that the planned copy platform was simple and direct: to use guilt to motivate their subscribers "to call home for just one minute each day to stay in closer touch with their mothers." But then she read the research that revealed that the target customer base was urban twenty- and thirty-somethings, most of whom were unemployed and underemployed.

Wondering, "What the hell am I doing with my life," Sharon quit to seek a different connection with young Africans. She spent the following couple of months as a student teacher with a class of ninety pupils in an orphanage adjacent to the city dump in Dar es Salaam. Her Swahili was negligible.

> One of the first words I learned was 'pole,' which means 'I'm sorry.' Every day, at least twenty of the kids walked by my desk or approached me on the walk home through the dump. They'd tell me they were sorry because I looked so tired (I was). Tanzanians repress their emotions, except for the one we repress in the West: compassion. And almost all thanked me at one time or another for coming to help them learn. I was hooked. In the ad business, I can count on one hand the number of times a client went out of their way to say 'thanks' for our all-nighters preparing a presentation to help them sell more soap, or cereal, or God knows what else.

Sharon is radiant and reports that she has never been happier.

Visions of Union

Our frequent lack of generosity to strangers is reinforced by our tendency to polarize. A prime example of dualism's sorting function is our distinction between strangers and familiars. Membership in one group automatically incorporates a built-in set of Outsiders. We think of, and treat, *them* as... well, *not us*. I personally needed a whole new way to think about, to re-imagine, familiars and strangers.

I think the ultimate ground of the spiritual ideals of love and compassion is our shared yearning for some kind of union. It may be a compensation for our physical separateness and isolation. On the other hand, our instinctive and cultural preference for independence is far more pronounced than a mere, vague longing. Our preference for independence is therefore very difficult to overcome. Annie Dillard talks us down:

> The religious idea, sooner or later, challenges the notion of the individual... Huston Smith suggests that our individuality resembles a snowflake's. The seas evaporate water, clouds build and loose water in snowflakes, which dissolve and go to sea. The simile galls. What have I to do with the ocean? I, with my unique and novel hexagons and spikes?... We know we must yield, if only intellectually. OK, we're a lousy snowflake.[164]

Like all utopians, Edward Bellamy imagined a future in which perfectible people would create a more perfect society. Even to this fourteen-year-old, the central economic planning required by his socialist vision seemed oppressive and even naïve. Yet his book was translated into twenty languages and many of his ideas were incorporated into the Progressive Party's Presidential platforms. The popularity of *Looking Backward* lay not in its practicality, but elsewhere: in the boldness of its vision of union.

———

Most types of unitive visions are religious and prophetic. The Christian notions of the Beatific Vision and the Communion of Saints envision an *otherworldly*, heavenly state. Others, like Pierre de Chardin and Roberto Assogioli, have imagined that we continually tend towards ever greater unity over time *in this world*, as part of God's evolutionary plan. This long-term process is sometimes poetically called the Supreme Synthesis.

Other visions imagine that we are *already* unified. Pantheists believe that we are each united with God and, thereby, everything else. Holographic Integration, another unitive idea, suggests that each part of the universe contains the whole. (Holographic means "the same as all"). Several decades ago, I experienced this transpersonal reality through holotropic breathing and through LSD. In one such an experience, I *was* a hawk. The most difficult one for me to accept (thus far) of all the ideas of union as a present-state reality is the Buddhist and Hindu conviction that our present separateness from one another is only an illusion, from which we are called to awaken.

Union as Connection—More or Less

My vision of union is more modest and less speculative than those mentioned above, but is still an important source of inspiration to me. Rather than imagining union as the ultimate or predominant reality, I'm inclined to believe we are *both* separate *and* connected. To synthesize our separateness and connectedness in a meaningful and useful way, we can employ some of the holistic tools mentioned in Chapter Ten. (These were peripheral vision, plurisignation, the golden mean, periodicity, and paradox).

I think the emphasis we personally choose to place upon one or another pole of this duality of self and others is spiritually significant. Since our separateness is so much more obvious and insistent, I believe our spiritual challenge is to keep ever mindful of our less widely accepted aspect: that of our interconnection. Ram Dass writes:

> What we have to offer others will come from our sense of unity. So we look for and cherish those experiences in which we feel ourselves connected to all things in the universe… Unity has to be what's most real in consciousness if it's going to have full power in action. Ultimately, it's got to be what we are.[165]

But how *are* we connected to others?

We are connected through the family of humankind. Science supports a reconsideration of our narrow views of the family. In Iceland, all three hundred thousand native citizens are related. And in humankind's entire family tree, we're *all* blood relatives, closer than fiftieth cousins.[166] Carl Jung posited the collective unconscious to explain his discoveries that a common shared historical experience seems imprinted in the psyche of all. Walking about in East and South Africa, I couldn't shake the notion that the landscapes in this cradle of humankind contained the bones, memories, and wisdom of all my ancestors.

Our devotion to our immediate and extended families can help lead us to imagine and embrace the idea of membership in humankind's larger family. At ten o'clock one night at the northern Tanzanian border, our team of fourteen was led to the most remote of the Maasai homesteads, a thirty-minute ride through ravines and thickets that would be impassable when the rains came in two weeks time. The team had been waiting for months for this invitation because the patriarch was the most influential man in the region.

We came to a plateau lit by the full moon, as bright as a Dali nightscape. Within the acacia- lined homestead lived forty-five wives of the headman, his brothers, and sons; a couple hundred children living too remotely to attend school; and, in the center of it all, one hundred and seventy cattle and countless goats. As we expected, the men were disinterested in our documentary films about HIV prevention. But we were surprised that the women and girls were also withdrawn and distant. They were unhappy because they thought we would pay them to watch the movie as other NGOs had done.

While others set up our solar generators and a portable large screen, I unfolded a large color photo and shared it with a small group of kids. The picture depicted the two-dozen folks of our family vacationing in the mountains of Wyoming. Their mothers became curious for the first time, noting the absence of cattle and goats in our homestead. But they identified with our large family and were especially interested in Christina as the matriarch. They became animated, interested, and engaged. As the photograph was passed around, there began a palpable shift from wariness and distrust to warmth and then, laughter.

It had taken a little while, but we had found that we were all connected through our large families and all our children. A group of about seventy mothers and children warmed to the idea of watching our four HIV prevention documentaries, even though very few understood any of the dialogue. While the movies ran, the photo continued to make the rounds inside the stockade and was reverently returned with scores of embraces and good wishes.

We are connected through our ancestors and descendants to the stream of life. In New York City, during a palm reading with a remarkable Chilean poet, I mentioned my regret that I'd not really mourned the death of my mother, six years earlier. David asked, "But why would you weep? She's always here, in this line, in the palm of your hand." William F. Buckley, Jr. reminded us that our connection to *our ancestors* deserves more acknowledgement.

> We are basket cases of ingratitude, so many of us…
> To live lives without any sense of obligation—to those who made possible lives as tolerable as ours…
> to our parents who suffered to raise us, to our teachers who labored to teach us, to the scientists who prolonged the lives of our children when disease struck them down—is spiritually atrophying.[167]

We're also responsible for the well being of *our descendents*. "According to a native American tradition, the chiefs are charged to think in terms of the next seven generations… Such a long view brings both a sense of responsibility for, and a new clarity about, the shared future."[168]

We are connected through our communities. Communities of mutual support come in all shapes and sizes. In the same week his sister died, our oldest son, Marc, created a Yahoo website—an electronic community for perhaps a hundred of Hilary's friends. This site became an oft-traveled transcontinental village of mutual support that connected her larger family in North America with those in South America, Africa, and Europe.

The feminist movement and the Internet have combined to create cyberspace communities of support as diverse as new mothers with breastfeeding questions; micro-finance for entrepreneurial women in developing countries; and professional networking. Charles Handy points out that without three gifts of community—"*a sense of continuity, a sense of connection, and a sense of direction...* we might feel disoriented and rudderless."[169] The community offers us its history, culture, institutions, protection, and constancy. Our spiritual challenge is to imagine that our own communities include the nation, the hemisphere, the planet.

Finally, we are connected through our acts of love and compassion.

CHAPTER TWENTY-SIX

THE VALUE OF EQUIVALENCE

More or Less Different—Or The Same?

Fifteen thousand Africans dying each and every day from preventable, treatable diseases—AIDS, malaria, TB... This statistic alone makes a fool of the idea many of us hold onto very tightly: the idea of equality... Deep down, if we really accept that their lives—African lives—are equal to ours, we would all be doing more to put the fire out. It's an uncomfortable truth.

—Bono[170]

In our culture, the proposition that "all men are created equal" means that all have the same rights of suffrage, the same access to government services, the same economic and educational opportunities, and equal protection under the law. In place of the idea of *equality of* human beings, I prefer the notion of *equivalence to* each other. To be equivalent means more than *equality of rights*. It also means to be *"the same in importance,"* that is, in value. As in our previous discussion of the polarity of separation vs. connection, we can rationally argue both sides of this proposition: "Are we more different from each other—or more the same?" I'll again urge us to emphasize the less obvious, and therefore the least favored, pole. To grow in compassion, my own task has been to imagine and remind myself to behave as if I am more, rather than less, equivalent to the others.

More Different

Many of the older adults I knew as a suburban adolescent freely articulated a vehement bias against Jews and African-Americans. These animosities were borne of their parents' struggles for economic status a generation earlier in New York City. This sort of bias is not a one-way street. A neighbor had been raised among the lower middle class in Manhattan early in the twentieth century. She was taught by her Jewish mother to fear (and therefore to dislike and distrust) all strangers. A stranger was defined as any person who is not white, female, and Jewish. By her eighties, her exclusionary definition of strangers was broadened to all persons who are not family. Since acceptable caretakers meeting all four of these criteria became limited, her remaining years were ones of self-imposed loneliness.

Several deep habits of mind and long histories of group conflict complicate the ability of humans to emphasize their identification with strangers. Our history of slavery, patriarchy, meritocracy, social hierarchies, and our aversion to outcasts, all seem intransigent.

Species Discrimination. Homo sapiens have always distinguished themselves as separate from, and usually superior to, other species. In Africa, the haunting reminders of slavery are everywhere. The slave prisons and auction houses in Zanzibar were the ancient demarcation point for slaves destined for Europe and the Middle East. I imagine that such enslavement could only have been justified and rationalized by whites by convincing themselves that Africans were not only inferior, but somehow subhuman.

Gender Discrimination. Discrimination against women exists on all continents. The version practiced by the rural Maasai seems particularly oppressive. The men do virtually no work except graze the cattle. Ever. When they reach fifteen, the adolescent boys help look after the cattle and goats and become unavailable to help their mothers and sisters with "women's work."

On the other hand, each headman's five or six wives are his servants. Besides shopping and cooking, "women's work" includes building their homes, hauling water on their heads each day (for miles), raising four or five children, and milking all the cows and goats. The herdsman sells his daughters for about a dozen cows. Even though it's against the civil law, female circumcision is still practiced in the rural villages. This fundamental inequality has been unchanged for four hundred years, and the males of the tribe see no reason to change the least aspect of this heritage for the next four hundred.

Economic Meritocracy. In all cultures the wealthy consider themselves superior to the less affluent. On pretty good authority, I'm told that in the drug cartel business, one is viewed in only one of two ways: you're either an asset or a liability, an appraisal subject to sudden change. As stark as that idea sounds, it's mostly mirrored in legitimate business as well.

Judgment of Outcasts. By definition, outcasts are unequal. Jesus called them "the least of these." Today, the least and most marginalized are the *diverse* others: women, people of color, gays, and the foreign-born; *our enemies:* sinners, prisoners, and political enemies in hot and cold wars; and finally, *the economic failures*: the poor and the homeless. None of us are eager to acknowledge that we've all felt at times: like refugees from somewhere, adrift, hungry for something, or just trying to do our time the best we can. No better, no worse.

Social Hierarchies. In polite company, our instinctive pecking orders and social status are impolite subjects, rarely discussed. But I believe the determination of social order for humans is as real and ubiquitous as it is to a pack of wolves or a troop of baboons. Most times, I feel equivalent to others. But if I'm feeling especially less or more secure, I occasionally notice an underlying sense of inferiority or superiority in my relationship to others in that space. Either position separates me.

To rebalance the hierarchical scale, it helps to remind myself that I now lack the qualities of courage, endurance, and fortitude of all those who endure long term hardships, like inmates, the disabled, the homeless, the desperately poor, or undocumented migrants. Conversely, I can always remind myself of the hundreds upon hundreds of mistakes, failures, and harm for which

I've been, and will surely continue to be, personally responsible as a parent, lover, friend, and supervisor.

If I'm still feeling superior to anybody or anything, I can choose to recall some humbling scientific realities. For the first 99.99999 percent of our history as organisms, I've been in the same ancestral line as chimpanzees, from whom I am genetically distinguishable today by only 1.6 percent of my makeup.[171] I can also remind myself of Richard Leakey's admonishment: Humans are the single worst extinction event in the history of the world, the direct or indirect cause of some 120,000 species lost each year.[172]

Identification with Others and the Value of Our Imagination

So how *can* we learn to identify with strangers, to see them as the same as ourselves? The key to broadening the circle of people who we might be able to see as similar, is to engage our imaginations. Dr. J. L. Moreno, the founder of psychodrama, writes that we can use our disciplined imaginations:

> ... to overcome the differences which hinder communication between the sexes, between the races, the generations, the sick and the healthy, between... the living and the dead... A man can play a woman... a black man can be a white man... an old person can take the part of a child... [The imagination] can return us to our lost unity with the universe and re-establish the continuity of life.[173]

During a weekend of psychodrama training, I played the role of an estranged, abusive husband for one protagonist. A couple of hours later, I assumed the role of a devoted husband in another drama. I was reminded of how fluid and creative our imagination is. In therapy once, I imagined a wonderful two-way conversation with my great-grandfather, dead for a century. I spoke about my need to distance myself from his long shadow as a writer and thinker in order to become more of my own person. He was most gracious and helpful.

When I condescend to "provide for the less fortunate," the trick is to imagine myself caught inside the web of *their identical circumstances*. This requires some willingness to understand the other *and* the willingness to empathize with them. Both understanding and empathy require imagination.

More Understanding. In the West, most of us take for granted our vastly preferential share of the earth's favorable geography, geology, political heritage, and economic institutions. Conversely, we tend to be critical of the third world for their slow progress, instead of trying to understand their enormous disadvantages. In subtropical Africa, for just one example, the apparently innocuous year-round warm climate has two devastating consequences. First, the perennial heat decomposes and leaches away the soils' organic matter. The result is that only eight percent of African land is cultivatable. Second, the constant warmth is hospitable to microbes that cause malaria, yellow fever, and sleeping sickness.[174]

Another example, closer to home, of our need to understand more about others' circumstances to imagine their challenges, are the chronically homeless in our midst. They are most usually handicapped by one or more of: mental illness, late-stage addiction, or combat-induced post-traumatic stress syndrome. Any one of these would make maintaining a permanent job, home, or relationship nearly impossible. Are we willing to imagine a life (our life) with one, two, or three such burdens?

More Empathy. Understanding another's circumstance is the first step. Our willingness to feel empathy is another. I vacationed with two different groups of millionaire business associates. One trip was a weekend sail on a yacht from Charlotte Amalie in the Virgin Islands; another was a fishing trip to the Pacific, staying in a Mexican hacienda overlooking Mazatlan. I was moved by the squalor of the slums in the midst of these idyllic vacationlands. Both sets of companions, to my consternation, responded to my concern by expressing their distaste for "the awful way in which these people choose to live." They were actually quite annoyed that the barrios blighted their otherwise pristine ocean views.

Their lack of empathy was a failure of imagination. They *could* imagine (given their present level of education, ambition, work experience, and energy) that they'd be able to escape the squalor of the barrio. But they were *unwilling* to imagine such a predicament had they'd been born into such poverty *without* the advantages they inherited and enjoyed as North Americans.

Bo Lozoff, the founder of the Human Kindness Foundation, created an exercise for prison inmates he called *Human to Human*. My partner, a former Columbian drug runner, sat across from me. We looked into and through dark brown and light blue eyes, set in our chocolate and pink skin, under black and white hair. Twins, we were. Another inmate-facilitator read the following words to ten pairs of men, each gazing into similar mirrors of themselves, challenging us to expand our imaginations:

> You can just be you, just human beings on the path, who have recognized each other. See all the common experiences you share. Your partner understands... You can allow him to see the real you... maybe for the first time... Look straight into the eyes of love across from you... Receive the compassion, understanding and forgiveness that are there. You can let go of those burdens now... your pain and shame and secrets. Let it all go...[175]

Now What?

Re-visioning a kind of *connectedness* and *equivalence* to all others helps me overcome my reluctance to "get involved" in the plight of others. In the next two chapters, we'll discuss compassionate expressions of these two visions. I'm especially interested in the practical ways we can more generously respond to the needs of the poor. The first avenue is the donation of some of our wealth. Some of this form of generosity may turn upon a more active involvement in the political process. The second type of compassionate generosity is the donation of some of our time and energy in service to others, which is an entirely personal process.

CHAPTER TWENTY-SEVEN

THE VALUE OF (ECONOMIC) JUSTICE: SHARING OUR TREASURE

The Value of Justice and the Enrichment Of Strangers

Part of the remarkable mission statement of *Forbes* magazine (of all places) says: "The be-all and end-all of life should not be simply to get rich, but to enrich the world." Matsushita, a wealthy Japanese industrialist, wrote in 1932:

> The mission of a manufacturer should be to overcome poverty, to relieve society as a whole from misery, and bring it wealth... This is what the

entrepreneur and the manufacturer should aim at: to make all products as inexhaustible and as cheap as tap water. When this is realized, poverty will vanish from the earth.[176]

The three following ideas might encourage us to make a commitment to help enrich others.

1) Equitable Justice. A body of law "at equity" originated in Britain. It was based upon a legal principle and public policy of encouraging fundamental fairness. It governs cases in which a plaintiff's wrongs, though clearly inequitable, aren't redressed under either statutory or common law. This idea of equitable justice is one way to rationalize a more even distribution of wealth, the disparity of which actually continues to increase. In one recent year, the annual per capita GNP in the United States was $29,000 versus $150 in the Congo, Ethiopia, Burundi, and Sierra Leone. The average residents of these African countries live on forty-one cents a day. For many of us, the discrepancy in these numbers violates any conceivable sense of fairness.

2) Religious Exhortations. Theologian Hans Küng reminds us that, "Wealth is extremely dangerous to salvation. In principle, Jesus is on the side of the poor."[177] The spiritual dangers of affluence include the concern that the love of wealth will distract us from the needs of others and from our devotion to the Divine. Are we spending too much of our time "laying up treasure in the last days?"

3) The Value of Redemption. A third way to rationalize a partial redistribution of our wealth is through the idea of redemption, which is defined as a "repayment." Redemption is the motive for many inmates who feel driven to find a way to make amends for their previously destructive lives. They are "trying to leave something of value to somebody before I die." But how can our own personal redemption become an argument in favor of a partial redistribution of wealth? One may interject: "Repayment for what? What do *I* need to repay?"

Our notions of redemption are clouded by theologians' zigzagging explanations for Christ's crucifixion over the centuries. The Church fathers thought of it as a *ransom* to be paid the Devil. I had been taught that Christ's death was a sacrificial *atonement* to propitiate His Father. A more up-to-date interpretation is that Jesus' death was *a reconciliation* of man with God, necessitated by "the actual personal guilt and universal burden of sin… the real enmity between man and God…"[178]

I prefer to think of redemption very differently: not about guilt, but about gratitude. Redistributing part of our wealth to the needy can be thought of as a repayment for the gift of our lives of comparative plenitude and good fortune. By his forties, Peter Baron had amassed great wealth in the telecommunications industry. He explained why he thinks most contemporary Americans should be very grateful indeed:

> Let me say this straight out because it's the big context in which my own life has been just a tiny part: our generation is the luckiest that ever lived. Way luckier than we did anything to deserve… It was as if history itself had given my whole generation a gigantic trust fund. It just fell our way, an inheritance from the amazing post World War II economic boom and the unprecedented prosperity of the American century.[179]

Generosity is our best opportunity to express our gratitude for the blessings we've received: the blessing of our surplus and of life itself. My meager monetary gifts to poor strangers is a royalty I'll happily pay for my enjoyment of the world's bounty. Gratitude expressed to whom? To all. To each other, to our ancestors, to the universe, to God, to life itself.

Money & The Value of Sacrifice

Whether we base our financial generosity to the poor upon rationales of equitable justice, religious morality, or of redemptive debt service, such acts of generosity call for sacrifice: Renunciation precedes offerings.

When considering sacrifice, it's appropriate to ask whether I have less or more than I need. Estate planners' general response to that question in the context of future retirement is usually unequivocal: "To maintain the standard of living to which you've become accustomed, assuming a three percent inflation rate and actuarially determined life spans, you do *not* have enough money. You'll need to earn and save more."

On the other end of the "enough spectrum," we find the criteria of a few saints, all of whom would have made lousy financial planners. St. Thomas Aquinas said that we do not need anything we own that we are not using today. "The bread which you withhold belongs to the hungry. The clothing you shut away, to the naked..."[180] Gandhi's formula of our personal needs is even more restrictive:

> The golden rule... is resolutely to refuse to have what millions cannot... One must not possess

anything that one does not really need. It would be a breach of this principle to possess unnecessary foodstuffs, clothing or furniture. For instance, one must not keep a chair if one can do without it...[181]

Francis's definition of our "needs" was more severe yet; he said his followers didn't even need the *first* chair or the *next* meal. Today, we're generally inclined to dismiss as unreasonable our saints' radical calls to transformation, certainly including their instructions about sharing resources with others.

In his *Writings on an Ethical Life,* Peter Singer, a ethics professor, offers another possible definition of "our needs" to help us think about that which we may wish to give away. His suggestion is less rigorous and not unreasonable, but still radical for most of us. His definition of "needs" excludes all of our assets considered luxuries.

> Each one of us with wealth surplus to his or her essential needs should be giving most of it to help people suffering from poverty so dire as to be life threatening. That's right! I'm saying that you shouldn't buy that new car, take that cruise, redecorate the house, or get that pricey new suit. After all, a thousand-dollar suit could save five children's lives. The formula is simple; whatever money you're spending on luxuries, not necessities, should be given away.[182]

Elsewhere, Singer suggests another, less stringent, formula regarding our sharing of income: "[R]oughly 5 percent of annual income for those who are financially comfortable, and rather more for the very rich." That seems reasonable enough and some have done it for years.

Domestic Offerings

Christina and I were raised in wealthy suburbs of Detroit and New York, in Grosse Point Farms and Larchmont. Our families had part-time "cleaning ladies." Christina recalls her mom giving bacon grease to the domestic help to take home for cooking. As an adolescent, I was embarrassed that our day laborer's lunch consisted of the family's warmed-over leftovers. I don't think it occurred to Mom to drive these older African-American women to their bus stop half a mile away. Today, this strikes me as an insufficient an insufficient level of generosity.

And yet, compared to the generosity Singer calls for, the kinds of monies that Christina and I have given to our favorite charities amount to a piss in a windstorm. These donations didn't affect us at all, or make much of a difference to anyone else. I have a long way to go before "giving until it hurts." I still struggle with my own versions of leftover bacon grease.

Domestically, charitable contributions to institutions amounted to $252 billion dollars in 2005. Half of these are donations to churches. The other half is given to secular organizations promoting the environment, the arts, universities, medical research and hospitals, youth services, and human services.[183] Only 15 percent was targeted specifically to this last category—to help address the needs of our nation's poor.

Foreign Aid

We've arrived at the second of the two ethical questions I earlier promised to explore a little more deeply. I want to draw attention to another of the ethical issues normally framed in an economic and political context. As with industrial animal husbandry, foreign aid is a two-fold challenge of governments and of individuals. As with our duty to provide more humane animal treatment, the proper amount of foreign aid hinges on our perennial ethical question: "More life for whom?" In this case, do we offer more life for our citizens, or more life for citizens of the world? We may need to become politically, as well as personally, more active to persuade our government to raise our levels of foreign aid.

Since 2002, the agreed-upon objective of the developed countries in the international community has been to reduce the burden of the 1.1 billion poor who subsist on less than a dollar a day. This task requires the concentration of capital and expertise available only through international cooperation.

The U.N. and World Bank propose to concentrate investments in the five most critical infrastructure bottlenecks in the poorest countries: their primary school education, nutrition, supply of potable water, sanitation, and paved roads. To finance this work, the wealthy nations have pledged to increase their annual foreign aid budgets from an average of 0.2% of their GNP to 0.7% by 2015. Seven countries, including the Scandinavian nations, have already met their targets.

The United States has *never* delivered on our pledges, and in a recent year we donated 0.2 percent of GNP—*the lowest in the developed world*. The long-term goal of donating seven-tenths of one percent of our GNP would require an increment of $60 billion dollars a year in foreign aid. But Americans have chosen to spend this money in two other ways.

First, we preferred to give this money to the wealthiest among us, by reducing their taxes by $50 billion dollars. Secondly, we've preferred to spend our money on national defense. According to the Stockholm International Peace Research Institute, we spend nearly as much on military power as every other country in the world *combined*. Each year, the U.S. spends $548 billion for this purpose, maintaining troops in 560 bases around the world. According to the authors of *The Three Trillion Dollar War*,[184] we'll spend $2.6 *trillion* dollars on the war in Iraq, compared to $15 *billion* annually on foreign aid in one recent year.

Actually, it's not *really* $15 billion. Part of that "aid" consists of American food surplus and American technical assistance. Furthermore, our aid beneficiaries exclude many nations we judge to be not democratic, Christian, or capitalist enough for our tastes. To assuage Congressional Catholics, for example, our foreign aid is earmarked to avoid family planning projects and countries with legalized abortion (like our own).

Finally, the U.S. will not work through the (fiercely independent) United Nations, where the bulk of international development expertise resides. We prefer the auspices of the World Bank and the International Monetary Fund, whose management, funding, and foreign aid agendas we do influence. Certainly, foreign aid is a political and economic question. But first and foremost, I think it is a spiritual and ethical inquiry inviting more public participation by each of us and more personal contributions to the non-profit agencies serving the world's poor.

Leftovers

Well-bred families
care for their own.
PlayStations and ski vacations,
for each other, of course.
To the Others, we bequeath our
used bikes in mint condition
and sweaters you wouldn't
be caught dead in.
All deductible donations,
swept from the garage
like crumbs from
the rich man's table.

For the poorest of the poor,
we solemnly pledge to leave
all our leftover cash,
trickling downstream
year after year,
with little leftover
of Santa's good wishes
but lumps of hard coal.

I pray someday soon
we'll make a brand
new bargain with
the imperiled,

perishable poor.
Perhaps fewer gadgets
and getaways for us,
in exchange for two pearls
of great price: the lessons
only the poor can teach us
about gratitude and sacrifice.

In the meantime, I suppose
we'll continue to leave
these least, leftover ones
alone to overcome
the incalculable anguish
of taking their leave
from nine thousand more
of their gossamer,
doe-eyed babies, dying
of hunger again, today.

Summary

<u>The Value of Justice</u> refers to enriching others. We spoke of three rationales for a redistribution of wealth to the poor:

> Equitable justice.
> Religious teachings.

<u>The Value of Redemption</u>, which I have interpreted as the repayment of our unearned share of the world's blessings, based upon our gratitude rather than our guilt.

<u>The Value of Sacrifice.</u> Religious figures discourage hoarding. I like Peter Singer's formulae, which urge us to avoid expenditures for luxuries, and/or to contribute 5 percent of our annual income for the benefit of others.

CHAPTER TWENTY-EIGHT

THE VALUE OF MERCIFUL SERVICE: SHARING OURSELVES

Inspiring Options

For most of us, our lives probably fall between two extremes: one lived entirely for the benefit of ourselves; and one lived entirely in service to others. Locating myself on this continuum between service and self-service helped prod me to commit to perform more service for others. I've long admired people like teachers, therapists, nurses, doctors, and social workers, whose daily roles provide opportunities for one degree or another of compassionate direct service.

The customer service issues I dealt with in business had much more to do with problem-solving than compassion. The exception was a stimulating time in my late twenties when I ran a small subsidiary of an international development company. We built rural homes for Cherokee families in North Carolina and Oklahoma and for African-American families in Virginia and South Carolina. The amount of satisfaction of delivering those sixteen-thousand-dollar houses to needy families was in inverse proportion to my later involvement with homes many times more expensive

———

There are countless non-vocational ways to be useful to others. Most fleeting are random and often spontaneous encounters. In a recent university study, adults in the twelve largest cities in the U.S. reported performing an average of 137 acts of kindness in the previous year. Examples of the fifteen kinds of measured acts were: donating blood; giving up a seat in a public place to a stranger; shopping for another; talking to someone who was feeling blue; and helping a person find a job.[185]

The sixty-five million unpaid and unsung people providing care for family members, relatives, or neighbors exemplify a much more committed level of servant. For an average of twenty hours a week, they assist with personal activities of daily living, transportation, housework, grocery shopping, meal prep, paying bills, managing meds, or advocating with health providers. Rosalyn Carter summed up our relationship with care giving: "There are only four kinds of people in the world: Those who have been caregivers; those who currently are caregivers; those who will be caregivers; and those who will need caregivers."

THE VALUE OF MERCIFUL SERVICE: SHARING OURSELVES

St. Matthew's most famous passage quoting Jesus' words in His Sermon on the Mount cites fourteen corporeal and spiritual works of mercy (25:34-36). Another author conveniently summarizes them for us: "Compassion leads to works—feeding, clothing, sheltering, setting free, giving drink, visiting, burying, educating, counseling, admonishing, bearing wrongs, forgiving, comforting, praying."[186]

More than one in four adults in the U.S. volunteer their personal time to nonprofit organizations, mostly for their church or their kids' school or after-school activities. Others volunteer for social and community service for the poor in many different ways: tutoring the young, keeping the elderly company, visiting the homebound, teaching in prison, helping the indigent find medical care, organizing clothing drives, arguing in court for tenants or undocumented workers, assisting in nursing homes, working in homeless shelters…[187]

The national awards from the Caring Institute honor remarkable people offering remarkable service, especially those who provide unique responses to community needs. One agency re-educates gang members in Des Moines; another provides financial assistance to ten thousand families of hospitalized kids. Also honored was a seventy-seven-year-old physician who still makes house calls *and* works twelve-hour emergency room nightshifts. One young person collects thousands of blankets and cooking pots for the poor. A thirteen-year-old has donated twenty-seven thousand books to young hospital patients. What do these "acts of mercy," in the language of Jesus, seem to have in common?

1) *Compassionate Service is Personal*

> I am done with great things and big plans, great institutions and big success. I am for those tiny, invisible, loving human forces that work from individual to individual creeping through the crannies of the world like so many rootlets, or like the capillary oozing of water, which, if given time, will rend the hardest monuments of pride.
> —William James[188]

Because it is so interpersonal, most service is very small in scale. Small communities, smaller groups. In *Building Peace*, John Paul Lederach writes that, in the aftermath of ethnic atrocities, the most effective international peacemaking is dependent, not upon political bodies, but upon the bodies and minds of individuals. He finds that public reconciliation *first* requires personal healing between enemies, face-to-face, in their local communities. In small groups, they're better able to hear each other's stories of suffering and validate each other's experience of the conflict.[189]

Personal service is not excused or replaced by making generous financial gifts. Speaking of donors of the Sisters of Charity, Mother Teresa writes:

> What I desire is the presence the donor, for him to touch those to whom he gives, to smile at them, for him to pay attention to them… I never asked them for money or material things. I asked people to bring their love and offer the sacrifice of their hands… After some time they feel they belong to the poor and they are filled with the need to love.

They discover who they are and what it is they themselves can give.[190]

I think I understand. Because the Maasai are undernourished after years of drought, the three or four lactating mothers in each homestead couldn't generate enough milk between them to adequately nurse all their young. When a baby started to fuss during our outdoor bio-intensive gardening lessons, I walked with the infants around the bush until they fell asleep on my shoulder or settled down. I perspired a lot more in the East African sun than did their ebony mothers, and the babies liked the salty taste of my skin. The kids suckled on every knuckle and finger and earlobe. You could almost see the wheels turning: "This furry, pink guy is soft like my mom; he smells funny, but *really* tastes good; and there's gotta be some milk in here somewhere." I cherished every salty moment. If their hunger returned and they began to cry, I delivered them back to their mothers, whose look of helplessness mirrored my own.

2) Compassionate Service is Hard Work

Giving of ourselves to help others looks as if it would be enervating. One might expect the activity of providing merciful service will diminish our own potential to thrive and be useful. Will not the compassionate companion absorb the sorrow of the other, unto herself?

The miracle of service is that it seems to energize and empower the servant. John Wesley said about his sermons that he set himself afire, week after week, and "people came to watch me burn." Saint Francis and Mahatma Gandhi were two paragons of this paradox of compassionate energy. Both were physically slight, had wasted in prisons for years, slept less than four hours a night, walked thousands of miles, and performed daily manual labor in their communities. Yet these tireless souls found the energy to transform millions.

Until his ninety-second year, my father sponsored scores of recovering alcoholics, six to eight at a clip. For two decades, the nexus of his life had become his thousands of hours of service. Until the very end, his psychic energy seemed to be refueled by all this work. Because we stand for six hours, I anticipated that helping in a soup kitchen would be tiring. Yet I'm never tired, and feel energized at shift's end. During the balance of those days, I always get a lot accomplished. Go figure.

There are two possible explanations for this paradox. First, the most conscious giver understands that he and the receiver are one. If I'm you, then nothing is lost in a transfer of my energies for your benefit. Second, the giver gives away her gifts—her resources of time and energy—all of which are expendable and renewable. She avoids feeling empty or deadened because she is not giving away her personal power, her will, or her self-expression. She is sharing herself, but *not giving* herself away.

3) Compassionate Service is Heartfelt: The Value of Heartbreak

Because compassionate service is hands-on, it involves emotional connection. Service is not for the faint of heart. Ram Dass says, "With doors closed to the pain of others we banish that which would release our compassion and engagement with

THE VALUE OF MERCIFUL SERVICE: SHARING OURSELVES

life. We need heart-to-heart resuscitation."[191] The caregiver's heart swings open to include the other, and by extension, the whole world. To locate the intersection of our heart and the world, Andrew Harvey suggests we ask ourselves just one question: "Which cause most breaks your heart?" Heart work is a softening. Mercy, an antiquated word, means tender-, soft-, kind-heartedness.

We are afraid that if we ingest even a tiny amount of the suffering in the world, our hearts will break. Bearing witness to the pain of others, our hearts, of course, *will* be broken. But that's the point. As Gibran pointed out, "How can my heart be unsealed unless it be broken?"[192] In 2002, a rock star and the Secretary of the U.S. Treasury visited Africa, concluding with "a view of the shadow land," the AIDS hospice in Addis Ababa, run by the Sisters of Charity:

> Bono knew that progress, if it was to be made, would happen in the slums where {Paul} O'Neil's heart would be engaged. His head, and all that value-added analysis would follow... All the ravages of earthly hell were on display. A little girl, maybe two, hugged O'Neil's leg and he picked her up and held her as they walked.
>
> The entourage was quiet, respectful. This is what they had come for. They knew it now—so that a man who could make a difference would hold a dying baby... This of course, is why leaders, people in power, don't spend too much time in dank hospitals and shantytowns. A person could lose his head...[193]

4) *Compassionate Service Blesses the Servant*

Service, then, seems pretty straightforward. We act generously and mercifully to help others enrich and enhance their lives and decrease their suffering. But it turns out that behaving compassionately also bestows some unintended benefits to the servant. The freely offered gift produces satisfactions unlike any other, and may even yield a return greater than the gift itself.

Acts of service propel me beyond myself and interrupt my incessant self-consciousness. And service is a blessing because it changes us. I recently shared a lunch with a busy executive in her forties who has been leading AA meetings in a women's penitentiary near Orlando twice a week, for *nine* years. I asked if she felt she was making a difference. She replied, "To them? Who knows? I *do* know that it always makes a huge difference to me."

We learn from those we serve. We are welcomed into a different culture, whether it is the culture of a hospital or homeless shelter, among folk who will teach us, if we'll let them. New graduates of Eckerd College joined a roundtable discussion with younger students who asked about their weeks of service in rural West Africa. "We were not trying to teach them or change the villagers, even as we were ourselves being changed… We were all learning—from each other."

Specifically, from poor people, I learn lessons long forgotten, like courage, trust, letting go, satisfaction, endurance, simplicity, sacrifice. One summer afternoon on the Equator, during a two-hour trip without air conditioning, twenty-eight people taught me about longsuffering. We were all sitting on each other's laps in a five-seat passenger van, with nary one complaint or sign of discomfort from a soul, even the children.

I've learned the value of thrift by watching poor people recycling everything from used light bulbs and nails to bent sticks used to replace broken shovel handles. A grandmother taught me resourcefulness. She stretched a breakfast of three fresh eggs and eight stale hot dog rolls over seven hungry pre-teens. I learned a new level of industry from diminutive Mayan men and women, less than five feet tall. Up and down very steep mountain roads in the rain, they carried bricks, water, groceries, and babies, weighing more than they did. And I learned generosity the morning I left Guatemala. For my last meal, the fatted chicken was killed and I was offered the choicest piece in the soup—a gristled hip joint.

"At least for older people, it really is more blessed to give than to receive. In old age when social networks are thinned due to the deaths of friends and family, the social benefits of volunteering are strongest."[194] Perhaps because we are like-minded folk, working with other volunteers is fun. I like their energy. A volunteer on the flood plains of Iowa writes: "Passing sandbags is a personal thing. The line may be one hundred yards long. But it's not long for you. It's intimate, a three person event, only you and the person on either side... You get to know people..."[195]

Mostly, personal service just *feels* good. Making fifty peanut butter and grape jelly sandwiches for homeless men and women feels as if my time can't be more effectively used. For 34 cents apiece, these 400 calories will keep on the street for a couple of days. I'm not sure who feels more nourished. It gives me pleasure and feeds my soul.

Summary

<u>The Value of Mercy</u> is characterized by service in action, which is always personal, difficult, and emotional work.

<u>The Value of Heartbreak</u> is one of the difficult blessings of service. We are asked to break open our hearts in the face of another's suffering. Our broken hearts will change and deepen us.

CONCLUSION

Life Raised to a Higher Power:
Benefits Of A Value-Based
Spiritual Practice

Enrichment

- After years of passivity, finding my own spiritual voice was empowering.

- I have thrived on a palette of broader ideals and values adapted from contemporary culture, including deeper insights into my own psyche.

- Values have opened new sources of meaning, purpose, and identity to me.

- The pursuit of my ideals of wisdom, inner peace, love, and compassion has been a constant source of pleasure.

- Transformation, through the long-term adoption of more spiritual values in place of secular ones, results in a life that simply works better.

- Character formation, through the intentional habituation of values over the long term, is very slowly helping me to become more of the person I wish to be.

More Balance

- Navigating between both secular and spiritual values has been twice as rich and interesting than a life spent in an almost exclusively secular dimension.

- Recalibrating the ratio of spiritual challenge to secular comfort is always stimulating.

- An increased acceptance of earthly reality in all its shades of light and shadow has added fresh perspective and depth to my spiritual experience.

I wish you an equally revealing and expansive experience as you seek to define your own most cherished ideals and values. I wish you—more life.

End Notes

INTRODUCTION

[1] Garrison Keillor, *Good Poems for Hard Times*. (New York: Penguin Books, 2005), xvi.

PART ONE
CHAPTER 1

[2] St. Augustine, *The Great Thoughts*. Ed. George Seldes (New York: Ballantine Books, 1985), 25.
[3] Carl Jung, *Modern Man in Search of a Soul*, (Abingdon: Routledge, 2005, reprint from 1933), 238.
[4] Stephen Batchelor, *Buddhism Without Beliefs*. (New York: Riverhead Books, 1997), 13.

CHAPTER 2

[5] Annie Dillard, quoted in *For the Time Being*. (New York: Alfred Knopf: 1999), 185.

PART TWO
CHAPTER 3

[6] Karen Armstrong, TED Lecture March 1, 2008.
[7] Jean-Paul Sartre. *Existentialism and Human Emotions*. (New York: 1995), 15, 22, 49.
[8] Peter Morales, UU World Magazine, Spring 2011, 7.
[9] [4] Robert C. Fuller, *Spiritual, But Not Religious* (New York, Riverhead Books), 1999, 8-9.
[10] Irving Singer, *Meaning in Life. The Creation of Value*, The Free Press, NYC, 1992.

CHAPTER 4

[11] St. Thomas Aquinas, *The Great Thoughts*, 15.
[12] Mark Twain, *Autobiography of Mark Twain*.
[13] F. Scott Fitzgerald, "The Crack-up," in *The Art of the Personal Essay* ed. Phillip Lopate. (New York: Doubleday, 1994), 528.
[14] Charles Jencks. "What is Post-Modernism?," in *The Truth About the Truth*. Ed. Walter Truitt Anderson. (New York: Penguin, 1995), 27.
[15] Lee Robinson, "The Rules of Evidence," in *Good Poems for Hard Times*, 152.
[16] Robert Foster, *Modern Spiritual Formation Movement*. (8/13/2010)? (http.wwwpatheos.com?).

CHAPTER 5

[17] Irving Singer, 91-93, 99.
[18] Heather McHugh, "A Physics," in *Good Poems for Hard Times*, 103.
[19] Clarissa Pinkola Estes, *Running With the Wolves*, (New York: Ballantine Books), 19.

CHAPTER 6

[20] Professor Leuba, quoted by William James, in *The Varieties of Religious Experience*. (New York: New American Library, 1958), 382.
[21] Eckhart Tolle. *The Power of Now*. (New York: Namaste Publishing, 1999), 5.
[22] Thomas Moore. *Original Self*. (New York: Perennial, 2001), 140.
[23] Very Reverend Alan Jones. *Spirituality is the Art of Making Connections*, at the 16th Annual Common Boundary Conference. (Washington: Sounds True, 1996).
[24] Dillard, 172.
[25] Moore, 141.

END NOTES

CHAPTER 7

[26] José Ortega Y. Gasset, "The Revolt of the Masses," in *the Great Thoughts*, 315.
[27] Abraham Verghese. *Cutting for Stone*. (New York: Random House, 2009), 7.
[28] Seldes, 228.
[29] James Hillman, *A Blue Fire*, (New York: Harper & Row), 85.
[30] Gregg Levoy. *Callings*, (New York: Random House, 1997), 6.

CHAPTER 8

[31] Soren Kierkegaard, Quoted in Richard Strivers. *The Culture of Cynicism: American Morality in Decline*, (Oxford, Blackwell, 1994), 7.
[32] Kate Chopin, in *Bloomsbury Chronological Dictionary of Quotations*. ed. Edmund Wright, (London: 1994), 215.
[33] David Brooks, "The Organization Kid," *The Atlantic Monthly*, April 2001, 53.
[34] Aristotle, quoted in *Ethics Applied*. ed. Keith Govel, et al. (Boston: Pearson, 2004), 141.
[35] Michael Pollan. *Second Nature*. (New York: Grove Press, 1991), 46-49.

PART THREE—I

[36] Sylvia Boorstein. *Pay Attention, for Goodness Sake*. (New York: Ballantine Books, 2002), 106.
[37] Thomas Moore. *Care of the Soul*. (New York: Harper Perennial, 1994), XV.
[38] Dietrich Bonhoeffer. *Letters and Papers from Prison*. Ed. Eberhard Bethge. (New York: Touchstone, 1997), 371.

CHAPTER 9

[39] Scott Peck, 44, 51.
[40] Anton Chekhov, quoted in *The Great Thoughts*, 77.
[41] Richard P. Sloan, "a fighting spirit won't save your life,", St. Petersburg Times, 2011.
[42] *New York Times*, March 15, 1999.
[43] John Huss, quoted in Seldes, *The Great Thoughts*, (SPT (2011), 196.
[44] Jon Babbs, "New Age Fundamentalism," in *Meeting the Shadow*. ed. Zweig & Abrams. (New York: Putnam, 1991), 161.
[45] "As We Forgive: The Story of Rwanda's Redemption," A film by Laura Waters Hinson, 2007.
[46] Teilhard de Chardin. *The Phenomenon of Man*. (New York: Harper, 1975), 31.

CHAPTER 10

[47] Seneca, *The Great Thoughts*, 377.
[48] Pema Chodron. *The Wisdom of No Escape*. (Boston: Shambhala, 2001), 33.
[49] Bertrand Russell. *Bloomsbury Chronological Dictionary of Quotations*, 323.
[50] Carl Sandburg, *Abraham Lincoln*. (New York: Harcourt, Brace, Jovanovich 1967), 594.
[51] Peck, 193.
[52] Carl Sandburg, 392.
[53] Charles Handy. *The Age of Paradox*. (Boston: HBS Press, 1994), 34.

CHAPTER 11

[54] Ludwig Wittgenstein, quoted in *The Best Buddhist Writing, 2006*. Ed. Melvin McLeod. (Boston: Shambhala, 2006), 96.
[55] *Myers-Briggs Type Indicator*, MBTI.
[56] Carl Sandburg, 668

PART THREE—II

[57] New York Times, November 16, 2010
[58] Eckhart Tolle. *The Power of Now*, 22
[59] Terry Hershey. *Soul Gardening*. (Minneapolis: Augsburg Press, 2000), 160.
[60] Wesley McNair. "The Future, *Good Poems*, 178.
[61] Batchelor, 70.
[62] Eckhart Tolle, *A New Earth*. (London: Penguin, 2005), 243, 244.

THE VALUE OF EQUANIMITY

[63] Marc Jan Barash. "Searching for the Heart of Compassion in *the Best of Buddhist Writing*, 2006), 28.
[64] Seng Ts'an, "Believing in Mind" in *God Makes the Rivers to Flow*. ed. Eknath Easwaran. (Tamales, California: Nilgiri Press, 1991), 96.

CHAPTER 12

[65] David Loy. "Ego Goes Global," in *the Best Buddhist Writing- 2006*), 226-227.
[66] Edward Bellamy. *Equality*. (New York: Appleton, 1897), 266.
[67] Seneca. *Letters From a Stoic*. (London: Penguin Books, 1969), 34.
[68] David Pogul. *The New York Times*, November 25, 2010, B7.

END NOTES

[69] Seneca, quoted in *the Great Thoughts*, 378.
[70] Ivan Illich, quoted in *Bloomsbury the Chronological Dictionary of Quotations*, ed. Edmund Wright, (London), 328.

CHAPTER 13

[71] Robert Frost, quoted in *Good Advice on Writing*, ed. William Safire. (New York: Simon & Schuster, 1992), 69.
[72] *The Death of Common Sense*, 4.
[73] Kahil Gibran. Quoted in "Sunbeams," *the Sun*, February 1998, 48.
[74] Mark Magill. "Passing It On" in *The Best Buddhist Writing – 2006*, 283.
[75] Eckhart Tolle. *A New Earth*. (New York: Plume, 2005), 213.
[76] AARP Bulletin, September 8.
[77] Lao Tsu. *Tao Te Ching*, translated by Jane English. (New York: Random House, 1972), 46.
[78] Meister Eckhart, quoted in Joel Kovel, *History and Spirit*. (Boston: Beacon Press, 1991), 159.

CHAPTER 14

[79] Goldstein, 77.
[80] Montaigne. *The Great Thoughts*, 298.
[81] Jeanne Marie Beaumont. "Afraid So," in *Good Poems for Hard Times*, 169-170.
[82] Frances Bacon, in *The Great Thoughts*, 28.
[83] Michael L. Crichton. *State of Fear*. (New York: Harper, 2009), 572.
[84] Donald T. Phillips. *Lincoln On Leadership*. (New York: Warner Books, 1993), 99.
[85] James Hillman. *Inter Views*. (Dallas: Spring Publications, 1983), 21.
[86] Seneca. *The Great Thoughts*, 38. (or Kazanzakis)

CHAPTER 15

[87] Eckhart Tolle, *The New Earth*, 102.
[88] Jane Kenyon. "Twilight After Haying," Garrison Keillor, *Good Poems*. (New York: Penguin Books, 2002), 411.
[89] Quoted by Barash, *The Best Buddhist Writing*, 2006), 27.
[90] Jonathan Haidt. *The Happiness Hypothesis*. (New York: Perseus Books, 2006).
[91] Gladys Taber, "Stillmeadow Sampler", J. B. Lippincott Co., 1957.
[92] Alan W. Watts. *The Wisdom of Insecurity*. (New York: Vintage Books, 1951), 117.
[93] Batchelor, 9.

THE VALUE OF HEALING

[94] Thomas Moore. *Care of the Soul*, xvi-xvii.
[95] Rainer Maria Rilke. *Selected Poems*, ed. Robert Bly. (New York: Harper & Row, 1981), 25.
[96] Anne Lamott. *Plan B*. (New York: Riverhead Books, 2005), 174.

CHAPTER 16

[97] John Bradshaw. *Healing the Shame That Binds You*. (Deerfield Beach: Health Communications, 1988), 10.
[98] Anne Lamott. *Bird by Bird*. (New York: Random House, 1994), 116.
[99] Bradshaw, Ibid. 15, 96.

CHAPTER 17

[100] Bradshaw, 9.
[101] Mircea Eliade. *The Sacred & The Profane*. (New York: Harcourt Brad, 1987), 208.
[102] Mircea Eliade. *Myth and Reality*. (New York: Harper, 1963), 89.
[103] Harry Crews. *A Childhood: The Biography of a Place*, University of Georgia Press, 1995, 154ff.
[104] Derek Walcott. "Love After Love," *Collected Poems 1947-1987*. (New York: Farrar, Strauss & Giroux), 328.
[105] Jack Kornfield. *The Art of Forgiveness*. (New York: ???Pub, 2002), 19.
[106] Scott Russell Sanders., "Under the Influence," in *the Art of Personal Essay*, 744.

CHAPTER 18

[107] Ibid, 72.
[108] Anne Lamott. *Traveling Mercies*. (New York: Random House, 1999), 68.
[109] Ibid, 68, 72.
[110] Jane Gignoux. *Some Folk Say*. (New York: FoulkeTale Pub, 1998), 47.
[111] Judith Anderson, in *Life Prayers*, ed. Elizabeth Roberts. (New York: Harpers' San Francisco, 1996), 350.
[112] W.H. Auden. "Precious Five," quoted in Steindl Rast, 81.
[113] David Steindl-Rast. *Gratefulness, the Heart of Prayer*. (New York: Paulist Press, 1984), 12.
[114] Quoted by Joseph Goldstein, 144.

PART FOUR
CHAPTER 19

[115] The Dalai Lama. *Ocean of Wisdom*. (Santa Fe: Clear Light, 1989), 38, 16.
[116] Alan Watts. *Behold the Spirit*. (New York: Vintage Books, 1947), 69.
[117] Barbara Defoe Whitehead. "The New Family Values," *UTNE Reader*, May/Jun 1993, 61.
[118] Oriah Mountain Dreamer. *The Invitation*, www.davidbrown.co.UK.
[119] Kabir, quoted in Steindl-Rast. *Gratefulness, the Heart of Prayer*, 7.
[120] Anne Lamott, *Plan B*, 260.
[121] Hans Kung. *On Being a Christian*. (Garden City: Doubleday, 1976), 256.
[122] Ibid, 262.

PART FOUR—I—MARRIAGE

[123] John Wellwood. "Fighting for Enlightenment," *New Age Journal*, July, August 1996, 76.

CHAPTER 20

[124] Kurtz & Ketcham. *The Spirituality of Imperfection*, 229.
[125] *Alcoholics Anonymous, 3rd Edition*. (New York: AA World Services, 1976), 64.
[126] Quoted by Katy Kelly. Recipe for Wedded Bliss: Lower Your Expectations," *US News & World Report*, September 29, 2001, 50.
[127] Boorstien. *Pay Attention*, 223.
[128] Joseph Campbell with Bill Moyers, *The Power of Myth*. (New York: Doubleday, 1988), 201.
[129] Ernie M. Williams & Robert B. Levine. *It's How You Play the Game*. (Boston: Pearson, 2004).
[130] Phillips. *Lincoln*, 82.

CHAPTER 21

[131] James Hillman. *A Blue Fire*. (New York: Harper & Row, 1989), 285.
[132] Michael McGill, The McGill Report on Male Intimacy
[133] Karen Hesse. *Out of the Dust*. (New York: Scholastic, 1997), 218.
[134] James Hillman. *A Blue Fire*, 284.
[135] Sam Keene. "Living the Questions," Lecture at Esalen, 8.
[136] Pier Giorgio Di Cicco, In the Confessional.
[137] Bill Holm. "A Wedding Poem for Shele & Phil," in *Good Poems for Hard Times*, 98.

PART FOUR—II—PARENTING

[138] Nikos Kazantzakis. *The Saviors of God*. (New York: Touchstone, 1960), 74.
[139] Rainer Maria Rilke. *Rilke on Love and Other Difficulties*, ed. John Mood. (New York: Norton & Co., 1975), 31

CHAPTER 22

[140] Claude Steiner. *Scripts People Live*. (New York: Bantam Books, 1975), 123-124.
[141] Ellen Goodman, Value Judgments, p. 126

CHAPTER 23

[142] Amitai Etzioni. *The Spirit of Community*. (New York: Crown Publishing, 1993), 61.
[143] Marilyn Ferguson. *The Aquarian Conspiracy*. (Los Angeles: J.P. Tarcher, 1980), 401.
[144] Etizioni, 61.
[145] Peck, 127.
[146] Theodore Roosevelt, "The Strenuous Life," a speech in Chicago, April 10, 1899.
[147] Alan Wolfe. *Moral Freedom*. (New York: Norton, 2001), 70.

PART FOUR—III—COMPASSION

[148] Taisen Deshimaru. *Questions to a Zen Master*. Trans/Ed. Nancy Amphoux. (New York: Shambala, 1985), 31, 65.
[149] Albert Schweitzer. *Out of My Life and Thought*. Trans. A.B. Lemke. (New York: Henry Holt, 1990), 158.
[150] "Help the Planet," *St. Petersburg Times*, November 15, 2010.
[151] Schweitzer, 156.
[152] *The Worlds of Gandhi*, ed. Richard Attenborough. (New York: New Market Press, 1982), 101.
[153] Jeremy Bentham, quoted in Peter Singer. *Writings On an Ethical Life*. (New York, 2000), 33.
[154] Singer, Ibid. xv.
[155] Matthew Scully, quoted in *Newsweek*, July 18, 2006, 66.

CHAPTER 24

[156] Eric Weiner. *The Geography of Bliss*. (New York: Twelve, 2008), 301.
[157] "The United Presbyterian Churches for Holy Communion," quoted in *The Sun* of January 1995, 40.
[158] Kung, 256.

END NOTES

[159] Matthew Fox. *A Spirituality Named Compassion*. (Minneapolis: Winston Press, 1978), 15.
[160] Bill Bryson. *A Short History of Nearly Everything*. (New York: Random House, 2005), 38.
[161] Annie Dillard, 107, 59.
[162] Mother Teresa, quoted in Jack Kornfield. *The Art of Forgiveness*. (New York: Bantam Books, 2002), 115.

CHAPTER 25

[163] Jonathan Haidt. *The Happiness Hypotheses*. (New York: Perseus Books, 2006), 235.
[164] Dillard, 120.
[165] Ram Dass & Paul Garman. *How Can I Help?* (New York: Alfred A Knopf, 1988), 38, 180.
[166] Guy Murchie. *The Seven Mysteries of Life*. (New York: Houghton Mifflin, 1978), 345, 346, 351.
[167] William F. Buckley, Jr. *Happy Days Were Here Again*, Ed. Patricia Bozell. (Holbrook: Adams Publishing, 1993), 438.
[168] John Paul Lederach. *Building Peace*. (Washington, DC: 1997).
[169] Charles Handy, 247.

CHAPTER 26

[170] Bono, quoted in Jeffrey D. Sachs. *The End of Poverty*. (New York: Penguin Books, 2006), xiii.
[171] Dillard, 74, 187.
[172] Bryson, 427, 551, 563, 588.
[173] Dr. J.L. Moreno. "Current Approach to Drama Therapy", quoted in a *Florida Psychodrama Workshop*, July 12, 2004.
[174] Kenneth Vickery. *The African Experience*. (Chantilly, VA: The Teaching Co., 2006), 8.
[175] B. Lozoff, quoted in *the Alternatives to Violence Project Advanced Manual*. [Pub date, etc.?]

CHAPTER 27

[176] Matsushita. *Fortune*, March 31, 1997, 107.
[177] Küng, 268.
[178] Ibid, 425.
[179] Laurence Shanes & Peter Barton. *Not Fade Away*. (USA: Rodale, 2003), 16, 87.
[180] St. Thomas Aquinas. *The Summa Theologica*. II-II Q 66A7.
[181] Gandhi, 17-18.
[182] Peter Singer. *Writings on an Ethical Life*. (New York: Harper Collins, 2000), 33?
[183] *Independence Sector Giving & Volunteering in the U.S.*, Westat, 2002.
[184] Joseph Stiglitz and Linda Bilmes, *The Three Billion Dollar War,* W Norton & Co., NYC, 2008.

CHAPTER 28

[185] University of Chicago Study, Reported in <u>The National Post.</u>
[186] Fox, 8.
[187] Robert Coles. *The Call For Service*. (New York: Houghton Mifflin, 1993), 40, 46.
[188] William James, quoted in *The Sun*, May 1996, 40.
[189] John Paul Lederach. *Building Peace*. (Washington, DC: US Institute of Peace Press, 1997), 23-26.
[190] Mother Teresa. *In the Heart of the World*. (Novato, CA: New World Library, 1997), 69-70.
[191] Dass, 57.
[192] Khalil Gibran. *A Spiritual Treasury*. (Oxford: One World Publications, 2001), 109.
[193] Ron Suskind. *The Price of Loyalty*. (New York: Simon & Shuster, 2004), ???
[194] Haidt, 174.
[195] Joe Blair, "Sandbagged", The St. Petersburg Times.

Acknowledgements

A special thanks to my dear friend, Bernice Tripodi. She patiently typed countless drafts of this manuscript. Her counsel, patience, and good nature have been almost as inspirational to me as her steadfast devotion to her own religious path. I think we've learned from each other.

I've been blessed to have two mentors who have been indefatigable sources of encouragement and have patiently helped me to uncover my writing voice. My brother, Mike Bellamy, has recently retired from a career as a Professor of English at the University of St. Thomas in St. Paul. His thorough, gentle, and informed criticism is always been stimulating and challenging. I'm an appreciative beneficiary of Mike's long experience as a teacher of students (like me) to think more rigorously. I've especially treasured his Socratic explorations, broad intellectual range, and delightful sense of humor.

In her role as chief domestic editor, Christina has been a paragon of support. She has tirelessly nudged me to be more authentic and self-revelatory; and less certain and didactic. I'm especially grateful to Christina for teaching me the wonder of story. We share abiding interests in many things, most especially the values of family, our mutual personal growth, and the need for service. Thanks for all of it pal.

Bibliography

* Refers to material that was most important and useful to me.

Alcoholics Anonymous, 3rd Edition. New York: A.A. World Services, Inc., 1976.

American Poetry: The Twenty First Century, Vol. 1. New York: The Library of America, 2000.

*Ardrey, Robert. *The Territorial Imperative*. New York: Cambridge Urius Press, 1992.

*Aristotle. *The Basic Works of Aristotle*. Ed. Richard McKeon. New York: Random House, 1941.

*Armstrong, Karen. *A History of God*. New York: Ballantine Books, 1993.

Aronson, Ronald. *Living Without God*. Berkeley, CA: Counterpoint, 2008.

Assagioli, Roberto. *The Act of Will*. New York: Penguin Books, 1973.

Auden, W. H. *Selected Poems*. New York: Vintage International, 1989.

*Batchelor, Stephen. *Buddhism Without Beliefs*. New York: The Berkley Publishing Group, 1997.
Bellah, Robert N. et al. *The Good Society*. New York: Alfred A. Knopf, 1991.
*Bellamy, Edward. *Looking Backward: 2000-1887*. New York: Penguin Books, 1960.
Bellamy, Edward. *Equality*. New York: D. Appleton and Company, 1897.
Bennett, William J., ed. *The Book of Virtues* New York: Simon & Schuster, 1993.
Blake, William. *Selected Poems*. New York: St. Martin's Press, 1994.
Bloomsbury Chronological Dictionary of Quotations. Ed. Edmund Wright. London: 1994.
Bly, Robert, et al., eds. *The Rag and Bone Shop of the Heart: Poems for Men*. New York: Harper Perennial, 1992.
Bonhoeffer, Dietrich. *Letters & Papers from Prison*. Enlarged Ed. Ed. Eberhard Bethge. New York: Simon & Schuster, 1997.
Boorstein, Sylvia. *Pay Attention, For Goodness Sake*. New York: Random House Publishing Group, 2002.
Boorstin, Daniel J. *The Creators: A History of Heroes of the Imagination*. New York: Random House, 1992.
Bradlee, Ben, *A Good Life*. New York: Touchstone, 1995.
*Bradshaw, John. *Healing the Shame That Binds You*. Deerfield Beach, Florida: Health Communications, Inc., 1988.
Brehony, Kathleen. *Ordinary Grace*. New York: Penguin Putnam, Inc., 1999.
*Browne, Harry. *How I Found Freedom in an Unfree World*. New York: Avon Books, 1973.
*Bryson, Bill. *A Short History of Nearly Everything*. New York: Broadway Books, 2003.

Buber, Martin. *I and Thou: A New Translation*. New York: Charles Scribner's Sons, 1970.

Buckley, William F., Jr. *Happy Days Were Here Again: Reflections of a Libertarian Journalist*. Ed. Patricia Bozell. Holbrook: Adams Publishing, 1993.

Calvino, Italo. *Invisible Cities*. Trans. William Weaver. New York: Harcourt Brace & Co.,   1974.

Campbell, Joseph. *The Hero With a Thousand Faces*. Princeton: Princeton University Press, 1973.

Campbell, Joseph. *Myths to Live By*. New York: Bantam Books, 1972.

*Campbell, Joseph. *The Power of Myth*. New York: Doubleday, 1988.

Camus, Albert. *The Plague*. Trans. Stuart Gilbert. New York: Vintage International, 1975.

Carlyle, Thomas. *On Heroes: Hero-Worship and the Heroic in History*. London: Oxford University Press, 1974.

Cherry, Keith. Dissertation. "Ain't No Grave Deep Enough": A Ethnographical Study of a Residential Facility for People With AIDS. USF: 1997.

Chödrön, Pema. *The Wisdom of No Escape*. Boston: Shambhala, 1991.

Coles, Robert. *The Call for Service*. New York: Houghton Mifflin Company, 1993.

Collier, James Lincoln. *The Rise of Selfishness in America*. New York: Oxford University Press, 1991.

Collinson, Diané. *Fifty Major Philosophers: A Reference Guide*. New York: Rutledge, 1990.

Cook, Albert. *Oedipus Rex: A Mirror for Greek Drama*. Belmont: Wadsworth Publishing Co., 1963.

*Covey, Stephen R. *The 7 Habits of Highly Effective People*. New York: Free Press, 1989.

Cunningham, Lawrence. *Saint Francis of Assisi*. Photography, Dennis Stock. New York: Harper & Row, 1981.

Cupitt, Don. *After God: The Future of Religion*. New York: HarperCollins Publishers, 1997.

The Dalai Lama of Tibet. *Ocean of Wisdom: Guidelines for Living*. Santa Fe: Clear Light Publishers, 1989.

*Dass, Ram, and Paul Gorman. *How Can I Help? Stories and Reflections on Service*. New York, Alfred A. Knopf, 1988.

*de Chardin, Pierre Teilhard. *The Phenomenon of Man*. New York: Harper & Row, 1975.

Deshimaru, Taisen. *Questions to a Zen Master*. Trans./Ed. Nancy Amphoux. New York: E. P. Dutton, Inc., 1985.

Dillard, Annie. *The Annie Dillard Reader*. New York: Harper Perennial, 1995.

*Dillard, Annie. *For the Time Being*. New York: Alfred A. Knopf, 1999.

*Durant, Will and Ariel. *The Lessons of History*. New York: Simon and Schuster, 1968.

Dwyer, John C. *Church History: Twenty Centuries of Catholic Christianity*. Mahwah, NJ, Paulist Press, 1985.

*Easwaran, Eknath, ed. *God Makes the Rivers to Flow*. Tomales: Nilgiri Press, 1991.

*Eckhart, Meister. *Meister Eckhart: A Modern Translation*. Ed. Raymond B. Blakney. New York: Harper & Row, 1941.

Eckhart, Meister. *Meister Eckhart, From Whom God Hid Nothing*. Ed. David O'Neal. Boston: Shambhala, 1996.

*Einstein, Albert. *Ideas and Opinions*. Trans. Sonja Bargmann. New York: The Modern Library, 1994.

Eisler, Riane. *The Chalice & The Blade: Our History, Our Future*. San Francisco: Harper & Row, 1988.

*Eliade, Mircea. *Myth and Reality*. New York, Harper & Row, 1963.

*Eliade, Mircea. *The Sacred and the Profane*. New York: Harcourt Brace, 1987.

*Eliot, T.S. *The Hollow Men, American Poetry: The Twentieth Century.*, Vol. 1, New York: Library of Congress, 2000.

*Eliot, T. S. *The Waste Land and Other Poems*. New York: Harvest/Harcourt Brace Jovanovich, 1962.

*Emerson, Ralph Waldo. *The Selected Writings of Ralph Waldo Emerson*. New York: The Modern Library, 1992.

Epstein, Greg M. *Good Without God*. New York: Harper, 2009.

*Erdman, Sarah. *Nine Hills to Nambonkaha*. New York: Henry Holt & Company, 2003.

Erricker, Clive. *Teach Yourself Buddhism*. Chicago: NTC Publishing Group, 1995.

Ethics Applied. 4th Edition, Ed. by Goree, Pyle, Baker & Hopkins. Boston: Pierson Education, 2004.

*Etzioni, Amitai. *The Spirit of Community: Rights, Responsibilities, and the Communitarian Agenda*. New York: Crown Publishers, 1993.

*Ferguson, Marilyn. *The Aquarian Conspiracy: Personal and Social Transformation in the 1980s*. Los Angeles: J. P. Tarcher, Inc., 1980.

*Fox, Matthew. *A Spirituality Named Compassion and the Healing of the Global Village, Humpty Dumpty and Us*. Minneapolis: Winston Press, 1978.

Frankl, Viktor E. *Man's Search for Meaning*. New York: Washington Square Press/Pocket Books, 1984.

*Franklin, Benjamin. *Poor Richard's Almanack*. Mount Vernon: Peter Pauper Press, 1987.

*Frost, Robert. *Robert Frost's Poems*. New York: Washington Square Press/Pocket Books, 1971.

*Gandhi, Mohandas K. *The Gandhi Reader: A Sourcebook of his Life and Writings*. Ed. Homer A. Jack. New York: Grove Press, 1989.

*Gandhi, Mohandas K. *The Words of Gandhi*. Ed. Richard Attenborough. New York: Newmarket Press, 1982.

*Gibran, Kahlil. *A Spiritual Treasury*. Oxford, England: Oneworld Publications, 2001.

Gibran, Kahlil. *Sand and Foam*. New York: Alfred A. Knopf, 1991.

Gleick, James. *Chaos: Making a New Science*. New York, Penguin Books, 1987.

*Goethe, Johann Wolfgang von. *Faust: A Tragedy*. Trans. Walter Arndt. Ed. Cyrus Hamlin. New York: W. W. Norton & Company, 1976.

*Goldstein, Joseph. *The Experience of Insight: A Simple and Direct Guide to Buddhist Meditation*. Boulder: Shambhala, 1975.

Goodman, Ellen. *Value Judgments*. New York: Farrar Straus Giroux, 1993.

Greer, Colin and Kohl, Herbert. *A Call to Character*. New York: HarperCollins, 1997.

Grof, M.D., Stanislav with Hal Zina Bennett. *The Holotropic Mind*. New York: HarperCollins Publishers, 1993.

Grudin, Robert. *The Grace of Great Things*. New York: Ticknor & Fields, 1990.

Grudin, Robert. *Time and the Art of Living*. New York: Houghton Mifflin Company, 1982.

*Haidt, Johathan. *The Happiness Hypothesis*. New York: Basic Books, 2006.

*Halberstam, David. *The Best and the Brightest*. New York: Random House, 1972.

Hall, Calvin S. and Nordby, Vernon J. *A Primer of Jungian Psychology*. New York: Mentor, 1973.

Halmgren, David. *Permaculture, Principles & Pathways Beyond Substainability*. Hepburn, Victoria, Australia, 2009.

Hammarskjöld, Dag. *Markings*. Trans. Leif Sjöberg and W. H. Auden. New York: Ballantine Books, 1993.

*Handy, Charles. *The Age of Paradox*. Boston: Harvard Business School Press, 1994.

Hanh, Thich Nhat. *Going Home: Jesus and Buddha as Brothers*. New York: Riverhead Books/Penguin Putnam, Inc., 1999.

Hauge, Eric. *A Chinese Legend, In the Shadow of Nine Dragons*. London: Highway Press. 1958.

*Hayakawa, S. I. *Language in Thought and Action*. 3rd ed. New York: Harcourt Brace Jovanovich, Inc., 1972.

Hemenway, Toby. *Gaia's Garden*. White River Junction, VT: Chelsea Green, 2009.

*Hershey, Terry. *Soul Gardening*. Minneapolis, MN: Augsburg Fortress, 2000.

Hillman, James. *A Blue Fire*. Ed. Thomas Moore. New York: HarperPerennial, 1991.

*Hillman, James, with Laura Pozzo. *Inter Views*. Dallas: Spring Publications, Inc., 1983.

*Hillman, James. *The Soul's Code*. New York: Warner Books, 1996.

Hillman, James and Michael Ventura. *We've Had a Hundred Years of Psychotherapy and the World's Getting Worse*. San Francisco: HarperSanFrancisco, 1992.

Hilton-Barber, Brett and Prof. Lee R. Berger. *Field Guide to the Cradle of Humankind*. Capetown, South Africa: Struik Publishers, 2002.

Holy Bible, The. King James Version. USA: World Bible Publishers, Inc., 1989.

Holzer, Harold, ed. *Lincoln as I Knew Him*. Chapel Hill: Algonquin Books, 1999.

Hopke, Robert H. *The Collected Works of C. G. Jung*. Boston: Shambhala Publications, Inc., 198.

Hubben, William. *Dostoevsky, Kierkegaard, Nietzsche & Kafka*. New York: Touchstone, 1997.

Hunter, James Davison. *The Death of Character.* New York: 2000.

*James, William. *The Varieties of Religious Experience*. New York: New American Library, 1958.

Johnson, Robert A. *Owning Your Own Shadow: Understanding the Dark Side of the Psyche*. San Francisco: HarperSanFrancisco, 1991.

*Jung, Carl G. *The Portable Jung*. Ed. Joseph Campbell. Trans. R. F. C. Hull. New York: Viking Penguin Inc., 1971.

Jung, Carl G. *The Undiscovered Self*. Trans. R. F. C. Hull. Boston: Little, Brown and Company, 1958.

*Kazantzakis, Nikos. *The Saviors of God: Spiritual Exercises*. Trans. Kimon Friar. New York: Touchstone/Simon & Schuster, Inc., 1960.

*Keen, Sam. *Hymns to an Unknown God: Awakening the Spirit in Everyday Life*. New York: Bantam Books, 1994.

Kegan, Robert and Lisa Laskow Lahey. *Immunity to Change*. Boston: Harvard Business Press, 2009.

*Keillor, Garrison. *Good Poems*. New York: Penguin Books, 2003

Keillor, Garrison. *Good Poems American Places*. New York: Penguin Group, 2011.

*Keillor, Garrison. *Good Poems for Hard Times*. New York: Penguin Group, 2005.

Kierkegaard, Søren. *Fear and Trembling and The Sickness Unto Death*. Trans. Walter Lowrie. Princeton: Princeton University Press, 1974.

*Kingsolver, Barbara. *The Poisonwood Bible*. New York: Harper Perennial, 1998.

Kipling, Rudyard. *Gunga Din and Other Favorite Poems*. Ed. Stanley Appelbaum. New York: Dover Publications, Inc., 1990.

Kornfield, Jack. *The Art of Forgiveness, Lovingkindness, and Peace.* New York: Bantam Books, 2002.

Kovel, Joel. *History and Spirit: An Inquiry Into the Philosophy of Liberation.* Boston: Beacon Press, 1991.

Kozol, Jonathan. *Amazing Grace: The Lives of Children and the Conscience of a Nation.* New York: HarperPerennial, 1996.

*Küng, Hans. *On Being a Christian.* Trans. Edward Quinn. Garden City: Doubleday & Company, Inc., 1976.

*Lao Tsu. *Tao Te Ching.* Trans. Gia-Fu Feng and Jane English. New York: Vintage Books, 1972.

Lappé, Frances Moore. *Rediscovering America's Values.* New York: Ballantine Books, 1989.

Lasch, Christopher. *The Culture of Narcissism: American Life in an Age of Diminishing Expectations.* New York: Warner Books/W. W. Norton, 1979.

Lasch, Christopher. *Haven in a Heartless World: The Family Besieged.* New York: W. W. Norton & Company, 1977.

*Lederach, John Paul. *Building Peace.* Washington, D.C.: United States Institute of Peace Press, 1997.

*Lévi-Strauss, Claude. *Structural Anthropology.* Trans. Claire Jacobson and Brooke Grundfest Schoepf. New York: Basic Books, Inc., 1963.

*Levinson, Daniel J. et al. *The Seasons of a Man's Life.* New York: Alfred A. Knopf, 1978.

Lewis, Hunter. *A Question of Values: Six Ways We Make the Personal Choices That Shape Our Lives.* San Francisco: HarperSanFrancisco, 1990.

*Lopate, Phillip, ed. *The Art of the Personal Essay: An Anthology from the Classical Era to the Present.* New York: Anchor Books/Doubleday, 1994.

Lüthi, Max. *Once Upon a Time: On the Nature of Fairy Tales*. Trans. Lee Chadeayne and Paul Gottwald. Bloomington: Indiana University Press, 1976.

Lyon, David. *Postmodernity: Concepts in Social Thought*. Minneapolis: University of Minnesota Press, 1994.

*Maccoby, Michael. *The Gamesman*. New York: Bantam Books, 1978.

Maclean, Norman. *A River Runs Through It and Other Stories*. Chicago: The University of Chicago Press. 1976.

MacIntyre, Alasdair. *A Short History of Ethics*. New York: Collier Books/Macmillan Publishing Co., 1966.

Maguire, Jack. *Essential Buddhism*. New York: Pocket Books, 2001.

*Manuel, Frank E. and Fritzie P. *Utopian Thought in the Western World*. Cambridge: The Belknap Press of Harvard University Press, 1979.

Maslow, Abraham H. *The Farther Reaches of Human Nature*. New York: Penguin Books, 1985.

*Maslow, Abraham H. *Toward a Psychology of Being*. 2nd ed. New York: D. Van Nostrand Company, 1968.

May, Rollo. *The Cry for Myth*. New York: W. W. Norton & Company, 1991.

May, Rollo. *Man's Search for Himself*. New York: Dell Publishing Co., 1953.

McCullough, David. *John Adams*. New York: Simon & Schuster, 2001.

McLuhan, T. C. *Touch the Earth: A Self-Portrait of Indian Existence*. New York: Promontory Press, 1971.

McNeill, Donald P. and others. *Compassion: A Reflection on the Christian Life*. Garden City: Doubleday & Company, Inc., 1982.

Meade, Michael. *The Water of Life*. Boulder: Sounds True Recordings. 1993.

*Miller, Alice. *Thou Shalt Not Be Aware: Society's Betrayal of the Child.* New York: New American Library, 1986.
Miller, Arthur. *The Death of a Salesman.* New York: Penguin Books, 1985.
*Moore, Thomas. *The Care of the Soul.* New York: HarperCollins Publishers, 1992.
*Moore, Thomas. *Original Self.* New York: Perennial, 2000.
Morris, Desmond. *The Human Zoo.* New York: Dell Books, 1976.
Morris, Desmond. *The Naked Ape.* New York: Dell Books, 1967.
*Mother Teresa, *In the Heart of the World.* California: New World Library, 1997.
Mumford, Lewis. *The City in History: Its Origins, Its Transformations, and Its Prospects.* New York: Harcourt Brace & Company, 1989.
*Murchie, Guy. *The Seven Mysteries of Life: An Exploration in Science and Philosophy.* Boston: Houghton Mifflin, 1978.
Niebuhr, H. Richard. *The Responsible Self: An Essay in Christian Moral Philosophy.* San Francisco: Harper & Row Publishers, 1978.
*Nietzsche, Friedrich. *A Nietzsche Reader.* Ed. R. J. Hollingdale. New York: Penguin Books, 1977.
Norman, Dorothy. *The Hero: Myth, Image, Symbol.* New York: Anchor Books/Doubleday, 1990.
Odom, Guy R. *Mothers, Leadership, and Success.* Houston: Polybius Press, 1990.
Patterson, James and Peter Kim. *The Day America Told the Truth.* New York: Penguin Books, 1992.
*Peck, M. Scott. *The Road Less Traveled.* New York: Simon & Schuster, 1979.
Phillips, Donald T., *Lincoln on Leadership.* New York: Warner Books, Inc., 1992

*Plotkin, Bill. *Soulcraft*. Novato, CA: New World Library, 2003.
Pollan, Michael. *In Defense of Food*. New York: The Penguin Press, 2008.
*Pollan, Michael. *Second Nature*. New York: Grove Press, 1991.
Praeger Special Studies. *Ending Hunger: An Idea Whose Time Has Come*. New York: 1985.
Prochaska, James O. *Systems of Psychotherapy: A Transtheoretical Analysis*. Homewood: The Dorsey Press, 1979.
Putnam, Hilary. *The Collapse of the Fact/Value Dichotomy and Other Essays*. Cambridge, Massachusetts: Harvard University Press, 2002.
*Putnam, Robert D. *Bowling Alone*. New York: Touchstone, 2000.
Radice, Betty, ed. *Buddhist Scriptures*. Trans. Edward Conze. New York: Penguin Books, 1959.
*Ray, Paul H. and Anderson, Sherry Ruth. *The Cultural Creatives*. New York: Three Rivers Press, 2000.
Rilke, Rainer Maria. *Rilke on Love and Other Difficulties*. Trans. John J. L. Mood. New York: W. W. Norton & Company, 1975.
*Rilke, Rainer Maria. *Selected Poems of Rainer Maria Rilke*. Trans. Robert Bly. New York: Harper & Row Publishers, 1981.
Robbins, John. *Diet for a New America*. Walpole, New Hampshire: Stillpoint Publishing, 1987.
Roof, Wade Clark. *A Generation of Seekers*. New York: HarperCollins, 1993.
*Roosevelt, Theodore. *Theodore Roosevelt: An Autobiography*. New York: Macmillan, 1913.
Rorty, Richard. *Contingency, Irony, and Solidarity*. Cambridge: Cambridge University Press, 1989.
*Rosenau, Pauline Marie. *Post-Modernism and the Social Sciences: Insights, Inroads, and Intrusions*. Princeton: Princeton University Press, 1992.

Russell, Bertrand. *The Conquest of Happiness*. New York: Liveright, 1996.

Rybczynski, Witold. *Home, A Short History of an Ideal*. New York: Penguin Books, 1986.

*Sachs, Jeffrey D. *The End of Poverty*. New York: Penguin Books, 2005.

Salzberg, Sharon. *Faith: Trusting Your Own Deepest Experience*. New York: Riverhead Books, 2002.

*Sandburg, Carl. *Abraham Lincoln: The Prairie Years and the War Years*. New York: Harcourt Brace Jovanovich, 1967.

Sanford, John A. *The Kingdom Within: The Inner Meaning of Jesus' Sayings*. New York: Paulist Press, 1970.

*Sartre, Jean-Paul. *Existentialism and Human Emotions*. New York: Citadel Press/Carol Publishing Group, 1995.

Schmidt, Michael, ed. *The Great Modern Poets*. Quercus, 2006.

*Schweitzer, Albert. *Out of My Life and Thought: An Autobiography*. Trans. A. B. Lemke. New York: Henry Holt and Company, 1990.

*Seldes, George, Ed. *The Great Thoughts*. New York: Ballantine Books, 1985.

*Seneca, Lucius Annaeus. *Letters From a Stoic*. Ed. Betty Radice. New York: Penguin Books, 1969.

*Senge, Peter, et al. *Presence*. New York: Doubleday, 2004.

*Shanes, Laurence and Barton, Peter. *Not Fade Away*. USA: Rodale, 2003.

Simon, Sidney B. and others. *Values Clarification: A Handbook of Practical Strategies for Teachers and Students*. New York: Hart Publishing Company, 1972.

*Singer, Irving. *Meaning in Life: The Creation of Value*. New York: The Free Press, 1992.

Singer, June. *Seeing Through the Visible World: Jung, Gnosis, and Chaos*. San Francisco: Harper & Row, 1990.

*Singer, Peter. *Writings on an Ethical Life*. New York: HarperCollins, 2000.
*Sowell, Thomas. *A Conflict of Visions: Ideological Origins of Political Struggles*. New York: William Morrow & Company, 1987.
*Spengler, Oswald. *The Decline of the West*. New York: Alfred A. Knopf, 1939.
*Steindl-Rast, Brother David. *Gratefulness, The Heart of Prayer: An Approach to Life in Fullness*. New York: Paulist Press, 1984.
*Steiner, Claude. *Scripts People Live: Transactional Analysis of Life Scripts*. New York: Bantam Books, 1975.
Stivers, Richard. *The Culture of Cynicism: American Morality in Decline*. Oxford: Blackwell, 1944.
Storey, John. *An Introductory Guide to Cultural Theory and Popular Culture*. Athens: University of Georgia Press, 1993.
Strong, James. *Strong's Concise Concordance of the Bible*. Nashville: Thomas Nelson Publishers, 1985.
*Suskind, Ron. *The Price of Loyalty*. New York: Simon & Schuster, 2004.
Suzuki, Shunryu. *Zen Mind, Beginner's Mind: Informal Talks on Zen Meditation and Practice*. Ed. Trudy Dixon. New York: Weatherhill, 1981.
Tanner, Michael. *Nietzsche*. New York: Oxford University Press, 1996.
*Tarnas, Richard. *The Passion of the Western Mind: Understanding the Ideas That Have Shaped our World View*. New York: Ballantine, 1993.
Taylor, Charles. *The Ethics of Authenticity*. Cambridge: Harvard University Press, 1991.
The Power of Character. ed by Michael Josephson & Wes Hanson. San Francisco: Jossey-Bass, Inc., 1998.
*Thoreau, H.D. *Walden*. New York: Barnes & Nobles Publishers, 2004.

Tillich, Paul. *Love, Power, and Justice: Ontological Analyses and Ethical Applications.* New York: Oxford University Press, 1954.

Today's Missal. September 7 – November 29, 1997. United States Catholic Conference, 1997.

*Tolle, Eckhart. *A New Earth.* New York: Plume, 2005

*Tolle, Eckhart, *The Power of Now.* Novato, CA: Namaste, 1999.

*Toynbee, Arnold. *A Study of History: The First Abridged One-Volume Edition.* Oxford: Oxford University Press, 1995.

Trow, George W. S. *Within the Context of No Context.* New York: Atlantic Monthly Press, 1981.

The Upanishads: Breath of the Eternal. Trans. Swami Prabhavananda and Frederick Manchester. Hollywood: The Vendanta Society of Southern California, 1963.

*Verghese, Abraham. *Cutting for Stone.* New York: Vintage, 2010.

*Watts, Alan W. *Behold the Spirit.* New ed. New York: Vintage, 1971.

*Watts, Alan W. *The Book: On the Taboo Against Knowing Who You Are.* New York: Vintage Books, 1972.

*Watts, Alan W. *The Meaning of Happiness.* 2nd ed. New York: Harper & Row, 1979.

*Watts, Alan W. *The Wisdom of Insecurity.* New York: Vintage Books, 1951.

Wilber, Ken. *The Essential Ken Wilber.* Boston: Shambhala Publications, Inc., 1998.

Wittgenstein, Ludwig. *Culture and Value.* Ed. G. H. Von Wright. Trans. Peter Winch. Chicago: University of Chicago Press, 1984.

*Wolfe, Alan. *Moral Freedom.* New York: W.W. Norton & Co., Inc., 2001.

Wolfe, Alan. *The Transformation of American Religion.* New York: The Free Press, 2003.

*Woodman, Marion. *The Pregnant Virgin: A Process of Psychological Transformation*. Toronto: Inner City Books, 1985.
*Yeats, William Butler. *Selected Poetry*. Ed. A. Norman Jeffares. London: Pan Books, 1974.
Zaleski, Philip. *The Best Spiritual Writing 2000*. New York: Harper Collins, 2000.
*Zipes, Jack, ed. *Spells of Enchantment: The Wondrous Fairy Tales of Western Culture*. New York: Penguin Books, 1991.

INDEX OF VALUES

Abundance 284
Acceptance 121, 229
Acquiescence 156
Authenticity 183

Balance 263
Blessing 232

Competence 278
Constancy 224

Discernment 85
Diversity 72

Encouragement 273
Equanimity 121

Equivalence 311

Forgiveness 233
Feedback 222
Fortitude 135

Generativity 249
Generosity 229
Gratitude 201
Grief 196

Healing 168
Heartbreak 336
Holism 92
Honesty 81
Humility 89

Imagination 315
Individuation 99
Integrity 77
Interconnection 303
Intimacy 243

Justice 319

Letting Go 163
Liberation 257
Listening 242

Magnanimity 228
Mediation 223
Mercy 331
Mindfulness 115

Novelty 86
Nurturance 219

Prudence 159

Quietude 109

Realism 78
Redemption 320

Regression 180
Renewal 234
Renunciation 139
Revelation 240
Re-visioning 300

Sacrifice 322
Satisfaction 136
Self-acceptance 188
Self-confidence 269
Self-discipline 134
Self-esteem 276
Self-forgetfulness 212
Self-forgiveness 189
Self-understanding 69
Shame 179
Suffering 156
Synthesis 93

Teaching 252
Temperance 134
Transparency 239
Trust 160

Uncertainty 90

Made in the USA
Lexington, KY
23 April 2013